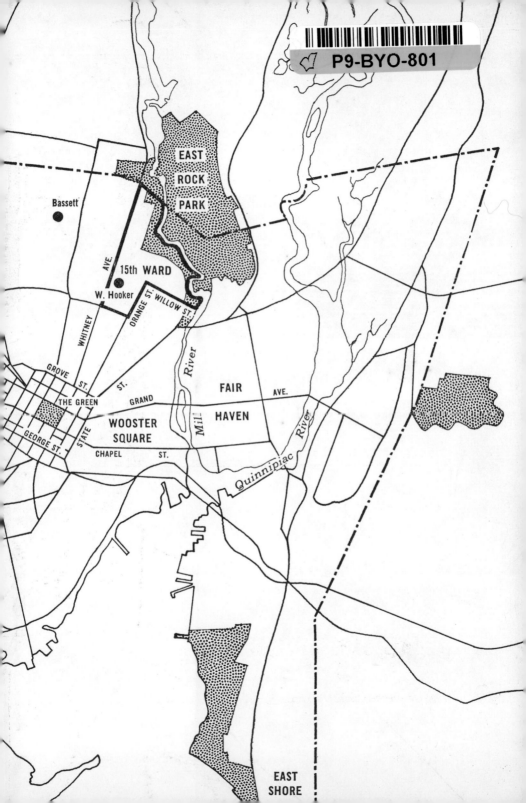

EAST
ROCK
PARK

Bassett

15th WARD

AVE.

W. Hooker

ORANGE ST. WILLOW ST.

WHITNEY

ST.

Mill   River

FAIR

AVE.

GROVE

ST.

ST.

THE GREEN

GRAND

HAVEN

WOOSTER
SQUARE

STATE

GEORGE ST.

CHAPEL   ST.

Quinnipiac   River

EAST
SHORE

The
Fifteenth Ward
and the
Great Society

Also by William Lee Miller

*Piety along the Potomac: Notes on Politics
and Morals in the Fifties*

The
Fifteenth Ward
and the
Great Society

An Encounter with
a Modern City

William Lee Miller

Houghton Mifflin Company Boston
The Riverside Press Cambridge
1966

for

L. Thomas Appleby

Contents

Introduction: A City

M‍Y FAMILY and I were spending the summer of 1963 in New York City, in an apartment at Broadway and 121st Street, when I received from New Haven an ironical telegram: THE PEOPLE HAVE SPOKEN AND INSIST THAT YOU RUN FOR ALDERMAN. It was ironical because the People had nothing to do with it. I sat there in New York listening to the taxis stop at the traffic light before they headed down the hill into Harlem, and I thought about this new assignment.

My New York City friends that summer would smile rather condescendingly at a mention of New Haven. One New York friend was being arrested for jumping in front of bulldozers at a Brooklyn construction site; another, serving on the board of Mobilization for Youth, was coping with drug addicts on the lower East Side; another, home from Taiwan, was looking for an apartment in East Harlem. A woman friend matter-of-factly described the problems of elevators and getting home at night; if somebody wants your purse you give it to him; don't try to fight back. There was some irresponsible talk about blood in the streets. A person from a place with no more problems than New Haven's was given a feeling of inferiority.

New Haven has only 152,000 people, and Greater New Haven with all the suburbs has only 450,000 people. New Haven's public school budget was then $11 million, which must be roughly what New York spends on erasers; the budget for the

Board of Education of the City of New York — one of the nation's sizable industries — has risen to a billion a year. New Haven has little drug addiction; New York is said to have 50,-000 to 60,000 confirmed heroin addicts, which is nearly New Haven's number of registered voters. The New York City school system was considering breaking itself into thirty subsystems, each of which would be larger than New Haven's.

Nevertheless, I thought as I sat there in New York and reflected, New Haven does in *some* ways represent real city politics: it is in the East; it has both Yale University and a large population of immigrant background; and it has recently had an unusual city administration.

Being on the Eastern Seaboard does make a difference. I come from Rocky Mountain and plains country, and although there are attractions in that vast region ("The Great Central West, the reee-jun that's the best," as we used to sing to the tune of "My Wild Irish Rose" in the Southwest Kansas Council of the Boy Scouts of America), advanced urban living is not among them. Cities out there are built, as Edmund Wilson somewhere stated, not on the eighteenth century but on the flat land. New Haven, by contrast, has more than three and one quarter centuries of history behind it. New Haven has always been within striking distance of New York, and if we had a railroad it would be close to Boston and Philadelphia and Washington, too. New Haven is a medium-sized city in the middle of that great eastern stretch of cities in which the nation began and in which 40 percent of the nation now lives, the main stem of America's urban life.

Yale University plus an industrial-immigrant base give New Haven a cultural spread. It is Bridgeport mixed with Princeton — from which latter place my family and I returned happily to New Haven in 1958, rightly expecting that New Haven would represent a bigger bite of modern urban life, and hence of reality, than does Princeton. The combination makes New

Haven: it is not a university town alone or an eastern industrial city alone, but both, with each part weighty enough to keep the other from overwhelming it.

New Haven has the spark of a city also because its mayor has been a leader in efforts to cope with city problems. Our handsome pamphlet for the 1963 city election campaign, of which I seem still to have a large supply in the closet, had this powerful title: "LET DICK LEE FINISH A GREAT REBUILDING JOB PULL THE TOP LEVER NOVEMBER FIFTH." That rebuilding job and Mayor Lee were the reasons — in addition to believing in politics and in the Democratic Party and in the city anyway — why one might be willing to run for alderman in New Haven. They were a good part of the reason, in fact, why my wife and I had wanted to live in the city itself and not in a suburb. The "rebuilding job" is the most extensive urban renewal program per citizen's head in the country, and Lee is the mayor who brought that about.

New Haven is far from being a "Great American City" like New York. It is also not Warsaw or Barcelona or Leningrad or Haifa or Hiroshima; it has not felt the crunch of the twentieth century with any sharp pain. Although a never-to-be-extinguished "freedom torch" burns constantly in front of City Hall, except when it goes out, the city's freedom is not beleaguered, and really never has been. New Haven is not comparable to London or Tokyo or Moscow, or Washington, or even Pittsburgh or Detroit (although it once just might have become something like this last). New Haven is not like Jackson, Mississippi, or Birmingham, Alabama, either. Several times during the events I will describe in the first part of this book some defender of the city would contrast New Haven, rather self-righteously, to those police dog places in the South.

One could argue, I suppose, that this New England university city is one of the privileged sanctuaries of the modern world. It has had an uninterrupted history of effective self-government for more than three and one quarter centuries — as a settlement, a town, a colony, a town in the Connecticut Colony, and a town in the state of Connecticut in the United States of America — without experiencing a forcible overturn or imposition of government, or any bombing, general strike, siege, riot, civil war, famine, massacre, exodus, boycott, lynching, revolution, military defeat, martial law, vigilante rule, mass unemployment, sitdown strike, or barricade in the street.

The city's most memorable moment in world history came back in the seventeenth century, when the citizens sheltered the regicides of Charles I after the Restoration. There has been no invasion of the city or major violence in the streets since July 5, 1779, when during the Revolutionary War a diversionary raid brought a company of British soldiers into the center of the city, despite the effort of a President emeritus of Yale to resist them with his fowling piece. They stayed only the one day. Violence since then has pretty much been confined to the occasional clashes between Yale students and New Haven police.

One of the best American novels about the Civil War, John William De Forest's *Miss Ravenel's Conversion from Secession to Loyalty,* takes place in considerable part in New Haven (thinly disguised as "New Boston") and the city represents the peaceful Northern haven to which Southern loyalists flee, and to which brave Union soldiers return, a placid and rather stuffy college town under the elms, dominated by professors, especially theological professors, and by Puritan habits. It is not like that anymore.

New Haven is not a metropolis or the scene of dramatic events, but it reflects a great deal of history, nevertheless, including recent history. That Yankee college town, important at least in what happened in its classrooms, has been completely overturned by industry and immigration. Then came a slow, steady, silent stagnation, and deepening problems. And now since the early fifties New Haven has had another kind of history, that of an extraordinary effort to rebuild the place.

The one main fact about New Haven is that it has been continuously since 1732 the seat of a famous college. The other main fact is that it became in the nineteenth century a successful New England industrial city, although then not quite making its way into the big leagues.

New Haven's economic and political history is in general a long and a happy one. It may also be seen as a series of near misses. Two ambitious early trading and shipping ventures in the first days of the settlement ended in failure. A larger jurisdiction over towns not only on the Connecticut shore but across the Sound on Long Island, and the dream of a Long Island Sound Colony with New Haven at its center, collapsed after the Restoration when the crown denied New Haven that authority. After 1701 New Haven was co-capital, with Hartford, of the Connecticut Colony and then of the state; later, after the Civil War, New Haven lost out in a bitter battle and Hartford became the sole capital.

In the years before the Civil War, New Haven was the Detroit of the carriage industry, but that position, for which the Southern market was important, was destroyed by the war. Eli Whitney instituted the first factory using interchangeable parts in New Haven in a gun shop on Whitney Avenue, just beyond the end of the ward in which I live — the fifteenth — and near the spot at which a connector to Interstate Highway 91 will begin if we are unable to stop the State Highway Commission from building it, but New Haven never became a major mass-production city. Instead, in the latter part of the nineteenth century it attracted smaller firms making paper, clocks, cigars, hardware, corsets, guns, men's clothing, razor blades, chemicals, Erector sets, shirts, bathing suits, bird cages, and tops for tennis shoes. One is always discovering some additional small firm that makes some additional product. The Winchester arms plant, now a section of the Olin Corporation, and the Sargent Hardware Company, now moved from its old red brick five-story nineteenth-century factory building on Water Street to a new streamlined one in the Long Wharf renewal project along Long Island Sound, have been since the latter part of the nineteenth century two of the largest industrial firms in the city. These two plus Yale University and the New Haven Railroad and the telephone company and the hospital are the largest employers in the city. The city's economic life is diversified and split into relatively small units; New Haven is far from being a big-industry town, let alone a one-industry town, or a company town, or a one-union town. The fragmentation of the city's economic structure perhaps is one reason that strong political leadership could move as effectively as it has to rebuild the city. There was something of a vacuum of power.

New Haven did not become a major center of industry. It grew gradually throughout the latter part of the nineteenth century until it was a city of well over 100,000 citizens — and then it pretty much settled back and stopped. Major new industry has not come in. At the turn of the century optimistic city fathers predicted that by now its population would be 400,000; that, however, has not proved to be the case. The suburbs of course have grown a great deal, especially in recent years, but not the city itself. And the economy and the physical setting of the city were not those of an expanding and enterprising place, until the redevelopment that began in the nineteen-fifties.

New Haven, as I have by now made clear, is not just the seat of Yale but is a New England industrial city. I was confused on that point when I first came east to New Haven in the fall of 1947. After I got off the train at the railroad station and walked up to the New Haven Green, my picture of the city was quickly clarified. It was not, as I had imagined in my Western naïveté, a pretty white-clapboard New England college town with Congregational churches on the green, with the harbor and the river and the Connecticut hills around it, and with college buildings all covered with ivy. It was that in a way, but set in deteriorating late nineteenth-century urban-industrial surroundings. The walk up Meadow Street to Congress Square, and then along lower Church Street to the Green, took me through a series of rundown businesses, fading shops, flophouses, and amusement parlors typical of streets around the railroad station in many urban centers, especially in the East.

All that had changed by 1963. Congress Square was gone. Lower Church Street had become a modern business street, with a new First National Bank building, and a new Malley's department store building; soon there was to be a New Haven version of Macy's next door to it. And many new plans for that central part of town, I knew, were in progress.

Exactly the section of the city through which I first had walked, in some disillusionment, had now been torn apart completely and was being put together again. Oak Street was gone. When my wife and I set out in 1949 by Connecticut Company Bus to go to an economy furniture store to buy our first big piece of furniture — a Hidabed — the man we asked for directions to Oak Street looked at us, innocent newlyweds, with a mixture of skepticism and pity. When we got there we saw why. Oak Street was then New Haven's most rundown and dubious slum. It was New Haven's version of that street in every industrial city, the street that had been successively the home of the most newly arrived immigrants — in this case, Russian-Jewish citizens, then Italians, and then Negroes — and of unsavory activities. "Down on Oak Street," wrote Sinclair Lewis, in his short story "Young Man Axelbrod," "a place of low shops, smoky lights, and alley mouths, they found the slum already astir." Oak Street many years later was the setting of the New Haven version of East Harlem's Protestant Parish — the new "group ministry" effort in the worst of the slums. Oak Street

was the scene of Richard C. Lee's intense commitment to rebuilding the city. "I went into the homes on Oak Street," Mr.
Lee once said, "and they set up neighborhood meetings for me."
(This was during his unsuccessful 1951 campaign for mayor.)
"I went to block meetings . . . three and four in one night.
And I came from one of those homes on Oak Street, and I sat
on the curb and I was just as sick as a puppy. Why, the smell
of this building; it had no electricity, it had no gas, it had
kerosene lamps, light had never seen those corridors in generations. The smells . . . It was just awful and I got sick. And
there, there I really began . . . right there was when I began
to tie in all these ideas we'd been practicing in city planning
for years in terms of the human benefits that a program like
this could reap for a city . . ."

Oak Street now survived only as the name of the new four-
lane highway connector that brings traffic from the Connecticut
Turnpike swooping into the center of the city.

Wooster Square had been transformed. When I first came to
the city the "Wooster Street gang" was spoken of with uneasiness, and when we went to Frank Pepe's on Wooster Street for
the first pizzas I had ever eaten the area around it was anything but prepossessing. Now Wooster Square had become one
of the nation's showplaces of rehabilitation and renewal. The
most notable feature in it was the Conte School — a new community school of the sort thinkers about the city hope to en-
courage: a beautiful, functional Gordon Bunschaft school
building, with an auditorium, a swimming pool, rooms for the
elderly, benches, open space, and a bocce ball court.

The physical rebuilding of New Haven was not the city's
only notable new feature. There was also the social rebuilding,
for which in New Haven the label was "human renewal." One
thing leads to another, in innovative city politics as elsewhere,
and New Haven's extraordinary urban renewal program and
extraordinary mayor had led the high bureaucrats in their

offices in New York and Washington to talk enthusiastically about the city's climate of change (a recurrent phrase) and to look upon New Haven as a likely setting for their programs.

The Ford Foundation in the spring of 1962 had given large sums of money to new agencies in six places (five cities and the state of North Carolina) to try news ways of overcoming poverty. New Haven was one of these, and proved to be the most successful. The New Haven antipoverty agency set up originally with the Ford money — Community Progress, Inc., or CPI — was to become a model for the national war on poverty. I didn't yet know that, of course, in the fall of 1963, but I did know that many interesting things in this line were going on in New Haven, and that national administrators were watching the city. Bright young planners from all over the country had been consuming quarts of coffee together in New Haven, talking about "opening opportunities," the title of the booklet they put together to outline CPI's plan. They discussed the community school (the school as a center for activities in the poor neighborhoods) and prekindergarten classes for slum children, and "higher horizons" doses of culture, and work crews training young dropouts in work habits, and work-study programs to keep youngsters in school, and neighborhood employment centers. When in the spring of 1963 I had talked with Wilbur Cohen, then an Assistant Secretary and now Under Secretary of Health, Education, and Welfare in Washington, for example, there was much head nodding and name swapping and local reference when he found out that I came from New Haven and wanted to talk about antipoverty. As on urban renewal, so on human renewal — New Haven, with an alert mayor, and with able people around him, had had good connections and an early start.

All of this had meant a significant change in New Haven's city politics and, I thought to myself, in that regard too New

Haven might be showing the way for other cities, even including New York.

A certain new attention was just then being paid to city politics. To find readable layman's books about this subject — city politics and city government — it appeared that one had to go all the way back to the Progressive era, to those of Lincoln Steffens and Jacob Riis, or, on rather the opposite side of things, to William Riordan's *Plunkitt of Tammany Hall*. Of course there had been considerable writing since then of a more technical nature about municipal affairs, and many books of a broader aesthetic and philosophical kind, and of a city-planning kind, about what the city ought to be and isn't. The grubby politics and government of the city, nevertheless, did not seem to have been examined with much imagination for the general reader from just after the turn of the century until the early sixties. I think this reflected the pattern of public attention. There was a great puzzling and worrying about city politics and city life back in the early years of this century, about *The Shame of the Cities,* and about *The Battle against the Slum,* about bosses and Tammany and whether reformers were on the right track and whether democracy was going to make it after all — but then attention shifted to broader fields. Steffens himself went on from the cities to the states, and then on to theories about the defects of society as a whole. There were the battles with the trusts, followed by world war and disillusionment and prohibition and depression and struggles over labor unions and the New Deal, and then war again and war's aftermath and the Cold War, and one thing and another. (So much for sixty years of history.) I thought we were just coming back round again — we ordinary mildly public-spirited American citizens — to focus on the city, its politics, problems, and government.

And New Haven had been ahead of other cities both in this new interest in municipal affairs and in providing an answer to its puzzles: a strong mayor who would make energetic use of federal programs.

There was also a new situation just coming over the horizon in state government, on which of course a city is very much dependent. Connecticut is certainly a more neatly arranged state than New York — or, in quite a different way, than Wyoming. I picture Connecticut as a trim and compact little state, square and tidy, green and hilly throughout, and pretty in every corner, with no jackrabbits, mountains, deserts, or sagebrush, and with four medium-sized and roughly equal cities distributed around in a balanced way among the hills, rocks, and rivers. These cities (New Haven, Hartford, Waterbury, and Bridgeport) provide — with some help from smaller urban clusters — Democratic balance to offset the small-town Republicans in the countryside and the rich Republicans in the martini suburbs and commuter places down around New York City. And although Connecticut was once heavily Republican, the depression and the coming of age of the immigrants changed that. From 1930 until 1958 Connecticut was the very model of the two-party system, with the real competition that American political scientists have desired. Either party could win; elections were close; and the Governor's chair and the Senate seats were divided about equally back and forth between the parties during that time. In contrast to an older day, when power companies plus small towns plus a Republican boss named Roraback dominated the state, the economic and partisan and demographic elements of the state were now diversified and fairly well evened out.

Except for one decisive point. The state legislature was grossly malapportioned. The Connecticut lower house was one of the examples in those catalogues of horrors then being exhibited in essays on malapportionment (in one view, it was "the worst of them all"). It gave one representative to each of

the 169 towns regardless of population, except that there were
to be *two* representatives for those towns in existence before
1818, or more than 5000 in population. Union (population 261)
had the same representation as New Haven (population 152,-
000). Less than 10 percent of the state's population could elect
a majority in the house. The small towns thus heavily favored
were overwhelmingly Republican; so the House was too, from
1876 until 1958. The cities suffered. Duane Lockard, a political
scientist, gave statistics in his book *New England State Politics*
to show the drastic results of this disproportion on state grants
for education: in 1948–1949, the towns with less than 500 population received $27.19 per capita for education and the largest
cities (over 10,000 population) received only $3.95.

The state legislature was surely not going to reform itself. I
remember a Yale professor thoughtfully remarking, in the early
fifties, that to change Connecticut's malapportionment would
take a "social revolution."

And yet it did not. In the spring of 1962 the United States
Supreme Court in *Baker* v. *Carr* had opened up to judicial ex-
amination what Justice Frankfurter thought was the "political
thicket" of the apportionment question. Connecticut thus
would be scrambling to make its legislature conform to new
rules. Although the suburbs might benefit from this as much as
the cities, there was not any doubt that it would make state
government more responsive to the cities, too.

The cities certainly needed attention. Even New Haven,
relatively manageable and fortunate, was still fully equipped,
in its smaller way, with the urban miseries possessed in such
abundance by New York. I remember a planner who had been
in Addis Ababa reporting how pleased his Ethiopian employers
were when he told them that they might have traffic problems.
Traffic problems! That would make them an advanced modern
city! Well, New Haven has traffic problems, and it has a pol-

luted and stinking river (near the Fifteenth Ward), and its harbor isn't what it ought to be, and the chaos of its railroad is beyond describing, and the central business district had been in trouble, and the city is even beginning to develop smog. Undirected technology, smoking and spewing and spilling its side effects, has sent this city, like all American cities, sprawling. The great symbol of all this is the Automobile. One joke has it that they are paving California. When Harrison Salisbury of the *New York Times* returned from Russia to do a series on American commuter-suburban problems he visited Los Angeles and began his article with a paraphrase of Lincoln Steffens: I have seen the future, and it does not work.

New Haven represented the future, too, in its way, and a future that might come nearer to working. The answer to the Automobile — to rampant technology plus masses of people — is government and planning. New Haven had had more and better examples of this than most other cities, and earlier. It had been a kind of a trial run city. It had become the country's priority center for urban renewal and the showplace for "human renewal"; it had one of the first and best of the country's new breed of mayors. It had been doing in the late fifties and early sixties what other cities were to begin to do in the middle sixties.

The core of the long list of urban difficulties is this double set: a contracting tax base combined with an expanding demand for services; an influx of new Negroes with an exodus of whites. The two are connected. The short summary of the connection would be, the suburbs. The incoming Negroes, poor and ill educated, provide little in the way of taxes and require much in the way of services. The retreating whites take with them to the suburbs, beyond the reach of the government and taxing power of the city, money, leadership, middle-class and white pupils for the schools. Industries move out but their unskilled workers must live in the central city.

And in the city the problem of the Negro was very much complicated by a heritage of ethnic politics.

The new ingredients in New Haven city politics had not caused the old ones to disappear: we were every bit as "ethnic" as New York in our smaller way. In fact, one problem about my running for alderman in New Haven was that I am a white Presbyterian from Wyoming, and thus a little irrelevant. An older Jewish ward worker asked me, "You have family? Relatives in the city?" He was obviously startled to learn that I had no kinfolk nearer than Omaha, Nebraska. I could almost hear him say to himself in bafflement, What kind of a candidate is this?

For its first two centuries and more New Haven, as I have said, was a small Yankee Protestant town. With the growth of industry after the Civil War, and the big immigration of the turn of the century, however, it was completely changed. In twentieth-century New Haven politics, according to a notable political science study, "nothing less is revealed than a massive invasion of the political system by the ethnics."

New Haven's large population of immigrant background was distributed rather clearly by sections of the city, in a way the politician's rules of thumb obviously acknowledge: Italian wards on the Hill and in Fair Haven, Negro wards in Newhallville and Dixwell, Jewish wards in Westville. When a new assistant corporation counsel was to be appointed, he had to be of the right ethnic background.

One might wish, perhaps, that ethnic considerations and balanced tickets and all of that would vanish from politics. Robert Bendiner once wrote that he became so disgusted with the careful ethnic and geographic balance of every ticket in New York State that he would be happy to vote for a party that would put forward five Cherokee Indians from Staten Island. But the ethnic identification, whether we like it or not, was obviously a fact with which any realistic politician still had to deal. A chief point Nathan Glazer and Daniel P. Moynihan made in their book *Beyond the Melting Pot* is that it didn't work: the ethnic ingredients in the American pot didn't melt the way they were supposed to do. The problem has hung on longer than anyone expected.

New Haven's waves of immigration corresponded to those of the eastern seaboard generally, except that the Italian wave is proportionately larger. The Germans as elsewhere had more or less disappeared. The Irish, the first big wave, came in New Haven as elsewhere to dominate the Democratic Party and city politics, and had tended to fade into the assimilated middle class. A large Russian-Jewish immigration had settled chiefly in Westville. As in the state of Connecticut, there used to be an implicit understanding that the congressman-at-large (before redistricting) was to be a Pole; so the city's alderman from the Thirteenth Ward was often of Polish background. There were a few Greeks and Hungarians and Czechs and others. The "foreign stock," which means the foreign-born plus those with at least one foreign-born parent, came to 64,000 of New Haven's 150,000 citizens even as recently as 1960, and that strict measure of foreign stock would seriously understate the number of white citizens for whom an ethnic identification was a fact of political life.

By far the largest ethnic group in New Haven was the Italian — 25,000 in 1960 by the foreign-stock test, and a great many more if the third generation is counted. Between 1880 and 1920 very large numbers of immigrants came from southern Italy to work in New Haven's industries. Some said the city had the largest proportion of citizens of Italian extraction of any city in the country. The chairmen of both political parties were of Italian background; the United States congressman from the district was of Italian background; the only successful Republican candidate for mayor of New Haven in this century was of Italian background; the best restaurants in town were Consiglio's and Papa Coppolo's.

And then, more recently, Negroes had come.

Glazer and Moynihan wrote that the mass migration from Italy after the eighteen-seventies "became modern history's greatest and most sustained movement of population from a single country." The Great Migration (as Gunnar Myrdal already called it in 1944, well before it reached its peak) of Southern Negroes to Northern cities — five million since 1915, two million since World War II — must be one of modern history's largest and most sustained movements of a people *within* one country.

Here in this once Yankee city these two great movements — Italian and Negro — were going to crunch against each other, one could be sure. (It would happen most notably, as things turned out, in the Fair Haven Junior High School on June 22, 1964.) In 1900 there were 3000 nonwhites in New Haven. By 1940 this had risen only to 6000; in 1950 it had mounted slightly to 9500. By 1960, however, there were 22,000, with the number still growing rapidly — 26,000 was the estimate in 1963. Fifteen percent of the city's population had been Negro by 1960, and it was rapidly rising. This was New Haven's version of the nationwide phenomenon, the great migration of millions of Southern Negroes to the Northern cities. "I'll be the first Negro mayor of New Haven," said one humorous Negro alderman, joking one day in Mayor Lee's office, "if my cousins keep coming in from the South." Only one New Haven Negro in ten now in the city was born here. During the middle and later fifties Negroes had come to New Haven at a rate exceeding 1000 a year.

Because Negroes were younger and poorer and have more children than the city's average, and sent very few children to parochial or private schools, they represented a disproportionate percentage of the public school population. During New Haven's school battle one white fellow would demand, indignantly, to know how come the Negro population, with only 15 percent of the city's population, had 35 percent of the public school children? I guess he thought it was some sort of unfair overrepresentation, like that of the rural areas in state legislatures.

As in other Northern cities, there was an older, established group of Negroes, many middle class, for a very long time residents of the city, once brought to the city as slaves or servants by Southern boys coming north to Yale or by the wealthy Louisiana families who once came regularly in the summer to New Haven as a northern seaside resort. These Negroes, many with more or less good jobs in Yale clubs and Yale dining halls, in some professions and even a few businesses, had been overwhelmed by the new arrivals from the South — poorer, younger, less educated, less experienced in city ways.

A politician could think of the 70,000 voters in New Haven (distinguished from the population at large) as being divided into seven ethnic parts: two of them Italian, one Irish, one Jewish, and one Negro, the other two parts composed of the smaller groups such as "Wasps," Poles, and Puerto Ricans, roughly in that order of importance. But of course this rule was rapidly changing. The Irish would become assimilated, the Italians would move out, the Jewish numbers would decline — and the Negro proportion would grow. Large numbers of potential Negro voters were still unregistered, and new ones were steadily moving in and coming of age.

New Haven was also a city of widely differing educational backgrounds.

Professor Robert A. Dahl of Yale wrote in his book *Who Governs?* that "the average parent of a public school child has had considerably less formal education than is now compulsory. In 1950 half the people twenty-five years of age or over had not gone beyond the ninth grade. Only a little more than a third had completed high school." That was in 1950, before the large Negro immigration. It is notable, by the way, how small a role the Negro plays in Professor Dahl's book; no one writing about New Haven politics a few years later would have

so little to say about the Negro voter and about issues connected with race. In 1960, in the six inner-city poverty areas
served by Community Progress, Inc. — which represent 55 percent of the total population of New Haven — 50 percent of the
adults had not graduated from the eighth grade; 72 percent
had not received a high school diploma.

At the same time, New Haven had a large slice of enlightenment and advanced education. Although many Yale faculty
lived out of town, many also lived in the city — the Fifteenth
Ward and the adjacent Eighteenth Ward were one area.
Younger faculty and students in the graduate and professional
schools lived throughout the city. Yale was no longer a rich
boy's college, but a university with worldwide scholars full of
strange and wonderful ideas. A university attracts other institutions, and people with cultural and scientific and scholarly
interests. And the programs of Mayor Richard Lee had brought
an influential group of new people with advanced training
into the city.

New Haven had large numbers of intellectuals, still more of
Negroes, and still more of "ex-plebes" — and that was about it.
There was not very much else. There was no large, moderate,
and secure nonethnic and nonegghead middle class. The suburbs had stripped the city fairly clean of this. In the subsequent
crisis it appeared that the city might fly apart. The segments
with their widely differing sets of values, would meet each
other head on, recoil aghast, and then proceed night after night
to rub salt in each other's wounds. As that experience would
reveal, New Haven is a difficult city to govern; but it had been
governed well for more than a decade, and that was the more
important part of the story.

 Part I

The Heat of a Summer

1. Election, 1963

"You can't keep the national issues out of it!"

When I started to campaign in that autumn of 1963, I rather assumed that the subject matter of the office would be local: local streetlights to be installed, local property taxes to be spent, local snow to be plowed. Some of my Yale colleagues assumed that too, and greeted the word "alderman" with amused and lofty references to the great issues of garbage collection. It turned out, however, that there is more to city politics than garbage collection — more large and national stuff than these Great Issues men realized, and more than I did.

There is in city politics, to be sure, considerable discussion of garbage, of streetlights, and of the removal of leaves, but these matters lead sooner than you would think into deep waters and large national controversies. Even the two-hour parking restriction turns out to be a class issue, one of people with garages against people without garages. Moreover, the detailed matters of streets, leaves, and variances are interesting in their own right. I didn't mind that the alderman dealt with matters that are small, local, and particular, such as putting the enforcement of the health code under the Division of Neighborhood Improvement; trying to rezone for the new apartments in Fair Haven; even coping with the difficulty of getting out of the garages on North Bank Street when it snows. You can see what you are talking about, and you can have an effect on it. The very particularity has a kind of interest —

this street corner, this place to park, this corner of the block.

And local politics has the added feature that you come to know the cast of characters personally. C. P. Snow distinguishes the large politics of headlines, national parties, and parliaments from the other, smaller, self-enclosed and face-to-face sort that he calls "closet politics": the politics, that is, of a handful of professors choosing a new Master for the college. This small-scale kind, in which everybody knows everybody else, in which the larger labels and ideologies are stripped away, shows plainly the strange-bedfellow intricacies of politics, and the interesting complexity of the human beings and human values that make it up. City affairs, needless to say, are full of closet politics.

It turns out that they are full of the other type too. One ward leader said in the middle of the 1963 effort, "I've never seen anything like this campaign. You can't keep the national issues out of it!" A year later one could almost say the reverse. One could scarcely keep the city issues — busing, mainly — out of the 1964 national election in New Haven. Local issues and national issues, in fact, have come to be mixed around together to a degree that is new.

One national issue that intruded itself briefly into the 1963 New Haven city election was that of school prayer. The Board of Education, to whom and from whom so many hot potatoes come, had taken action in early September in accordance with the decisions of the United States Supreme Court of the previous June, and had eliminated official prayer-saying from the New Haven schools. There were many complaints. At the time another candidate for alderman and I had our picture taken with the Mayor for the campaign pamphlet we argued about the New Haven board's decision. The other candidate insisted, "There is leeway, there is leeway," and the Mayor agreed with him. We stood facing the photographer, smiled for the picture, and then turned right back to the argument. Happily this issue (which has the danger of antisemitism in it) faded as the campaign went on.

Another large national matter, having to do with conservation, natural beauty, open space, outdoor recreation, and Stewart Udall, had a local manifestation right in the ward in which I was running, the Fifteenth. A new interstate highway was to go swirling along overhead not far from our ward, headed toward Hartford and Springfield; 90 percent of the cost would come from federal funds, as part of the nearly $50 billion federal highway program started by national legislation back in 1956. The State Highway Commission, a very powerful body, planned to build a long four-lane connector to this interstate highway; and the connector would slash through the city's most interesting parks, East Rock Park and College Woods Park, which lie partly in the Fifteenth Ward. One feature of my aldermanic campaign was to oppose that connector, so we started a "Save the Park" committee centering in the East Rock area. (This problem — a national one — is that highways and automobiles have more money and power than parks do.) A ward worker and I visited the State Highway Commission in Wethersfield to talk about the connector. On the wall there was an idealized picture of the park, Norman Rockwell style (a rendering, they called it), with the two lanes of the connector on either side of a clear blue river. The state highway man who talked to us about the "facility" explained, as though this were a virtue, that the connector would straighten out the river, which now meanders through the park. Perhaps it is the highway engineer's view that rivers ought to move in a direct and efficient manner toward their destination.

City politics is now bound in with national politics at almost every serious point. Great sums of money for all the big enterprises — urban renewal, warring on poverty, highways, schools, libraries — come from Washington (usually, although not in the case of urban renewal funds, by way of Hartford). Federal Court decisions, on school prayer, on segregation, on reapportionment, reverberate in city politics. Congressional decisions (on the funds for a regional federal building) and national bureaucratic decisions (on the location of the regional airport) heavily affect the city; national legislation (on housing, for example, and now on education) gives shape to the city. And at the same time the city government is much more visible and important in national matters than it has been before. Urban renewal depends upon local decisions, and so now also does the community-action part of the antipoverty program. If new steps are to be taken in public education, local districts one by one will have to take them.

The most evident of the domestic issues — Negro rights — brought many citizens to a new focus on local government. Two public institutions directly connected to that matter, the schools and the police, are under local control by a kind of fundamental American principle. The sheriffs of counties in Alabama and Mississippi and the policemen of New York and Chicago are central figures in the drama of civil rights and, like the schools, they are dependent upon the decisions of local agencies, one by one. Local decisions about public housing and urban renewal markedly affect the situation of Negroes. Debates about welfare have a strong undertone of attitudes toward Negroes. In fact there were moments during these months, when the whole range of issues in the modern city seemed overtly or covertly to have to do with Negro-white relations.

Almost all citizens have a conscious relation to the civil rights revolution, both in the nation and in the city. Yale people who otherwise ignore the merely local scene, who subscribe to no New Haven paper but only to the *New York Times,* who testify in Washington but don't know which ward they live in in New Haven suddenly *do* focus on the city when an issue of civil rights arises. Workingclass townsfolk, on the other hand, whose life and interests are entirely local, who do not care about NATO, the World Bank, and the conservation of wilderness areas, *do* pay attention to national news about civil rights.

The first, indeed the only, question about any issue that was put to me by any ward Democrat when I started "going for alderman" was this one: "Where do you stand on the colored?" I was not altogether surprised. One could not help knowing that there were apprehensions and negative feelings about the Negro among some of New Haven's white citizens. During my first connections with the politics of New Haven, back in the late forties, I was startled to hear party workers speak in a derogatory way about "the colored." When my wife went to her first Democratic Party ward meeting in New Haven in the early fifties, she came home nonplused because the gathering had started off with anti-Negro jokes and remarks. That did not correspond to the way we had been brought up, as liberals out in the West, to think of the Democratic Party.

The New Haven Board of Aldermen had considered in its previous term an ordinance prohibiting racial discrimination in the sale or rental of housing. This effort had failed, but the alderman from the Fifteenth Ward — the Republican I was running against — had voted for the ordinance. It was explained to me by my Democratic confreres that many Republicans and swing voters in the ward were eager to support somebody who would take a contrary position; they were offering their votes, as it were, to the Democrats if the leaders of that party would just put up somebody who would stand against these housing ordinances. It was a considerable frustration to these ward Democrats, as well as to a sizable group of voters, that this was not to be. A new Republican ward chairman explained to me in the middle of hot issues six months later that many of his friends were saying, "We had a Republican alderman and we didn't get what we want; now we have a Democratic alderman, and we don't get what we want. What do we do?"

"Where do you stand on the colored?" I was asked. "God put 'em on this earth," it was conceded, "and they have to live too, you know"; but still, it was said, people in the neighbor-

hood objected when just two days after the moving in of Negroes there were "bottles and unmentionables in the street."

The Democrats held their city convention on an August evening two days after the March on Washington, at which Martin
Luther King made the memorable speech about his dream.

Rather to my surprise, I found campaigning for office en-
joyable. I had rung doorbells in political campaigns many
times before, but always for somebody else's candidacy; to tell
the truth, I hadn't liked it. It had for me something of the psychological difficulty of door-to-door salesmanship. Campaigning for myself, however, proved to be different; it gave me a
solid reason for being there on the voter's porch, and an easy
opening line. Also, the popularity of the head of the ticket,
Mayor Lee, yielded a generally favorable atmosphere. "Anybody on Dick Lee's team is good enough for me." There were,
of course, some tight-lipped ladies who abruptly turned away
a Democratic candidate with angry barks about taxes, and
there were even a few fierce partisans who wanted to argue.
Another group were those lonely and dislocated souls who
would seize the opportunity to take up some large topic not
strictly relevant to the office under consideration — the reck-
less speed of teen-age drivers, for one. Most voters, including
Republicans, were just noncommittally cordial.

I believe my favorite doorstep encounter was with the nice
lady who on being told that I was the Democratic candidate
asked, "The President's a Democrat, isn't he?" I assured her
that the President was indeed a Democrat and she replied,
"Well, it would be good to have an alderman of the same party,
wouldn't it?" That was so nice that I didn't want to disturb it.
I backed down her stairs without even giving her my pamphlets, assuring her that if she voted for me there would certainly be no conflict at all between the Fifteenth Ward alderman and the White House.

The Fifteenth Ward, which is east of Whitney Avenue in

the neighborhood of East Rock Park, includes among its now about 2400 registered voters a richer variety of the components of the city than the picture of it among local politicians sometimes allows. Politicians, like other people, develop stereotypes that often oversimplify life's complexity and often hang on past the date of whatever relevance they may originally have had. "This is a snooty ward," one ward leader remarked, and Yale Professor Dahl's study of New Haven politics referred in passing to the "wealthy fifteenth." That is not the whole story. It is true that the ward has some large old houses across from East Rock Park and on Everit Street that were once, quite a while ago now, the homes of the business elite of New Haven. It is true there is in the very center of the ward a big block of newer apartments, many of which are moderately high-priced. The average income in the ward would certainly make it relatively wealthy, if not snooty, compared to New Haven as a whole, which is not a rich city. There are almost none of the poor, of whom there are considerable numbers in other New Haven wards. There is only the barest handful of Negroes, and these included at that time the young doctor who became the new president of the NAACP and the lawyer who fills the Negro slot among the assistant corporation counsels — a very elite token of integration. In fact — one of the harbingers of the Great Society that is to be — one encounters occasionally a Poor Little Rich Girl note in the Fifteenth Ward: we don't receive any of these good things, such as new schools, new cultural programs, new libraries, antipoverty benefits, because we don't have enough poor people; we are deprived because we are not deprived enough. This is the kind of thing on which you simply can't win.

The ward is not any longer unequivocally Republican, conservative, Yankee, or rich. The movings-out and movings-in of recent years and the breakup of big, old frame houses into apartments have meant an increase in the number of second- and third-generation Italians especially, but also Irish

and other national extractions. There is a section once known
as Goatville (there were goats), on the "other side of Orange
Street," with less expensive houses and with workingclass or
lower-middle-class families, which furnish the core of the Democratic voters in the ward. Many new Yale people, who are not
the same as old Yankees, also have moved into the old frame
houses and apartments of the ward, which is now a jumble of
such various ethnic and educational backgrounds, religions
and incomes, and of old residents and new ones as not to be
subject to any easy characterization. In 1962 Democrat Giaimo
and Republican Alsop carried the ward for congressman and
governor respectively, and Democrat Ribicoff and Republican
Seely-Brown finished in a tie in the contest for Senator.

The Fifteenth Ward has sizable representations of the two
great contrasting attitudes that run through all the literature
about American city politics. At one door a woman launched
into a tirade about the failure of the city to fix the sidewalk in
front of her house; at another door a man, talking to the candidate while changing his baby's diaper and pointing to
framed copies of the Gettysburg Address and Declaration of
Independence on the wall (believe me, this is the way it was),
complained that the candidate's propaganda (about a park,
school, and library in the immediate neighborhood) is "too
parochial"; "Dixwell needs it worse than we do." One young
woman lit into me because I didn't want to discuss my position
on nuclear war. Another woman told me she disapproved of a
previous alderman because he made a large point about so
small a matter as the blinking traffic light installed through
his efforts at a nearby corner; the very accomplishment he
thought would commend him to this voter had the opposite
effect.

How shall I identify these two attitudes? They appear in
every book and every article about American city politics. They

used to be called, in the days of Lincoln Steffens, the reformers or the good-government people, on the one side, against the machine, or the professional politicians, on the other. That set of terms no longer applies, at least in New Haven. The erstwhile middle-class reformers are at least as strong supporters of a professionally political mayor as are the nonreformers, and some of the latter now have a cynical, or at any rate negative, view of parties, professional political leaders, and City Hall. And yet there is still an unmistakable division.

In a recent book about *City Politics,* Professors Edward Banfield and James Wilson of Harvard describe these two attitudes that cut across the cities of the nation as the "working-class, immigrant ethos," which is "private-regarding," and the "Anglo-Saxon Protestant middle class ethos," which is "public regarding." I think they are right to tie division to a difference in the ethos, and to connect that in turn with social background. One might quibble, however, about the Anglo-Saxon Protestant part; Mr. Banfield and Mr. Wilson get themselves in the awkward position of having to say that much of the Jewish community has adopted the Anglo-Saxon Protestant ethos. I would rather say it is middle-class, associated with Anglo-Saxon Protestantism in the past largely because that was the dominant group.

Campaigning at least gave me a reason to go outdoors. New Haven's best season is the fall, and one is often frustrated by having to spend a colorful autumn day inside one's office or classroom, staring in a glum educational effort at students' papers or students' faces. In my previous campaigning it had always seemed to be raining and cold, but in 1963 it was pleasant football weather every day. I had a fine time going up and down Avon and Whitney and Anderson and Cottage and Willow and Orange and Canner and Everit while the trees were changing color.

There were difficulties, of course. At the university it happened that I was having political science literature inflicted
on me at this time, and so I made notes in the form of

REPORT ON EMPIRICAL RESEARCH IN
THE FIFTEENTH WARD.

I believe that I have data substantiating the following generalizations:

No apartment-to-front-door speaker system in any apartment building in the Fifteenth Ward in New Haven, Connecticut, actually works.

Citizens of all streets in that ward, with statistically insig-
nificant exceptions, regard traffic on their street as too heavy
and dangerously fast (correctly in every case), and strongly
desire a traffic light, four-way stop signs, a policeman, cross-
walks, "Drive Slow" and "Watch for Children" signs, plus perhaps an under- and overpass, at the intersection nearest to
their houses.

No matter at what time doorbells are rung three out of eleven
voters will be eating, and will still be chewing when answering
the door, and will continue chewing noncommittally during
the presentation of the issues.

All housewives in that ward wear hair curlers and house-
coats throughout the Saturday forenoons of October. Typical
housewife behavior in the time period 10:30 A.M. to noon on
Saturdays, in response to doorbell ringing, is as follows: a long
delay; eventually the opening of the door to a distance of two
to four inches; the slow projection of the upper portion of the
head, curlers first, around the corner of the door; the utterance,
in a querulous voice with rising inflection, of one of these two
Housewife Responses, "Ye-es?" or "What *is* it?"

Media participation in the area is high. On a Sunday afternoon, especially during a New York Giants football game, and
more especially still during the game between the New York
Giants and the Cleveland Browns, many voters will strongly

prefer media participation in sports to direct participation in the political process as represented by a candidate for alderman at the front door. This preference often will be forcefully expressed.

The apartment-communication problem obviously is a weighty field for contemporary urban political science. Recent work has highlighted COMMUNICATION and COMMUNICATION-FLOW in the political process. In the speaking-tube problem I believe we have isolated a significant variable. We can suggest its importance by this impressionistic recapitulation of a typical case. The candidate, having entered the apartment lobby (6 ft. x 3 ft.), finds on his voters list the names O'Halleran, Merriweather, and Kuzinski, whereas the apartment doorbells have the names O'Brien, Olson, Percelli (Mrs. Esther), and BLANK. Now he is faced with Candidate's Choice A: Should he take the coward's way out, toss his pamphlets on the table, and leave? Or should he bravely ring the doorbell of BLANK, and hope? (Hope rather ambivalently in most cases, one might observe.) If he takes the second course, the importance of the broken speaker system is apparent. Mrs. BLANK cannot call down through it "Ye-es?" or "What *is* it?" like any housewife, but must make Voter's Choice A, whether or not to push the buzzer allowing the unknown visitor's entry at the front door five floors below. If she does so she immediately regrets it, and fears that she has let Jack the Ripper into the building; the candidate regrets it too, for he, gratefully, was just about to leave when the sudden buzz startled him into a great leap backward (dropping his Lee buttons) for the apartment-access door and allowed him now to puff glumly up the five flights of stairs to the BLANKS' apartment. The two will confront each other at last in an inadequate state of communication-flow. Sometimes Mrs. BLANK has retreated behind her chain-fastened door; sometimes the candidate, puffing speechlessly, simply hands her his pamphlet without a word and turns back down the stairs.

Internal apartment politics also are complicated by the same phenomenon. The voter-scaring, or *Boo!* effect illustrates this point. Some apartment buildings have a button at the apartment door that rings the same bell rung by the button down in the lobby. The candidate, now roaming inside the building with his inaccurate list and his dog-eared pamphlets, rings such a bell at one of the apartments. The voter inside rings the lobby admission bell and, expecting Aunt Mabel to be making her way slowly up the stairs, comes at leisurely pace to open the apartment door. *Whango!* A large, dark, unknown, unprepossessing figure with pamphlets, lists, and buttons is standing right there at her face. Voters have turned Republican for less.

Ordinarily it has been assumed in political science literature that the Time-Energy Resource available to politicians includes only the waking hours, but in this election there appeared an interesting sort of Wee Willie Winkie campaigning. A Democratic worker, weaving home from ward work at two-thirty in the morning, was startled to see a lively figure running around putting papers under the windshield wipers of cars parked in the street; in the morning voters discovered these to be Republican campaign material. On another occasion a voter who on coming home at midnight had found nothing at his door found there the next morning at seven-thirty, when he came down for the paper, the Republican candidate's potholder. With it there was the candidate's handwritten message, unsettling under these conditions, saying, "Sorry I missed you."

Another campaign device, not altogether new, involved wife and baby, or at any rate the baby-stroller. On election day the Republican candidate's wife stood on a corner near the polls with a baby-filled stroller (I assume that there was a baby in there; I didn't check) on the sides of which were homemade signs saying, "Please Re-elect My Daddy Alderman." It was necessary to station three handsome grade school children and an extraordinarily attractive and visibly pregnant wife on the opposite corner in order to re-establish the Balance of Power in the ward.

When "busing" was first mentioned to me, in the middle of the campaign, I did not know what it was all about. We Democrats in the Fifteenth Ward were holding what the handbills called a Monster Rally in the basement of the Worthington Hooker School at the time. There were red and blue political banners on the school basement walls; there was a generous supply of refreshments; there were special Democratic Party napkins, with a donkey and the mayor's name and mine; and there was even a three-piece orchestra ("The Royals — music for all occasions"). The high point of the rally had passed with the appearance of Mayor Lee. The other candidates on the city ticket — for town clerk, city clerk, registrar of vital statistics, city sheriff, and tax collector — had come trailing in behind the Mayor and had been introduced and had each made a brief speech explaining that he did not make speeches and urging everyone please to vote Democratic, et cetera. As the candidate for alderman in the ward I had been introduced, too, and had made a few remarks along those same lines.

Then after Lee had spoken and the city-wide dignitaries had all departed we Fifteenth Ward Democrats, rather a mixed collection, had settled down to our raffle. There were many old-line Democrats — men who worked for Winchester Arms, Marlin Blades, the Rockbestos plant, the post office, and the city supply house, many of whom lived "on the other side of Orange Street." There were also the wives of two law school professors, the wife of a school board member, and the wife of the city's development administrator, together with some CPI employees, and lawyers and a scattering of additional Yale people. Bob Reilly, a gas company employee and a devoted Democrat who was once an alderman and now my campaign manager, was

picking the numbers out of a hat. Pat Cassidy, the Irish patriarch of the ward Democrats, was dispensing the door prizes —
bottles of perfume, bottles of wine, and two dollars worth of
cleaning — along with jokes. (A visiting French political scientist who came to the meeting with a professor from Yale won
the two dollars worth of dry cleaning; I wonder what he made
of that sample of the American political process.)

In the middle of these raffle festivities two women — wives
of workingmen and mothers of children in Worthington Hooker
—signaled that they wanted to have a word with me, their al-
derman-to-be. We then conferred at the back of the room in
earnest whispers contrasting with the partisan gaiety around
us. They had a disturbed, intent, and serious air that impressed
me and stuck in my memory. They wanted to know, they said,
about this "busing." I said I did not know what that was. They
explained it to me: busing-in the colored, busing white children
to the colored schools. I said I had not heard about any such
thing. They insisted earnestly that something like that was being talked about — and, as it turned out, they were right.

The New Haven Board of Education, as we were all to learn
later, had had conversations that fall about "de facto segregation" in the city's schools. Although the city had had for ten
years an enlightened city administration, an urban renewal
program including careful relocation, and a model "human
renewal" program, and although the city had well-integrated
high schools, a Negro among the members of a progressive
Board of Education, some good new school buildings in the
Negro areas, and many good intentions, yet, since there were
"Negro areas," there were schools — grade schools and a junior
high school — that were more than 90 percent Negro. Thus
we were guilty of de facto segregation and racial imbalance.

The New Haven school board had had a meeting early that
fall of 1963 with June Shagaloff, who is the special assistant for
education for the national NAACP — which means the person
in charge of efforts to desegregate Northern school systems.

Miss Shagaloff had been chosen for this post back in September 1961, after the first nationally publicized efforts to desegregate schools in New Rochelle, New York, and in Englewood, New Jersey, when it was felt by some that the NAACP had been outdistanced in militancy by other groups. After its meeting with Miss Shagaloff, the New Haven board adopted a resolution, not much noticed at the time, declaring that "racially imbalanced schools are educationally unsound." It also committed itself to produce a plan to end this unsoundness in New Haven by one year later, September of 1964.

But in October 1963 few New Haven citizens knew anything about this. I admitted my ignorance to the two mothers at the Monster Rally; educational matters, after all, are decided by the Board of Education, not by the Board of Aldermen. Although that hardly satisfied the two anxious mothers, I turned my attention back to the raffle.

On election night, after a hard campaign, we waited for the results in the polling place, the basement of the Worthington Hooker School. Hooker, as it is called, is a squat two-story red brick school built in 1905 which stands at the corner of Livingston and Canner Streets. Its basement meeting room was later to be the scene of many agitated gatherings.

This time we did not have much agitation or a very long wait. The last straggling voter — a professor of drama at Yale, wearing white tennis shoes and bursting in just under the wire — pulled his lever and departed. At six o'clock Bob Reilly, moderator of the polls that year, shut the two doors into the Hooker basement and officially declared the polls closed. For a few pregnant minutes the Republican and Democratic workers who were allowed inside the polls and the Republican candidate for alderman and I stood around self-consciously looking calm and making small talk. The wife of the Republican candidate prepared a piece of paper on which to write the results. Mr. Reilly announced that first they would call off the results for each machine on line one for mayor and then, skipping over the rest of the city ticket, those for alderman on line eight. He moved to the back of the first of the three voting machines and began to open it. The waiting group, never very noisy, fell silent. Mr. Reilly had generously given the privilege of calling out the results to an old party worker, who shortly began to call out letters and numbers.

One notable fact about elections conducted on voting machines is the speed with which the results are known; there is no long night of waiting but, rather, an abrupt moment of truth. The polls close in city elections at 6:00; the machines are opened at 6:05, more or less, and by about 6:10 it is all over. A seasoned politician, in fact, pretty well knows the story when he looks at the back of the first machine. Indeed, he may feel that he knows it when the absentee ballots are counted in the middle of election day. For some unaccountable reason the percentage on each voting machine seems always to be nearly the same, so that the first machine tells the story for all of them. In 1952 the numbers on the back of the first machine in the normally Democratic ward in which I then lived, the Twenty-ninth, immediately told the story of the big national Eisenhower victory. John Golden, for many years the Democratic National Committeeman for Connecticut, and also chairman of the Twenty-ninth New Haven ward, said gloomily at that election he had not seen anything like it since the Harding victory of 1920.

There are voting machines throughout the state of Connecticut, so that in the big elections the statewide results are tabulated very quickly, too; Connecticut is always one of the first states to list final results in a national election. In that 1952 election Connecticut had gone for Eisenhower, and Democratic Senator William Benton from Connecticut had already conceded his defeat before we even had time to get from the polls to the home at which we were to watch the results. We were greeted at the door with the news that it was all over. It was a dreary evening for Democrats, but at least there was no suspense.

Now, in 1963, the results in this much smaller city election were also speedily known, and they were much happier ones for New Haven Democrats. First machine: line A1, 463; B1, 376; C1, 4; A8, 450; B8, 387. "A1" was the Mayor; "A8" was myself. The Republican candidate for Alderman looked at the figures on his wife's paper and made a negative gesture. "But that's just the first machine!" said his wife. "Oh, no, that's *it*," said the candidate. I was subtracting and adding vigorously as the totals on the second and third machines were called. Before I could finish my arithmetic, a group of the poll watchers and party workers gathered around me and began to shake my hand. The Republican candidate put his hand through the crowd and congratulated me, and quickly withdrew. Democrats in the group stayed around for a few minutes, beaming with satisfaction, while Mr. Reilly prepared the official count on all the offices. The Mayor had won the ward by a plurality of 150 votes, and I had won by 125. After a last buzz of congratulations, I went out to my two older children, who were waiting on the corner to hear how Daddy did, and then we went home to wife, younger child, television set, radio, and victory party.

By the time I got to the radio it was clear that the story throughout the city was like that in the Fifteenth Ward: the Democrats not only were winning but were winning by a larger margin than had generally been expected. The heavily Negro wards — the Sixteenth, Seventeenth, Nineteenth, Twenty-second — about which some had been concerned because of the Paige campaign, were supporting the Democratic mayor overwhelmingly. During the parties and hurrahs that made up the rest of the evening it became clear that the Democrats would carry all but three of the city's thirty-three wards, elect all but three of the city's thirty-three aldermen, and give Mayor Lee a quite comfortable plurality.

It had not been certain that this would happen. Although

Mayor Lee in his decade in office had come to have a national reputation, and although he won big victories in previous city elections, it was thought by some that this time he might stumble. Urban renewal requires much tearing up and moving around of buildings, streets, business, and people, and adds to the normal accumulation of hurts and resentments for which an administration long in power comes to be blamed. In the city elections of 1961 Mayor Lee's plurality had fallen to 4000 votes, well below the comfortable, not to say extravagant, margins that the New Haven citizenry had come to expect him to gain, from his large pluralities in 1955 (20,608), 1957 (23,331), and 1959 (13,884). (Something over 70,000 votes are cast in a New Haven city election.) Mr. Lee's opponent in 1963 was once more the Republican member of an old New Haven family — a man named Henry Townshend — who had come respectably close to beating him in 1961, and it was thought by some that 1963 might be the year in which even Mayor Lee would prove the political rule that, given enough time, all incumbents at last defeat themselves. But that did not happen. The returns coming in the radio made clear that his 1963 plurality would bounce back up again, and would be larger than almost everyone — probably including the Mayor himself — had expected. Arthur T. Barbieri, the Democratic Party's town chairman, had predicted that Lee would win by more than 10,000 votes, but that was widely regarded, in private by Democrats as well as Republicans, as just the inflated professional optimism for public consumption that goes with Mr. Barbieri's post. When the totals were completed, however, he proved to be right; the Mayor had defeated Mr. Townshend by 33,150 votes to 21,805 — a plurality of 11,345.

Mr. Barbieri was beaming with understandable satisfaction when, after a very quick supper, I went with the ward chairman to Democratic Party headquarters, up the stairs to the second floor in a building on Chapel Street. A Negro politician with a bullhorn amused the roaring mass of Democratic work-

ers with remarks about "a prophet, and his name is Arthur."
We stood around in the crush of happy Democrats, looking at
the figures on the blackboard, pushing up against the Lee buttons and the Lee posters and the Lee stickers, until after a while
a sudden efficient bustle of aides and police at the door began
to clear a path. Mayor Lee himself, laughing, joking, and shaking hands, made his way through the crowd to the wobbly
platform. He was understandably jubilant. The victory was
particularly sweet because it was larger than almost anyone had
expected, and represented a vindication and a comeback after
the close election of 1961.

Things did look good that night. We couldn't know that that
was a high point, and that the year to follow would bring a series of blows.

The assassination of President Kennedy was the first blow.
This happened just two and a half weeks after the victory in
the city election, and was especially hard for the New Haven
Democracy to take.

Whatever his political deficiencies in the Protestant and unsophisticated provinces, Mr. Kennedy was the perfect candidate
and the perfect President for New Haven, Connecticut: he was
Catholic and Irish, but also New England and Ivy League; he
was liberal, cultured, and intellectual, but he was also a regular
organization Democrat and a descendant of immigrants. He
was grandson of two ward politicians of the Eastern city's
streets; he also was young, glamorous, and rich, and he had
great style. He carried every one of the city's thirty-three wards
in the election of 1960. Had he been alive to run against Mr.
Goldwater in 1964, he would almost certainly have received a
majority beyond even the very large one that Mr. Johnson received, and have set a record for all the forseeable future.

The Irish, of course, loved him. Although the Irish are not as
visible or numerous as they once were in New Haven, they are
still evident in the Democratic Party. Pat Cassidy, for one, a

big, humorous laboring man — formerly a blacksmith — is
something of a patriarch of the Democratic Party in the Fifteenth Ward. He was an immigrant from Ireland as an adult.
He speaks with a brogue and has a Mr. Dooley or George
Washington Plunkitt humor. "It used to be," he said to a fellow
humorist one day when we were out campaigning, "that they
didn't make y' stop votin' till y' was dead five years; now these
reformers have got in and they have cut it down to two."

It was in the circles of the Democratic Party in the ward
that I first heard "God rest 'im," or "God ha' mercy on his soul,"
spoken as a quick phrase after the name of someone who had
died; in its proper setting it is rather a touching custom.

In the August when I was nominated I paid a visit to Cassidy's Restaurant and Men's Bar to discuss my candidacy. The
restaurant was founded by the late Martin Cassidy (they would
say, "God rest 'im"), brother of Pat Cassidy and once chairman
of the Fifteenth Ward, and now was run by the chairlady of the
ward. I found it to be a forthrightly political place in which the
waitresses wore Lee buttons. I also observed there upon the
wall behind the bar a large shamrock, and on the shamrock a
giant picture of President Kennedy.

After the ward committee meeting at which I was nominated,
Pat Cassidy looked me in the eye as we stood under a street-
light on the corner of Orange and Canner Streets and asked
me pointedly what I thought of President Kennedy, and then
Attorney General Kennedy, and in general the Kennedy family.
It was his litmus paper, I gathered, to test whether I was really
a genuine and acceptable Democrat. Fortunately my convictions were such as to enable me to pass that particular test. He
also asked how large a family I had, and I didn't do too badly
on that test, either. To have Kennedy be President of the United
States represented a vindication for all the years of precinct
work by these Irish Democrats of the American city. Mr. Kennedy made great gains in popularity once he held the great office, although he had been quite popular without it. The other

Catholic immigrant groups became more attached to him, and so, for somewhat different reasons, did the Jewish and Negro voters.

Much of Yale also liked, or came to like, Kennedy. He gave one of the notable speeches of his short Presidency when he was given an honorary degree by Yale University at its commencement in 1962. He sat on the platform — out-of-doors, on the old campus, on a perfect June day — busily revising his manuscript up to the last minute. His speech came a month after his blunt confrontation of the steel executives over the increase in steel prices, and featured an appeal to discard outmoded economic shibboleths.

Again in October of the following autumn he visited New Haven, to help the Democrats in that year's congressional elections. He came down Elm Street past the freshman dorms and some of the Yale residential colleges, on the sides and windows of which were signs that were by no means pro-Kennedy. Along with "Kennedy for King" and "Hell, I even miss Harry" were some that had to do with Cuba, such as "CASTRO LOVES DEMOCRATS." What none of us knew on that October night, as President Kennedy went down Elm Street past those signs, was that at this moment he had on his mind something even more important than the congressional elections: Russian missiles in Cuba. That New Haven visit came on the Tuesday of the first week, the unpublicized and silent week, of the Cuban missile crisis. On Monday, the day before he came to New Haven, Mr. Kennedy had been shown the photographs of the missile installations in Cuba. Even while he traveled and gave his speeches his advisers in Washington were holding a remarkable seminar on what the United States ought to do. On the day after his New Haven visit he canceled further campaign trips (the press was then told that he had a cold). On the following Monday he made the television speech that revealed the Cuban crisis to the world. Thinking back, one cannot avoid the irony of his coming down Elm Street, his mind no doubt back in Washington with that historic seminar, and reading signs saying "Castro loves Kennedy."

A year and a month after that last visit to New Haven President Kennedy was shot. Mayor Lee, who an aide said was "numb like Bobby Kennedy," went so far as to propose that the city build some kind of a memorial to President Kennedy on the spot on the New Haven Green where he had spoken; this proposal did not get anywhere — the Green has been protected for three hundred years against statues, memorials, and other incursions. Mayor Lee had been a friend of John Kennedy's when he was a Senator and when he was President. Just four weeks before the assassination Mr. Lee had been with the President at a ceremony in the White House Rose Garden at which he accepted an $800,000 grant to New Haven to combat juvenile delinquency. (The announcement of this grant, with a picture of Lee standing with Kennedy, had been well timed; it came during the last weeks of the city election campaign.) The Mayor had a close tie politically as well as personally with President Kennedy, which was not true with respect to the new President. During the city election of 1963, in fact, New Haven Democrats had more or less boycotted a fund-raising dinner for Senator Thomas Dodd, held in a New Haven suburb, because they resented its timing, while their own city campaign was in full swing. The then Vice-President, Lyndon Johnson, a friend of Dodd's, had been the guest of honor.

In the study at his new house on McKinley Avenue Mayor Lee has a shelf of Kennedy books and memorabilia and a bust of Kennedy. On the base of the bust, after Kennedy's name and dates, there is inscribed the text of the congratulatory telegram Lee received from Kennedy after his 1963 election victory: "Your re-election is a source of great comfort to us all."

On the Monday of President Kennedy's funeral, a local radio station taped a long discussion about Kennedy which turned out to be somewhat cathartic, at least for me. The participants included Mayor Lee, Mitchell Sviridoff, who was director of New Haven's antipoverty agency, and a few professors, one of whom was myself. Another was James Tobin, who had been a member of President Kennedy's Council of Economic Advisers; I remember that he said wistfully, "I wanted to see the flowering of the New Frontier." Among the Mayor's reactions were contradictory feelings, as a fellow city official, about the city administration of Dallas. He was angry at their inefficiency, and especially at their not having known about Oswald and taken precautions. Whenever the President comes to the city we always "make a sweep," Lee said. But then, on the other hand, as an official who feels a kind of personal responsibility for everything that happens in his city, he had an outburst of compassion for his Dallas counterparts, "God! Think what they must be going through!"

John F. Kennedy was the first thoroughly urban American President. Out in farm country, on his last tour of the nation in the fall of 1963, he described himself as "a city boy from an Eastern state who has never milked a cow or plowed a furrow, straight or crooked." He was the first American President to give urban affairs top priority. He was also the first President to make explicit — in his speech of June 11, 1963 — a full moral commitment to racial integration. Did he bring people along? Not as much as one would want. Kennedy was, and is, a celebrity; his popularity is to a considerable extent independent of the national issues with which he was identified. Nevertheless, I do notice now some quiet shifts of attitudes (on Negro rights, on money for city schools, on Catholic and non-Catholic relations, on the possibilities of politics) that are a heartening surprise. I think that one important cause of the hopeful present period in American domestic affairs was the life and death of John Fitzgerald Kennedy, God rest 'im.

The next blow to Lee and the New Haven Democrats had to do with the Mayor's own health. In the spring of 1964 he missed the St. Patrick's Day dinner for the first time in his political career. At the Yale commencement in early June he leaned on a friend and said, "I don't feel good." After shaking the hand of the most newsworthy of the persons receiving honorary degrees — Martin Luther King — Mayor Lee collapsed.

The city was full of rumors and worry and gossip about his health throughout the spring and summer. People continually asked an alderman "How is Dick?" "How is the Mayor?" There were fears and rumors that the Mayor's illness was something worse than was being reported; his friend, A. Whitney Griswold, the President of Yale, had died of cancer, in the spring of 1963, after being in and out of the hospital. The Mayor himself had the analogy of "Whit" on his mind. It turned out, however, that what he had was acute diverticulitis, a tension-related difficulty in the lower intestine.

When he came back to his office in the following September Mayor Lee explained that on the advice of his doctor he was now going to be "detached." I remember riding with him to his office one day. As he talked about the great detachment he planned to cultivate, he became passionate and articulate and colorful — and attached — in describing the things he wasn't going to let disturb him.

This illness kept him out of his office throughout the summer; the summer during which the downtown centerpiece of his renewal program finally reached its clinching point, and during which also the city had its fiercest row in recent history over the "busing" of schoolchildren to achieve racial balance. The story of that row might have been different had the Mayor been well.

2. The Board of Aldermen

"All right, Joe, put your teeth in
and make a speech."

Meanwhile I had become an alderman.

At first that office seemed mainly to consist of going to parties; people are always selling you, or trying to sell you, tickets
to luncheons, dances, dinners, and benefits — and soon you
are selling, or trying to sell, tickets yourself. In December
Arthur Barbieri, the town Democratic chairman, held a caucus
and a (free) party for the thirty Democratic aldermen; it
turned out to be about one part caucus to nine parts party.

The Democratic nominations for aldermanic offices — obviously equivalent to election since we Democrats controlled the
board 30 to 3 — were made with unanimity and dispatch, de-
layed only by a few friendly jokes ("All right, Joe, put your
teeth in and make a speech"). Then we had drinks, hors
d'oeuvre, food, more jokes, political conversation, and accor-
dion music for the rest of the evening. "How about some Irish
songs?" "No," said Barbieri, joking about his own role in New
Haven's heavily ethnic politics, "let's have nothing but Italian
songs all evening."

The Victory Ball of the city Democrats in the armory on
Goffe Street on January 6, 1964, was a splendid affair on a much
larger scale. At the height of the Grand March we all stopped
for a moment of silence in memory of the late President, but
otherwise it was a gay and partisan evening. The Governor of
Connecticut, John Dempsey, was there, and the Mayor was in

good spirits. The ward committees and prominent Democrats had paid for booths around the sides of the armory, out from which the dancing ones would sally onto the dance floor and the circulating ones (the larger number) would booth-hop around the armory, stopping to gossip and drink and chortle over the happy state of the city's Democrats and the sad state of the Republicans.

I like the social events accompanying city politics. Would I enjoy the same group under other, nonpolitical circumstances? Probably not. But linking the variety of human types with the shared interest and dramatic edge of politics makes it engaging.

I also like the word "alderman" better than substitutes like "city councilman." A city councilman is just a — well, a member of the city council, and there is obviously no mystery in *that*. It sounds like a boring "I second the motion" committee-meeting job, which is probably about what it is. Although being an alderman is the same thing, the word at least seems to have a certain weight and roundness. "In shape no bigger than an agate-stone/On the fore-finger of an alderman," Shakespeare wrote. "On the forefinger of a city councilman" wouldn't sound the same. "Alderman" has echoes of the long struggle of the human race to govern itself; also, in this country it has acquired a certain distinctive odor, as of old cheese. The old Board of Aldermen in New York City, before they changed in 1938 to the present shadowy city council was called — not without reason, one senses — the "Boodle Board" or the "Forty Thieves."

Speaking of odors. The association of cigar smoke with city politics holds absolutely true in my experience, as does also that of pipe tobacco with the higher reaches of academic life. On the first Mondays of the month my life recently has been a pleasant alternation of these two smells: university smells in the morning until eleven; City Hall smells in the Mayor's large and pleasant office from eleven to twelve, when the Democratic aldermen meet with the Mayor to discuss the items on the evening's agenda; university pipes again in the afternoon and in the evening at Morse College (one of Yale's residential colleges); then at eight back to the cigars at City Hall for the Democratic Party caucus and the aldermanic meeting itself. They make a nicely balanced day.

One professor with whom I had studied made a particularly grand and lengthy business of loading and lighting his pipe, tamping down the tobacco, sucking on the pipe, smoking a puff or two, and soon starting the whole thing over again (there was never very much actual smoking, so far as my memory records it), all of this closely intermingled with mulling and hemming and hawing and thinking and questioning over some large question in moral philosophy or social thought. When I return to that world after being away from it the smell of pipe tobacco brings it all back — the hedonistic paradox and Kierkegaard and dialectical materialism and the Nicomachean Ethics and the Summum Bonum and the Categorical Imperative and Plato's *Republic* and the nineteenth book of *The City of God* and Bentham-and-Mill and all the great questions that got smoked over in the book-lined office.

Cigar smoke in City Hall evokes quite a different set of associations: waivers, tax abatements, easements, and variances; unanimous consent (U.C. for short); first reading and second reading — WHEREAS, WHEREAS, WHEREAS; NOW THEREFORE, BE IT ORDERED; IT IS FURTHER ORDERED; NOW, THEREFORE, BE IT RESOLVED; "Your honorable Board"; "be given leave to withdraw"; lighting petitions, ordinances, and communications received. All smoked over in a rather different manner.

The New Haven Board of Aldermen chews cigars together once a month, on the first Monday. There are also special meetings held at the call of the mayor, and there are in addition meetings and hearings held by the several committees.

I was a member of the Committee on Sewers and Sanitation and the Committee on Manufacturing and Industry, neither of which ever met.

You may think of a board of aldermen or a city council as being roughly comparable at its own level to the legislature of the state and Congress of the United States; however that is not quite accurate. A council often has less relative power within its government than these sister bodies, and in any case along with the city government as a whole it is severely circumscribed by state law.

The governments of American cities vary widely not only in their formal arrangements — city manager, weak mayor-council, strong mayor-council, city commission — but also in the *real*, or informal, arrangement of power by which they are run. At least in the large and heterogeneous cities several trends run toward the reduction of the power, both on paper and in fact, of city councils: the strengthening of the office of mayor, the increased role of expert technicians and administrators, the growth of independent boards and commissions, and the heavy involvement of federal programs in city affairs.

Even on paper the New Haven Board of Aldermen is not the weightiest of the organs of city government. The way the city budget is enacted, for illustration, testifies eloquently to its lowly place. The annual budget is not primarily the work of the Board of Aldermen but rather of the Board of Finance. The Finance Board, except for the one aldermanic member whom the aldermen choose from among their own number, is appointed by the mayor, who serves as its chairman. It is traditionally the more conservative organ of city government. Throughout the months of summer the serious work is done; hearings are held and decisions are made with respect to the departmental requests. In September the budget composed from these decisions is presented to the Board of Aldermen for adoption — but with this decisive and rather revealing limitation, they are allowed only to lower, and never to raise, any appropriation. They are also allowed only to raise, and never to lower, proposed taxes. The fact is that action by the aldermen is a formality. They enact what the Board of Finance presents.

The aldermanic hearing on the budget is a formality, too, although a colorful one. It is the one occasion in this modern middle-sized New England city on which any citizen can speak his piece about city government, or any part of it — any part of it that appears in the budget, at least, which is about everything. We aldermen sit as a troop in the front of the public hearing room in the Hall of Records at 200 Orange Street, and listen to a long and varied string of testifiers, and then we enact the budget as it was presented to us.

Governing New York City, by Wallace Sayre and Herbert Kaufman, says that the work of New York's city council consists of "an abundance of trifles." "In the period from 1938 to 1956 approximately 2,100 local laws were passed by the City Council . . . Roughly 30 per cent of these dealt with naming streets, parks, and playgrounds; 25 per cent were detailed alterations of the Building Code (changes in specifications for values of certain kinds, for example); another 12 per cent transferred property from the jurisdiction of one city agency to another or to a borough office. These minor or fundamentally administrative acts thus made up two thirds of all local laws. . . . There can be no question that the great majority of Council actions either relate to its internal operations, minutiae, or trivia."

But Sayre and Kaufman also say, "Interlarded among the trivialities were a number of important acts: laws on rent control, garage and parking regulations, fire safety for multiple dwellings, traffic control, smoke control, the office of City Administrator, discrimination in housing, and others."

Both of these points are true also of New Haven's Board of Aldermen. A great part of what is done, either by the passing of ordinances (on which we take a roll call vote) or by the passing of resolutions or votes of approval (with a voice vote), is minor or routine or internal (we pass resolutions congratulating members on marriages and births — including the birth of a son of mine — in response to which cigars and candy are passed around). But interlarded among these are a few more substantial items: the Equal Opportunities Ordinance, an open-spaces program, the setting up of a charter commission on an elective school board.

The ordinances we pass are not world-shaking yet they may have some importance, such as those requiring swimming pools to be fenced, and food vendors to be licensed.

The ordinances passed in other cities generally have this same character of minor but worthwhile efforts to manage the complexity of modern urban life: in Duluth, levying a 50-cent per capita tax for rat extermination; in Lansing, forbidding sale or possession of model glue for sniffing purposes; in Toledo, prohibiting use of bicycles whose handlebars are fixed at above-shoulder levels; in San Bernardino, permitting unaccompanied minors to patronize poolrooms if they have parent's consent; in Akron, prohibiting operation of motor vehicles "in such a fashion as to spin or squeal tires" (tires are to be treated with respect in Akron); in Sheboygan, prohibiting keeping of chickens for commercial purposes; in Dallas, restricting smoking in large retail stores (this not long after a Neiman-Marcus fire). One could write a social history, I suspect, based on the laws and ordinances passed by American cities. The restriction of glue-sniffing and the permission for minors to patronize poolrooms turns up in more than one city just now. Airplane glue and the poolroom each has changed its significance. Although many of the recurrent ordinances might have been passed at other times — like tightening dance hall restrictions in Colorado Springs, or resetting penalties for prostitution and gambling in Rochester — a great many others reflect more recent efforts by cities to cope somehow with the new and spreading effects of technology: regulating disposal of junked automobiles in Sheboygan; requiring removal of doors of unused refrigerators in University City, Missouri; forbidding aircraft landings except in emergencies at points other than airports or heliports in Detroit; providing for continuity of municipal government in the event of enemy attack in Toledo.

The boards and councils in the recent years of urban renewal, and especially in New Haven, have had this new and potentially significant additional responsibility, that of passing on the renewal projects, piece by piece. We approve the steps in redevelopment. In the early summer of 1964, smack in the middle of the busing furor, we acted on the complicated $15 million "front block" project, with its hotel and office building and underground garage and shops, and with its three participating corporations. We held a hearing, and examined it and discussed it and queried the administrators about it, and had the majority leader draw a diagram of it in chalk on the board. But then, of course, we passed it as they had presented it to us. We examine what the city administration is doing and although we may ask a question or two we rarely change anything.

The board's passivity comes in for occasional negative comment. It is sometimes said to be merely a rubber stamp. Aldermen defend themselves by saying that there may be in some cases negotiation with aldermen *before* the administration presents its proposals; and that when one is in general agreement with the line of an administration's policy to vote regularly in favor of it is not to be a rubber stamp. Many aldermen would also like to say that the actions of the board are not the main part of their work. "Those League of Women Voters ladies just see us at the meetings," one long-time alderman said to me. "They don't see the service we do for our constituents. That's what I think the job is — service." By service he meant

getting sidewalks repaired and streetlights put up and variances granted, and being available to constituents as a kind
of contact man with city government. Much time was spent
on the great matter of lighting petitions. One new Republican
alderman conceived it to be his job to increase the light in his
ward, and steadily petitioned for streetlights, street by street.
We Democrats were thrown into paroxysms of strategy and
tactics to try to cope with this flood of Republican lighting petitions.

There is no pay, and the job is done in such hours as one
can spare. Most of the big issues are complicated, and one is
dependent upon the full-time experts from city departments —
most often from the Redevelopment Agency — to explain what
they are all about. Some professional city administrator regularly sits with the aldermen in the Mayor's office on the mornings of the Mondays on which the board meets, and answers
questions, and administrators are often called into the Democratic caucus in the evening to explain some action the board
is about to take.

On a night on which the honorable board is to meet, you
come out of the rain and darkness, through a revolving door
into New Haven's filigreed red nineteenth-century City Hall.
There on your left is a creeping antique iron elevator for those
who don't want to walk. For speedier ascent there directly
ahead is a very broad metal staircase. At the top of this staircase, standing around talking in little knots smoking their
cigars, stand the aldermen. There are scattered others — one
or two newsmen, the representative of the taxpayer's council,
perhaps one of the League of Women Voters, an occasional
extra-aldermanic politician or even a member of the public.
Going up this broad staircase — built for what grand entrances
and exits I cannot imagine — you join one of these little groups
and begin to talk about the affairs of the evening ("Nothing
much up tonight, is there?") and about politics and politicians.

Politics is an interest, like baseball, that a man can follow in the papers and talk over continually with his cronies. A fellow alderman suggests that a good ballet for some musical comedy like Fiorello could be made out of the premeeting shifts and groupings and regroupings of the aldermen getting ready to start the meeting.

Later than anyone intends, after floating conferences among the president of the board and the majority leader and perhaps the minority leader and the city clerk (who serves as a secretary to the board), somebody says "Okay, let's go." And we go, not into the aldermanic chambers but — we Democrats — upstairs to the third floor of City Hall, into an overheated and inadequate room, full of tired public health materials, where we hold a party caucus. This institution keeps the Democratic members often for longer than an hour, while the three Republicans occupy themselves somehow downstairs. Usually this caucus includes more substance than the actual board meeting which follows it. The majority leader stands at the head of the table and brings up for discussion each item that is to come before the board. Most of the time there is not much argument but sometimes, as in the days of the racial items, there is a sharp exchange or two. If there is a question we cannot answer, the sheriff is sent down to capture some administrator to explain it to us. Where there is disagreement the majority leader may ask for a vote, to see what the proportions are. Then, having worked over the agenda in our fashion, we go down to the aldermanic chamber and the meeting starts — at 9:15 or 9:35 or 10:20. Sometimes it is over in twenty minutes.

The aldermen in New Haven during this time included a private detective, an ambulance driver, a mattress salesman, a band leader, the driver of a beer truck, a machinist at Winchester's who is also a labor union official, the driver of a diaper service truck, a Negro waitress who was going to night school, a physical education instructor with bulging shoulders, a liquor store operator, a swimming suit maker, a time-study man, a

teacher of marketing at Quinnipiac College, a Linotype operator at the *Register,* an insurance agent, a real estate man, a
housewife, a secretary, two professors at Yale Divinity School,
and of course several lawyers. There were three Negroes and
there were almost certainly soon to be one or two or three more.
More than a third of the aldermen were of Italian extraction
and one — as is traditional from the Thirteenth Ward — was
of Polish background. About five were Jewish and seven or
eight were of Irish background.

The casting of votes in a legislative assembly is one of
those few institutions in real life which do approach the possibilities of drama on the stage, like the climax of a jury trial.
It must have been quite a moment in the United States Senate
on June 10, 1964, for instance, when after 75 days of filibuster
the clinching vote for cloture on the civil rights bill was cast,
and Hubert Humphrey, counting the votes at his seat, raised
both hands above his head in a silent sign of victory. On
weighty matters in such an august body there is an expectant
hush as the tally starts, and a quiet and concentration as the
feeling passes through the watching people that the moment
of decision has come. As the yeas and nays are called out
each is received with a murmur of appraisal. Sometimes there
is a gasp, as at the first loud Nay vote by the as yet uncharac-
terized new Senator from Arizona in the Eighty-third Congress.
When the voting is close unofficial tallies are kept, with a
steady, breathless mathematics. Then there is a bustle and
whispering when the tally is complete, before the result is announced; in the Senate there are also the latecomers who call
out to get themselves recorded.

To make an abrupt descent — even votes on the Board of
Aldermen of New Haven offer a certain piquant interest, at
least to those involved. We have had in my time two
complicated series of votes on which the outcome was in doubt.

One was on three amendments to an open-spaces bill, in which one parcel of land was voted out and another voted in, and a resolution against the East Rock highway connector was defeated. Another series was on questions asked us by the charter commission that was to reapportion the city's wards.

On the reapportionment matter we were asked whether this commission could reduce the number of Aldermen (New Haven's number is regarded as excessive by good-government people) and whether it could recommend compensation for the aldermen. It was thought that answers to these two questions would go together, since realistically the city probably could afford to pay the aldermen only if there were fewer of them. Nevertheless, the board in its collective wisdom gave this pair of answers: No, you may not reduce our number, but yes, you may give us pay.

I voted with the minority to allow the charter commission at least to consider the reduction in the number of aldermen (their decision would then come back to the aldermen, and then go to the people, for decision), but I do not necessarily think that the board's unwillingness to allow that to be contemplated is as obtuse as it may sound.

Of course, a parliamentary body like this one is not the best judge of itself. A club spirit develops, as in the United States Senate, one traditionalist, conservative, easygoing, inclined toward logrolling and back-scratching, resistant to change and especially change that would endanger any fellow club member's seat. Those who adopt this club spirit — reflected, with respect to the Senate, in the book by William S. White called *The Citadel* — tend to put the internal convenience of the members, in particular the senior members, and the smooth operation of the parliamentary body, above any service to the public that might make a strain. These parliaments ordinarily are not going to be able to take an objective look at themselves, or to generate internally the strength for reform. That is one reason why it is good for the courts to have taken up the matter of reapportionment. Legislative bodies aren't going to reapportion their own members out of their jobs. And that is why it would have been good to have had a charter commission outside the Board of Aldermen consider the whole range of questions about its composition. However, as to the merits, the conservative aldermen are not without their points.

Three closely related questions are asked about the arrangements of city councils. First, should they be chosen by *partisan* election, as in New Haven, New York City, Philadelphia, St. Louis, and Chicago (in fact), or by *nonpartisan* elections, as in Detroit, Boston, San Francisco, Denver, and especially many other cities in the West? Second, should they be chosen at large, from the city as a whole, as in Pittsburgh, Dallas, Detroit, Boston, and many cities especially of the nonpartisan type? Or should they be chosen from subdivisions of the city — wards, precincts, districts — as in New Haven, New York, Chicago, Cleveland, and Milwaukee? Some cities, most notably Philadelphia, have a combination, with some members at large and some from districts. New York's council president is chosen from the city as a whole. Third, should the number of councilmen be large, as in Chicago with its 50 aldermen and New Haven with its 33, or small, as in Minneapolis with 13 or Los Angeles with 15 or Philadelphia with 17 or Gary, Indiana, where the vote on its open-occupancy ordinance was 5 to 3?

Answers to these three questions cluster somewhat, although there is also much mixture and variety: nonpartisanship, at-large election, and small councils tend to go together and tend to be favored by good-government forces. New Haven, therefore, with a large, partisan, subdivided board is "wrong" from that point of view, on every count. Its board, however, is not as bad as that might make it seem.

Partisan elections seem to me at least desirable in large cities, where there are diverse interests and groups. Party competition, by giving the masses organization, helps to keep the middle class and the newspapers and the business community from running everything. Party life in local affairs helps the parties to be alive when state and national elections come around; for that matter, with the large role of Washington and the state capital in city affairs, larger national party connections are no longer irrelevant to local issues. Reformers of another day wished above all to disconnect local affairs from national party labels. Even if they were right in their own day they aren't right for today.

One argument in favor of city-wide election and a small paid council is that "better people" will be more willing to run in that circumstance; I would want to examine that idea of better people for its implicit class bias. It also is argued, and this is perhaps the crucial point, that such a council will take a broad rather than a parochial view, and will be in accord with the mayor, since it is elected from the same city-wide constituency and is not beholden to one small neighborhood. Is it altogether undesirable to have one organ of government that does represent the neighborhoods? Most wards in New Haven are small enough so that an energetic alderman can ring every doorbell in his ward, and can know the people fairly well. That seems to me a virtue.

Smaller bodies are supposed to be more efficient and businesslike, too. But the larger number of aldermen isn't all that cumbersome, and with subdivision into wards you gain a rather clear reflection of the actual state of public opinion and popular values in the city. The middle-class reformer may unconsciously — or perhaps even consciously — want everyone on a city council to be like himself, and is impatient with the parochialism and narrow neighborhood interest, and perhaps also sometimes the lack of polish and education, of many aldermen chosen under this old New Haven system. The views and characteristics the aldermen so chosen reflect are in fact genuinely present in the body politic. Should we shape institutions to *avoid* their expression? Or work with them as they are? *

Most of the significant decisions for New Haven city government are worked out in the mayor's office and in the city departments and agencies, not in the Board of Aldermen. The aldermen can participate, at least, in some significant decisions, as they did in the Equal Opportunities Ordinance. I was completely in favor of the ordinance myself. FEPC had been part of my earliest political upbringing. The only time I had ever appeared before any parliamentary body, prior to these aldermanic adventures, was before a committee of the unicameral legislature of the state of Nebraska on Good Friday of 1947 in behalf of a proposed state Fair Employment Practices Commission. Other university students who testified on that day included the co-ed whom I later married and Theodore Sorensen, who was later to be employed by John Kennedy.

That was an extraordinarily futile time and place for such a venture, but since then, with the civil rights history of the intervening years, the prospects for FEPC legislation have gradually brightened. By the time New Haven came to consider its city ordinance in 1964, 25 states, including Connecticut, had state laws in the fair employment field, and 17 states, also including Connecticut, had fair-housing laws (additional states are now considering such laws). About 60 municipalities had civil rights ordinances, including New York, Philadelphia, Pittsburgh, and Baltimore. New Haven became the first city in Connecticut to enact one.

This enactment began, significantly, with a speech by President Kennedy. In the summer of 1963 Mayor Lee, the outgoing chairman, had presided at the annual meeting of the United

___

* In the spring of 1966 another charter commission, set up to reapportion, proposed that the Board of Aldermen be reduced to ten members, with salaries of $2500. But would the board, and then the people in a referendum, enact that change?

States Conference of Mayors in Honolulu, to which meeting President Kennedy gave an address. This happened exactly at the time of the crisis in Alabama in which Governor Wallace tried to block the door at the University, and immediately before the President's notable civil rights speech on television. In Honolulu Mr. Kennedy asked the assembled mayors to bend their efforts to the securing of human rights in each of their cities, at which local level, city by city, the battle against discrimination would in large part have to be won. ". . . What happens in Birmingham or Chicago or Los Angeles or Atlanta depends in large measure upon the leadership of those communities." He specifically suggested that local governments enact ordinances to protect equal opportunities. "Such measures are not the exclusive concern of the federal government."

Mayor Lee responded to this presidential request when he returned home by appointing a New Haven Human Rights Committee, with Louis H. Pollak of the Yale Law School (and the Fifteenth Ward) as its chairman. This committee held hearings, gathered data, and presented recommendations to the Mayor and to the Board of Aldermen in the spring of 1964. In their letter of transmittal the committee referred immediately and explicitly to the late President Kennedy as the originating impulse.

The finding of the Pollak committee, to no one's surprise, was that discrimination existed in New Haven. The recommendation of the committee was, chiefly, the setting up of an agency to promote fair employment and fair housing in the city. The arguments against it were the same ones used in Nebraska in 1947 — it won't work, it is unconstitutional, and it relies on Force to do something that should be done voluntarily. It interferes, that is, with Freedom. The defenders of these actions ask in return: Whose freedom? And *which* freedom? "Freedom for the shark is death for the minnow." These so-called freedoms compounded create a pattern that is freedom-destroying for the victim, and the point of these laws, of course, is to alter that pattern. Fair-employment and fair-housing laws are intended to put the law on the side of the men who want to act justly. One lone employer or one realtor or developer may feel that he alone cannot violate the pattern, even if he wants to; the law gives him a chance (and an excuse). A thousand times those of us who support such laws have had to answer the notions that "you can't change men's hearts by law" and that what is needed is the "slow process of education" rather than law and force.

The immediate point, obviously, is not to change men's hearts but to change their actions (hiring, firing, selling, renting) and those can be changed by law, to give Negroes rightful opportunities for jobs and houses, even if hearts are not changed. But then — on the second round, so to speak — one may change some hearts and actually do some education by changing the objective social situation: seeing and knowing Negroes in what the sociologists call "equal status contacts" (neighbors, co-workers) helps to break stereotypes and to put real people in place of fearful imaginings. Whitney Young, Jr., of the Urban League, speaking in New Haven in that same spring, said, "If you want to know how race relations are, don't ask your maid: 'Oh, jes' fine, m'am, jes' fine.'"

The fear of force in the New Haven ordinance centered chiefly on the powers of subpoena and injunction. The notion of the subpoena power seemed to be particularly frightening. The agency was to have this power in two regards: in the routine investigation of specific complaints, for which it would obviously be necessary, and in the investigations on its own initiative of fields in which patterns of discrimination are suspected to exist. The second is a more unusual step. The agency also was to be empowered to ask for a temporary injunction against allegedly discriminating landlords — an essential device for preventing a sale or rental before the agency can resolve a case.

There was considerable anxiety about the subpoena and the injunction; these sounded like fearful powers, by which the agency could keep a small businessman or landlord tied up in litigation over alleged discrimination, "drag him into court," and do him great harm. We had an informal meeting of some of the aldermen in the basement of one alderman's home to talk this over. Then before we brought the ordinance to a vote the controversy over the general subpoena power had a curious outcome, an apparent compromise that was not a compromise at all. In place of the specific language in the proposed ordinance which said exactly how the subpoena power was to be used, and how it was limited, the aldermanic committee on ordinances — at the suggestion of the *New Haven Register* — simply incorporated language from the city charter granting to the agency, the Equal Opportunities Commission, exactly the same subpoena powers that are granted by the charter to all city commissions. This had a reassuring sound to it: the agency had only the powers possessed by all other city commissions. It meant the same thing as before, though, except that the specific limitations on the use of that power had been removed!

The other large argument struck at the ordinance as a whole and had to do with legal propriety. Since the state had taken action in this field, it was held, the city could not constitutionally take action in the same field. Our American cities are not independent governmental entities but are creatures of the state, with only those powers that the state governments grant to them. Constitutionally, the cities do not exist; there are only the states, the "people," and the federal union. One long chapter in local-government books has to do with home rule — that is, with what powers the states do and what powers they do not grant to the cities and towns. Characteristically cities have been frustrated by the narrow bounds within which they must move. Much of the importance of the reapportionment of state legislatures rests here. It should give cities a voice proportionate to their size in a state government that very much affects their life.

May a city enact legislation exactly in a field in which the state has laws? Connecticut does have state laws in both of these fields — fair housing and fair employment — that go well beyond anything in the federal Civil Rights Act, and they are among the most satisfactory in the nation from a civil rights point of view.

There *had* been some legal questionings about earlier efforts to pass a fair-housing ordinance in New Haven, because the standards for application of the New Haven ordinance differed from those in the state laws. But this time the drafters of the ordinance carefully made those standards precisely the same as those of the state, which had since been tightened, so that ground for a legal challenge was removed. The Connecticut state law now prohibits racial discrimination in the sale of any house and in the rental of any unit except in a two-family house that is occupied by the owner (the federal civil rights law, after the famous discussion of "Mrs. Murphy" and her roominghouse, allows a wider immunity, of four units). Connecticut state law prohibits discrimination in employment by any firm with 8 or more employees (the federal law specifies 100 or more employees at first, reducing the number gradually to 25).

The New Haven ordinance simply takes over those provisions of the Connecticut state law and sets up an agency to apply them within the city. The reason for this apparent duplication is to provide more funds and people, in order to apply the law that is on the books. Although the formal provisions of the Connecticut law are good, from a Negro rights point of view, there is a catch in the provision, or nonprovision, of funds and personnel to enforce the law. The Connecticut Civil Rights Commission had only four full-time investigators for the entire state — 169 towns, 3 million people, ½ million Negroes. The state legislature, which until the reapportionment was dominated by the small towns, was not perhaps as passionately concerned about this largely urban matter as it might have been, and though it passed the law, it did not provide the kind of money and staff that would make the law fully effective. The regular experience was that, in the housing field, for example, houses were sold or apartments were rented before the investigations had been made, the hearings held, and decisions reached. The case had become, as lawyers say, moot. New Haven's city ordinance was intended to help, mainly by providing another agency to enforce the existing state law within the city. Also, the agency would be nearby, and not up in Hartford.

Legal experts bloomed on every hand, however, to insist that the city ordinance was not constitutional; the state, they said, had pre-empted the field. This position on a rather recondite point was forcefully put forward by persons who were not lawyers at all, and who, I think it would be safe to guess, had not had an opinion on the constitutionality of any other matter in their lives. They persisted in their constitutional opinions despite the testimony of the Attorney General of the state and the Corporation Counsel of the city, both of whom said that in their opinion the New Haven ordinance was valid, and that in fact many cities located in other states with such state laws also have laws of their own.

The hearings held by aldermanic committees are usually rather cozy affairs. A handful of people affected by the matter sit mumbling their case across the table to a sleepy handful from the honorable board. Sometimes the citizens have a certain fire in their eyes, but they rarely kindle any in anybody else's. The two commercial fishermen who still use it don't want the board to demolish the city dock, which has been declared unsafe by the Public Works director; the city's garage operators want the board to enact stiff fines against car owners who sneakily recover their own cars, towed when illegally parked, without paying the towing fee; the lady who owns a house on a busy corner wants an exception made to the zoning laws so that she could sell her house to a gas station outfit, but the residents of the street vigorously object. Usually those who testify have distinctly the aspect and the sound of the common man.

When the Blakeslee Construction Company or the United Illuminating Company comes in to defend some interest of its own, the smoothly glib and well-dressed lawyer, flanked by eminent corporation vice-presidents, creates quite a contrast.

The hearing on the Equal Opportunities Ordinance was a contrast, too: a different, bigger room, a microphone, large crowds, applause, cheering, barely suppressed booing, a passionately interested public. I went to that hearing, one night late in April 1964, expecting the opposition to the ordinance to be strong. One could not help knowing that some white citizens of New Haven were racially prejudiced and that others, whether prejudiced or not, were much worried by the ordinance. This new proposal was stronger than the two fair-housing ordinances that had failed to pass and, since it involved employment as well as housing, it covered more territory.

I expected a clash, but there wasn't much of one. The room was packed. A large part of the audience were Negro, and another large part were white civil rights people, who gave their testimony on behalf of an assortment of religious, educational, labor and brotherhood groups. Sprinkled in among the official presentations were some unofficial and individual ones, and many of these, especially by Negroes, were effective.

The testimony against the ordinance, on the other hand, was dreadful. I remember a Kennedy man saying after the struggle at the 1960 Democratic convention in Los Angeles that if they had gone down to a casting agency and picked the people they wanted for Stevenson supporters they couldn't have done any better — from their point of view as opponents — than the bearded, sandaled Southern California kooks who actually cast themselves for that role. Similarly, if we who supported the New Haven Equal Opportunities Ordinance had been able to pick our own opponents we couldn't have selected better adversaries than the people who served in that capacity at the public hearing. They were dull, legalistic, and long-winded. They had to give their addresses, which regularly proved to be out-of-town ones. They were lawyers paid to speak for the Real Estate Board and the Chamber of Commerce or officials of the Republican Party. The Chamber's opposition, by the way, was not total. The president of the Chamber, in fact, had been a member of the committee that proposed the ordinance. The Mayor's appointing of this Chamber of Commerce man and of the publisher of the *New Haven Register,* both of whom gave some people a surprise by signing the committee's report, doubtless helped the ordinance to pass.

The testimony alternated on each side in half-hour allotments. As the testimony wound along I noticed, standing over by the wall and not exactly seeking out my eye, a close associate from among the Democrats of the Fifteenth Ward: my former campaign manager, Bob Reilly. When the time for opponents came around for the third time he went forward and testified against the ordinance.

After the hearing the committee on ordinances brought its favorable report, with the change about the subpoena, to the board meeting for a vote. The aldermen sit at schoolboy desks in three rows, with the president (a senior alderman), the city clerk, and the sheriff at a high desk in front. Much of any meeting is taken up with those noncontroversial matters — petitions, resolutions, votes of approval — on which there is the unanimous consent that allows the board to act immediately, without waiting for the procedure of first and second readings, and going over to a subsequent meeting, that is otherwise required. To grant U.C. the aldermen stand, although the standing becomes rather feeble. Then the matters granted such consent are dealt with by voice vote. On ordinances there must be a roll call vote. The city clerk calls the wards successively. Sometimes one doesn't quite know how one will vote, even when the roll call begins, and sometimes there is a chuckle when an alderman wiggles a moment before he says Yes or No or (occasionally) Abstain.

When we came down into the aldermanic chambers after our caucus on the night of the vote on the Equal Opportunities Ordinance we found a small crowd waiting. This was unusual, since ordinarily only a handful watch our sessions from the benches in the back. (To tell the truth our public sessions are mumbly and unimpressive). The question was by how large a margin the ordinance would pass. There were a few very brief speeches, although we don't go in much for speeches on the New Haven Board of Aldermen, and then the city clerk began to call the wards. The Yes votes sounded along the front row — the wards on the Hill — in heartening fashion, and kept coming along the second row and the third row with only the most certain exceptions, the three Republicans plus only three conservative Democrats. The tally was 26 to 6, an impressive margin.

One of the men who voted No whispered rather embarrassedly to a Negro alderman, "Congratulations, Bruce," when the result was announced.

Why did this ordinance, in spite of the failure of two less inclusive ordinances in the recent past and in spite of considerable public resistance, now pass so easily? Why did this civil rights effort go so smoothly, when in contrast the subsequent effort to integrate schools met nothing but bumps, blocks, and resistances? Most importantly, because the political leadership was aggressively in favor of it. The Mayor's was the first testimony for the ordinance to be presented at the public hearing. Mr. Barbieri actively supported it, and is generally credited with having helped along some aldermanic votes; perhaps the fact that the Registrar of Vital Statistics had died and an appointment to that post was pending was not altogether without its enlightening influence. At the private preparatory meeting in the basement of an alderman's home I asked innocently, as a new alderman, what the chances of passing the ordinance in its full strength were. "If the Mayor and Barbieri really want it," I was told, "they can pass it even if it puts these fellows in chains." To this one wit responded, "We had that in the earlier version, before we softened it."

There was careful preparation, and objections were met in negotiations before the actual joining of public battle and vote. Laymen underestimate, I think, the amount of prevote politicking in legislatures. And fair-employment and fair-housing agencies have a far wider acceptance and a longer history than busing. Then, too, I think the ease with which the Equal Opportunities Ordinance passed was deceptive. There was more resistance to it in the public feeling than showed itself either at the public hearing or in the aldermanic vote. Frustrated opposition stored itself away to burst out doubly strong on the school integration question.

3. De Facto School Segregation

"It's the buses over the hill in the winter."

I HAD BEGUN TO REALIZE during the winter of 1963–1964 that something was coming on the school integration question, and there surely was. There were anticipatory sprinklings throughout the school year, and then in the late spring a cloudburst.

The New Haven Board of Education had hired two capable women to make a study and suggest alternatives for New Haven's school system, in order to meet the antisegregation commitment that the board had made in September 1963. These two women worked throughout the winter visiting schools, talking to teachers, traveling to Princeton and New York.

There was already a considerable collection of ideas about "de facto segregation" in Northern schools. A month after the Supreme Court's decision on May 17, 1954, against legally segregated schools, Kenneth B. Clark, the psychologist whose work had been cited in a footnote to that decision, underlined the significance of the decision for the North as well as the South. The Supreme Court, he said, held that segregation damages human personality, and this would apply to Northern segregation-in-fact as well as to Southern segregation-by-law. Since that time, and especially with the acceleration of the civil rights movement in the sixties, efforts had been made to integrate the schools of many Northern cities. Each city had its own little tale to tell.

New Rochelle, New York, was the first city in the North to

have a court order against its segregated schools, in 1961. In that case, however, the New Rochelle school board, according to the judge's decision, had deliberately frozen the Negro children into one elementary school (the Lincoln School). In cases — like New Haven's — in which school segregation-in-fact arises not from deliberate school board policy but from residential patterns, the courts have not *required* that school boards act to correct it. But they certainly may.

Princeton had "paired" two schools, one primarily white and one primarily Negro, sending all the children of a given grade from both schools to one school, all the children of another grade from both schools to the other school. My oldest daughter went to one of these Princeton public schools for her first grade, but we didn't know until we had moved away from Princeton that she had been participating in a significant social experiment. Although we had seen a number of Negroes in the school it was not until we moved to New Haven and began to read about the integration of Northern schools that we realized what it was all about. I daresay there are parents moving to New Haven right now who will innocently send their children off to public school completely unaware of the spiritual blood that has been spilled over those schools.

The two women in New Haven examined the mysteries of de facto school segregation and made a report to the New Haven board. Among the measures that have been used to integrate Northern schools are these: changing of school zones; open enrollment or free-transfer arrangements; pairing as in the Princeton plan; and strategically locating the sites for new schools. This original New Haven plan combined the first two of these. It proposed the rezoning of one junior high and the creating of subsystems — clusters of schools — within which there could be free transfer from one school to another if the receiving school had room.

Those proposals could be said to have been, as their proponents kept insisting, moderate. Miss June Shagaloff, in fact, said — getting out her copy of the blue-covered New Haven booklet, in NAACP headquarters at 20 West 40th Street in New York, and remembering how she had felt when she first saw the thing — that she was very disappointed by New Haven's proposals, because they were so minimal and insufficient. "We expected more of New Haven than, say, Gary, Indiana," Miss Shagaloff said, rather reproachfully. The proposals probably sound, in calm cold print read by a reader in his armchair in another city, like a quite unexceptional and minor change of school districts and nothing at all for anybody to become excited about. The main item and the only really controversial proposal would have changed merely the "feeder patterns" (as the school people call it) of only two of New Haven's thirty-one grammar schools — Worthington Hooker was one of the two — to reroute their children to a different junior high school. That was almost all. There was not even to be much busing, in reality. Most of the rerouted children could walk, and some of them were actually nearer to their new junior high than they had been to their old one. That great and terrible "bus," nevertheless, sprang instantly into minds of fearful parents as a symbol of the menace of the whole idea. The two grammar schools (Worthington Hooker, whose top two grades were to be abolished, had actually been an eight-graded school; the other, Beecher School, has six grades) were almost entirely white. The junior high school to which the children were newly to be sent, Bassett Junior High, was 91 percent Negro, was located in a now predominantly Negro section, and had a negative reputation among many of the white parents.

This set of proposals was presented, before its public release, to a committee of citizens. It also was presented to another committee, one made up of teachers and administrators, but not much was heard from this one.

As it turned out, having a citizens' committee, unfortunately sometimes called a blue-ribbon committee, was a mistake. Apparently the intention had been to employ the same device that had been used in New Haven's redevelopment program with great success: to gain acceptance from leading and representative citizens on an advisory committee before the plans were presented to the broad public. Although that worked well in redevelopment, it did not work at all in the racial-balance plan. Instead, the composition of the committee was sharply and instantly attacked as soon as the names were known. "There's nobody at all on it from east of the river," said one opponent.

The committee appeared to the opponents to be composed primarily of persons of liberal leaning and of a generally favorable predisposition in civil rights matters. And it was not felt to be representative either of the city as a whole or of the people most affected. Mothers could take the list and name off which blue-ribbon citizens had their own children in private schools and which ones did not live in New Haven but in white suburbs, which ones when you called them turned out not even to have read the proposals, and which ones were such established and professional civil rights people as somehow not to count. Listening to one woman ticking off this list reminded me of pious Republican maiden ladies in my Midwestern childhood disdainfully naming all the divorces in the Franklin Roosevelt family.

The New Haven newspapers printed the proposals before their release time, so the angry discussion had a head start on itself. Imbedded in a list of thirteen new proposals for the schools — many of them good ideas which mostly got lost in the shuffle — was the redistricting of the Bassett Junior High School and also some cluster arrangements that would allow voluntary attendance on the part of Negro children at previously white elementary schools like Worthington Hooker. These caused a furor. For some Hooker pupils the proposals meant that, having gone for seven grades to this school and expecting to go to the eighth and final grade, with a small graduation flourish at the end, they were sent abruptly to a different school for the eighth grade. It also meant that these pupils would be going to a predominantly Negro school. The blue booklet that set forth the proposals stated that when they "were fully in operation" the Bassett Junior High School would be 50 percent white. However, in the first two years they would not yet be fully in operation, and the proposals did not allow for such withdrawals as might be made by white students.

The PTA's of the two predominantly white schools that were to send their pupils now to Bassett — Beecher and Worthington Hooker — reacted early and strongly against the proposals. Both had angry meetings, even before the plan was officially put forward; at both a vote was taken to oppose the redistricting.

Our meeting took place, of course, in the basement of the Worthington Hooker School. It was nominally a meeting of the school's PTA, but it was a much bigger and more electric gathering than any PTA meeting had been before. There was a crowd, and many new faces. There were catcalls and loud heckling from the people standing in the back. People I had called on and worked with in the fall were scattered throughout the crowd, on opposite sides. As I sat down a man sitting behind me, who had voted for me in the election, said, "You'd better vote right on this!" From his point of view, I didn't. At one point somebody said, "You people just don't want your children to go to school with Negroes," and that brought shouts of protest. The crowd obviously had been touched where it hurt. One woman managed to call out repeatedly her contrary point, in a metrical refrain: "It's the buses over the hill in the winter." Other objections did not scan as well, but they had the same general effect. They opposed the school integration plan on grounds having nothing to do with race. It's the traffic on Whitney Avenue; it's the danger in that other neighborhood, where there is broken glass all over the playground; it's the convenience and desirability of the Neighborhood School; it's the friends the kids have made; it's the quality of their education; it's the money we paid to buy a house in this school district.

Many civil rights people greeted all these efforts at argument with complete cynicism, as being nothing but rationalizations of racial prejudice. At a city-wide meeting of racial-balance defenders somewhat later in that turbulent month, I listened with sympathy while one survivor of the Worthington Hooker PTA meeting, a supporter of the busing plan, tried in vain to convince the integrationist group that not all the opposition was racism. This effort was greeted with instant snorts of complete and derisive unbelief.

Some civil rights militants refuse to grant any motive other than racism to the opponents of any civil rights action. They are very quick on the trigger with epithets like "bigot," and they spot hypocrisy on every side.

And not without reason. Because the civil rights advocate has encountered so much hypocrisy and nonsense, he expects it every time. Just as the Negro, whose color is perforce a fact in his life, has a difficult time discerning which disadvantages accrue to him from social injustice and which are part of his individual life or the common life, so also the civil rights person, having encountered endless runarounds and sleights-of-hand, has a hard time believing that there is any other kind of response. His well-founded skepticism makes it difficult for honest argument against any civil rights proposal to make itself heard. The ordinary white person struggling through his life without much sense of community responsibility feels hard pressed to resist anything that comes with a civil rights label. His inarticulate self-interested protests are heard as a wholly reprehensible racism. "I can say that I don't want my children sent to Fair Haven Junior High, because of the element there, but I can't say that about Bassett."

In June 1964, while Yale boys were heading south to join an effort to register Negroes, called the Mississippi Summer Project, New Haven had an unusual summer project of its own. The citizens gathered for two long, hot series of meetings, at which these school proposals were shouted over. The first series was to be informational and the second series of four was the official set of public hearings, at which opinions could be expressed. The so-called informational meetings in general turned into attack and defense, too, rather than requests for information (some of the questions were like this: "Is this Communist Russia or Cuba? Or What?"), and as a result the meetings were fairly similar throughout both series. Some of them had to be shifted from junior high schools to high school auditoriums because of their size. Rarely has there been such widespread citizen participation in a civic proposal in New Haven. The school board sat on the platform at each of these gatherings, and one of its members served as chairman. Throughout the so-called informational hearings the antagonism simmered and boiled and gathered steam. Then with the formal public hearings, especially the first one, the opposition blew off the lid. There were four hearings proper, one at each of New Haven's junior high schools, on the nights of June 22 through June 25. The speaking time was divided between those opposed and those in favor, a half hour for one side and a half hour for the other.

In the huge old auditorium of Fair Haven Junior High, on the night of Monday, June 22, the proponents, speaking first, were mostly university types, and Human Relations Council people, and individuals from various professions, and League of Women Voters ladies. The opponents waited for their turn, grumbling and angry, and when it came they burst out at these "people who live up around the high-class areas" with jeers and boos. There were sizzling arguments among different groups in the audience, policemen striding around in the back of the room, and booing and cheering and hissing and electricity in the air. There were extracurricular arguments out on the stairway.

Inside the auditorium comments like this could be heard:

"Our local universities are producing many fine intellects that will help carve our nation's growth. They are also harboring some unusual ones who should confine their displays to the university grounds alone (*loud cheers*). If they have any excess energy that has to be released, I suggest that they release it in their home towns."

The evening ended, after much emotion had been spilled, with a powerful speech against the proposals by a popular alderman of Italian background who comes from the Fourteenth Ward — a ward just next to the Fifteenth but a sociological world away, entirely "on the other side of Orange Street." His speech was at once slow and sober in manner and passionate in content, a combination that his followers appreciated. He referred back to the Sargent Report.

As one of the progressive efforts of the Lee administration, New Haven had had in 1960–1961 a thorough study of its school system made by an educator named Cyril Sargent. His report formed the basis for the rebuilding of the system that had been under way since that time: 15 new schools — 40 percent of the system — were to be built. Included in this Sargent Report were sentences about the advantages of the "neighborhood school." In New Haven as in New York the antibusers seized on the concept of the neighborhood school as their positive symbol ("the neighborhood school seems to become more sacred the nearer Negroes move to it," one student of these matters remarked). But in New Haven this concept had a kind of official endorsement in the city's school study.

It is notable, indeed, that as recently as 1960–1961 an enlightened city like New Haven should have made a thorough study of its school system without raising any question about racial balance, and with a quite explicit commitment to the neighborhood school, at least for the lower grades. The antibusers now triumphantly and angrily brandished this Sargent Plan commitment. The alderman, quoting it, said that there had been a "breach of faith," and a large part of the Fair Haven audience stood and cheered.

To attend the four hearings was to make a sociological tour of New Haven. The city's four junior high schools had a predominantly ethnic identity: Fair Haven Junior High, Italian; Bassett, Negro; Troup, recently, half Negro; and Sheridan, where the second hearing was held, Jewish.

Occasionally, in the old days before the district lines became important, a Jewish parent from a distant district like Hooker's could receive permission to have her child go all the way to Sheridan Junior High. One source of anguish in the school board's proposed redistricting came from this ethnic source: Beecher, a Westville grade school, had fed, along with other schools having many Jewish pupils, into Sheridan Junior High and thence into Hillhouse High School — once one of the nation's outstanding high schools. Generations of Jewish parents with high educational standards had helped to make this educationally the best set of public schools in the city. The proposal to rip Beecher loose from this and to send its children instead in another direction, to Bassett, caused much ethnic hemorrhaging. "You can't expect people to *sacrifice* their children's education," a Beecher parent, a Yale professor, said to me. "And then — you have to admit it — part of it is *ethnic*."

By the time of the Sheridan hearing Westville had already had its first and most virulent outbursts, an angry meeting from which rabbis were excluded and an "information" meeting with the school board at which the crowd insisted that each board member tell where his children went to school, and then booed openly when one told of a child in private school. It was after this fierce encounter that some of the board wondered whether they could hold out through this ordeal. Now a certain reaction against the virulence of the first outburst had set in, and a certain cooling off — to the point where there could be humor.

One man introduced himself, with effective irony, as "residing in the heart of the Beecher school area, better known these past two weeks as the Friendly Village, and the place of instant friendship." When this brought a laugh he went on, "I am elated to see so many people laughing, and our good superintendent of schools also for the first time in two weeks . . . I speak as a representative for a group of thirty-six white, realistic, ordinary, nonpressure parents . . . We support the Board of Education's proposals . . ." He said further along: "I think . . . that your board should . . . point out very positively that this matter of transportation does not assume transcontinental proportions (*applause*) but is about as far as it takes to drive to the pool clubs . . . the distance involved, in this day and age, with red lights . . ."

> VOICE: How small are your kids?
> CHAIRMAN: We have been courteous so far. Let's keep it that way.
> MAN (*continuing*): . . . that the distances are safe and sane ones.

In the public hearing that was held at Bassett Junior High School, with a predominantly Negro and liberal audience (the only one of the four hearings of which this was true), one unsophisticated white woman opposed to the plan tried rather pathetically, as the opponents regularly did, to establish her lack of prejudice. "Some of my best friends," she said, in exactly the established words, "are Negroes." She did not understand the hoot of laughter that greeted this sentence; unaware that this is a cliché, and an offensive one, she assumed that the laughter must mean unbelief. She insisted, "Yes, they are, too," and went on rather petulantly to spell out something about her great friendship with Negroes, while many in the crowd listened in contempt.

These hoots, together with the snorts and shouts I have mentioned before, illustrate the great gulf that opened in New Haven during those months.

Troup is the junior high school for the section of New Haven called the Hill. If the city has places that are becoming slums, while the rest of the city is being rebuilt, they would be spots up in this Hill area, not far from Grace–New Haven Community Hospital. Although there are stable neighborhoods on the Hill, parts of it might be called New Haven's Bedford-Stuyvesant, as Dixwell is its Harlem — the new slum, with less of a history and settled organization. Troup was, and is, the most nearly "racially balanced" of New Haven junior highs, with about half its students Negro; it was not included either in the original or in the eventual integration proposals. A problem with such a school, though, is to keep it from "tipping," from becoming more and more Negro, that is, and reaching a point at which whites move out.

By the time of the public hearing at Troup the city was exhausted with the subject of racial imbalance, but the list of people who wanted to speak was much longer than could be accommodated. Many handed in written statements.

Then came a wait. It was expected that the school board would announce its decision on the following Monday night, June 29 — but it did not. There was a week of waiting and intense rumor-passing. The integration forces became uneasy. They had expected the progressive board to come thumping through with the original plan — but they did not. Inside the Board of Education there was more debate than most citizens had expected. The board had stood together until the hearings were over. Then, when they had to decide, they had an internal argument of their own.

The delay came as a surprise. The antibusing forces were a bit startled that there was any disagreement among the board, whom they had cynically assumed to have closed minds; the probusing forces were unpleasantly surprised, since they had more or less assumed the board to be altogether on their side. It was now the liberals' turn to be unhappy.

National events furnished added emotional prodding to all sides throughout these months. The Senate had been considering the Civil Rights Act of 1964 all through the period during which New Haven was enacting its Equal Opportunities Ordinance and then debating busing. The Senate voted cloture on June 11 after a seventy-five-day filibuster. On June 17 the bill passed the Senate; and on July 3, while New Haven citizens were waiting for their board of education to make its decision, President Johnson signed it into law. Some resisters, both of the Equal Opportunities Ordinance and of busing, kept suggesting — confusedly, since the Act was not relevant — that we "wait and see" what the federal Civil Rights Act achieved, before taking action in New Haven.

On June 23, during the hearings in New Haven, three civil rights workers were reported missing in Neshoba County, Mississippi. Their burned-out station wagon was referred to in New Haven's hearings.

Over the Fourth of July weekend the probusing forces held a rally on the New Haven Green to try to show their strength and impress the board. Some members of the board and Superintendent Lawrence Paquin attended that rally, and a memorable photograph showed Paquin and the board president arm in arm with Negro leaders, singing Freedom songs. Telegrams and telephone calls urged aldermen and other city fathers to attend.

One Negro leader said, in disappointment, about the rally, "I knew everybody there." Although there was a moderately good attendance, the masses of Negroes did not show up. Middle-class Negroes, established civil rights leaders, and local liberals did come. The class division among Negroes was evident. The mass of low-income Negroes by and large did not indicate that they felt strongly about the busing plan, whereas the middle-class leaders became united behind it. Out of this rally, however, came an organization for voter registration that did good work registering voters in the predominantly Negro wards in the following fall.

On the next night the board announced its decision. There had been throughout the previous week and especially over the weekend intense negotiation, discussion, and argument behind the scenes, involving not only the board itself but representatives of the Mayor's office, high figures in the Democratic Party, and some representative citizens, and featuring at one point a long group telephone conversation with a gathering of Westville mothers around a swimming pool. Many plans were proposed. It had become clear the week before that those who did not want the original proposals had the greater strength. In addition to substantive objections to those proposals there was this point: that to have enacted the original proposal promptly would have confirmed the feeling that the board had already made up its mind and that the hearings were simply for show. Change in the plan as such had come to have a certain desirability. Then, too, the original proposals would have left Bassett in the first year a predominantly Negro school in a predominantly Negro section, with a fraction of new whites brought in against their will.

The board finally decided on pairing Bassett and Sheridan, the latter being located in the Westville area. This pairing would give each of the two junior high schools enough white children to keep the whites from feeling swamped. The change from the original plan had the effect of mollifying enough of the Westville parents to keep the protest within bounds.

But the argument did not go away. The opponents had formed themselves into a "Parents and Taxpayers" organization to resist all busing, and they initiated a court case that meandered on through the rest of one summer. There was an argument over money for the buses. Most important, there was a serious effort to obtain an *elected* school board to replace the un-popular appointed board.

I confess that there were times during the hearings and the arguments and especially during the last hectic days of ne-gotiations, trial balloons, and decisions when I said to myself, This is madness. That feeling was strongest on the evenings we spent with school statistics: the number of children in each school, the classrooms and capacity of each school, and the race of children now attending each school. "You get enough white kids over here to go with the Negroes over here, and that opens up the rooms to bus Negro kids in here." It did seem a curious kind of numbers game.

At the same time I remembered a conversation with a middle-class New Haven Negro woman who had gone to New Haven public schools and had received from them a good education, and an education in what we would now call an "integrated" setting (that word and concept were not then prevalent). Her children were going to 90 percent Negro schools, receiving what she regarded as an inferior education — one "pulled down to the economic level," as she put it, of the new Negro population of New Haven. Her situation illustrated to me the plight of the middle-class Negro, compared with the middle class of other ethnic groups. It represented one of the many ways that the Negro's situation is different from that of the white groups, and one strong point against the Northern city's pattern of de facto segregation. The Negro middle class can't escape. Because of racial discrimination in housing it cannot follow with the same success and in the same numbers the "old tenement trail" — up and out. This woman sees her section of town inundated with new arrivals, many of them very poorly educated and newly up from the South, with whom the white community in-sists on connecting her. These newcomers fill the schools of her neighborhood; the whites move out; largely as a result of real estate discrimination, she can't move out. She is stuck. The ed-

ucation in the neighborhood school deteriorates, chiefly because
of the changed educational atmosphere created by the changed
student body, and partly also as the result of the way teachers
and officials and the community at large now interpret this
Negro slum school.

Another incident brought home what this could mean. A
remedial reading teacher was shocked to find the children in
a class she visited at nine o'clock dancing around the room to
music from the record player. "When do you teach reading?"
she asked. "Oh, these children can't learn to read," the teacher
replied.

Overwhelmingly Negro schools are — if not exactly "educationally unsound" — at any rate educationally undesirable. The
most important reason for this undesirability is the effect on the
Negro child. Given the American pattern of discrimination,
the Negro slum school may reinforce the Negro child's sense of
exclusion, inferiority, and hopelessness. It may *interfere* with
his "education." What he "learns" from his effective confine-
ment to a Negro school may outweigh anything his teacher
may teach him. Granted that at least in some more or less enlightened cities like New Haven the school board does not
intentionally gerrymander Negroes into segregated schools, still
it can be argued that the schools should not simply accept the
prevailing pattern but counteract it.

The realities are, also, that the attitudes of teachers and administrators and parents are affected by a racial pattern: a
largely Negro school often becomes a Siberia of the system to
which the inexperienced and undesirable teachers are sent.
Some teachers, not all of whom necessarily are free from prejudice themselves, may have their own ideas about how little
Negroes can be taught. Boards of education and city governments are more responsive to articulate middle-class white parents who have both more political power and higher educational standards and demands — so the slum Negro school,
which needs the best, usually has received in fact the worst.

The probusers make another point, which seems lower down on the scale to me; that is, the effect on the white child of the mixed as over against the homogeneous school. It is of course desirable to have a diverse school population, simply for the social effects of it, but that is not the kind of *necessity* that would require sudden and drastic community-rending steps. Some of the argument on this point is sentimental, idealizing the actual effects of mixed schools. The results are not necessarily very lasting or unequivocally good; it depends upon the kind of experience and the interpretation somebody teaches you to make of it. I don't know that in Omaha Central or Wichita East, or in inner city high schools of Chicago, Detroit, or Cleveland, or for that matter in Troup Junior High in New Haven, the experience of "integrated" schooling is necessarily an enlightening one for all of the white students. Liberals should not overstate their case, or simply assume points to be universally accepted which in fact are not at all accepted by their hearers. This "how good it is for us all to be together" kind of thing is a sample. I hear an Italo-American sitting behind me at a meeting saying, in a loud stage whisper, "Ree — diculous!" when he comprehended that it was being argued his daughter should be removed from Hooker and sent to Bassett, in order to sit beside Negroes. The argument that education will be improved thereby is another sample. It isn't convincing; it sounds as though the people in charge aren't leveling with you. Better education indeed!

Sometimes, too, the argument that integration is good for the whites has in it a tinge of grim retaliatory moralism. I think that should be avoided. Retaliation in social affairs is morally questionable to start with and, besides, it usually hits the wrong people anyway.

4. Turmoil

*"First we had this big hate session, and then
we broke up into individual lynch mobs."*

THE BUSING BATTLE had a startling effect upon the social atmosphere, filling it with electricity and bringing out the worst
in everybody. Rumors sped around the city with the swiftness
that is always a little hard to believe, and were made of whole
cloth and gross exaggeration in larger proportions than usual.

There is clearly a sociological axiom that the greater the
tension the larger is the flow of rumors, the swifter is their passage, and the further is their distance from the truth. Citizens
flocked to meetings. PTA presidents and educators made wry
comments about the rather sudden increase in citizen interest
in education. The newspapers were read with unusual attention. The city buzzed with telephone calls and with street corner and supermarket conversations. Some traces of nasty business appeared: anonymous telephone calls; an informal boycott
or two; much name-calling; snarling, rude, unpleasant meetings. One civic leader, bruised and wobbly, humorously described one of the early informal gatherings during which he
had been hooted at. "First we had this big hate session, and
then we broke up into individual lynch mobs." "Wait until they
hear about this over in Fair Haven and the East Shore," he
added, referring to two parts of town most heavily populated
with workingclass and lower middle class Italian-Americans.
"They will be coming out of there with tanks and guns." Fig-
uratively speaking, he proved to be correct.

Friends fell out, and husbands and wives came to the point of angry silence with each other. People talked about almost nothing else. "I'm glad that the topless bathing suit came along," said one participant. "We had to have *some* other topic of conversation." In private, no holds were barred, and even in the big public meetings the normal restraints of politeness dropped away. Pointed *ad hominem* attacks were standard procedure.

All of the Fifteenth Ward was then in the Worthington Hooker School district. The streets on which I had had such a pleasant walk in the fall were now — not so pleasant. Democrats who worked together in the party battles of the fall now found themselves on opposite sides. Republicans were split, too. The battle divided people less along lines of party than of the ethos to which I referred in Chapter 1, the "community-wide" people against the private-interest people. The general level of articulateness on this subject is very high, and becomes higher still under emotional pressure.

The angry argument produced touchiness on the part of all participants, which often expressed itself with respect to minor matters of procedure. Many of the opponents instantly assumed that there was a powerful cabal supporting the plan, full of unfair tricks; they seized on every statement and new development, even every misprint in the newspaper, and assumed these showed some sinister purpose on the part of opponents. Why did proponents get copies of the blue booklet before they were available to the opponents? Who set up that "human relations" meeting at Conte School?

New Haven contains widely divergent groups. There is a dedicated civil rights minority. There is also a conservative majority of immigrant background. This majority felt forced to do something it did not want to do with respect to a very important value, education for their children. ("They say that those of us who are against this thing are emotional, but if we don't get emotional about our kids what should we get emotional about?" one man said, jumping up and down.)

They felt forced by the sudden alteration of their expectations. "Do not let the Board of Education take our children and use them as cattle, to transport them from one end of the city to the other, just to satisfy pressure groups." "This intergroup relations covers a lot of territory; and I feel at this time we are not ready to be led by the hand to force upon us who we may choose as a bosom friend, or to whom we would like to relate ourselves." "Is this the United States of America? No one has the right to tell us where we should send our children."

Usually the citizen feels the coercion of law rarely, and in a minor way, and mixed with elements that receive his consent. He does not like to pay his income tax or his property tax, but although grumbling he does not seriously doubt that these are necessary evils, and in any case they are long established and he expects them. The codes for housing and legal limits on his business have something of the same mixture of coercion, his consent, a general consent, and long acceptance. But this school redistricting had none of these; it was a new departure entirely, contrary to expectations, largely unsupported by the individual's consent or by a climate of consent.

The abruptness added to it, too. Moderate opponents of the busing kept wanting the thing postponed for a year, put off, developed more gradually.

The Negro community, by contrast, reacted in the opposite direction. Though New Haven Negroes in general were not particularly insistent about any school plan at first, they did come to be so as the battering of the opposition drove them emotionally back against the wall. There was no strong original initiative from the Negro community, but when lines were drawn and the opponents spoke, Negroes spoke out in reaction. The Negro member of the school board said that as he heard some of the opposition he could hear again the terrible chant of the crowd, when in his youth he played professional football: "Kill the Nigger! Kill the Nigger!" Several times in the month-long, or summer-long wrangle, a Negro would stop all the detailed arguments on this side and arguments on that side with some great cry from the heart, "What all this really means is — you don't want your child to go to school with my child!"

Some Negro parents were stung and hurt by certain things that were said, and inclined to a return backlash of their own. Many who sent their own children there said that Bassett wasn't a slum school unless you looked at it with a racial bias. As to inconvenience, "millions of Negroes go to bed inconvenienced every night." One unfortunate feature of this whole episode in New Haven, it seems to me, was the way it set up increasingly rigid reactions and counterreactions. The mass of ordinary white parents greeted the racial-imbalance plan with hopping fury and fear. As Negroes heard this opposition (much of it unruly, uninformed, and foolish) they became more and more united and insistent and uncompromising on their part, with angry speeches about a "sellout" because of "political pressures."

The articulate middle-class Negro leadership, that is, came to be united and vigorous in support of the proposals. The mass of impoverished Negroes in New Haven, however, was not much involved in the busing crisis. The really poor and uneducated and disorganized, indeed, in any city and of any race, tend not to be involved in any kind of community affairs. They have no connection, and have enough problems of their own. A middle-class Negro politician said, with some contempt, of the mostly Negro residents of a low-income housing project, "You can't get those people in Elm Haven out for *anything* — you'd have to *blast* them out."

There were reservations, not much noticed in the larger battle, on the part of some Negro parents, about what the plan would mean specifically for their children. Pupils from the predominantly Negro Winchester grade school were to have been bused across to the Fair Haven Junior High School in a pre-

dominantly Italian and poor section, in order to improve its
"racial balance." Once they had seen the hostility exhibited
in the public hearing at that junior high, some of these parents
were reluctant to send their own children into that atmosphere.
A critic remarked that Negroes want to be integrated only with
the middle-class whites, not with the poor or lower middle class.

All of this was a minor note. The major note in the articulate
Negro reaction, on the part of all who spoke out, was an endorsement of the proposals often coupled with a criticism of
them for not going far enough, for being just a small step, for
being inadequate. The Negro leaders, who tend in New Haven
as elsewhere to be individual and divided, with much vying
for position, came in the racial-imbalance struggle to be
"united on this as we've never been united before," as one Negro observer said.

A good education for one's children is a value for a disadvantaged group almost beyond every other value. The public
school system is the most important institution shaping daily
life that is directly under public control. An FEPC can try to
prevent job discrimination, and fair-housing efforts can try to
break up housing discrimination, but the centers of decision in
private businesses and unions and real estate boards and private sellers of houses are difficult to bring around to a pattern of
fair treatment. The school board, though, is a single and a public agency. It can by its visible decision right away alter patterns. It may be, therefore, that simply because of their vulnera-
bility the public schools are being asked to bear a disproportionate share of the change required to rectify the incrusted
injustice to the Negro.

Then there were the "white liberals," targets for criticisms
from every side and especially from among themselves.

I may have given the impression that the heat in New Haven
came chiefly on the side of those who resisted the busing. That
is not so. The proponents and semiproponents probably devel-

oped a more intricate pattern of internal antagonisms. There were factions and nuances and varieties and they were all unhappy with each other.

Social movements that are working for some ideal not yet achieved tend to be factional and sectarian, splitting into ever more refined divisions — like the Marxists, with all their Internationals, and varieties of socialism, communism, Trotskyism, revisionism, Stalinism, and so forth. Presumably it is easier to coordinate people if one is defending something real, especially a tangible self-interest, than if one is promoting some change toward an ideal and future state. One's troops keep falling apart with their differing ideas about that future, and that ideal, and the way to get there. In addition, on this matter, in the civil rights year of 1964 there was a heavy moral content; no American issue has been moralized, cast into doctrine, hardened into principle, covered over with guilt to any extent like that of Negro-white relations. Now came a civil rights question, in their very neighborhood, and liberals leaped into it with speeches ready. But then — not everybody agrees. Very refined distinctions and gradations in fact begin to develop. "It's all very well for her, with just her little toddler" . . . "We have three children to give to a *cause*" . . . "She's critical of me because we have our child in a private nursery school."

When the series of events was over it left a small number of shell-shocked liberals, wounded to have discovered, as it seemed to them, "the rotten core of prejudice" in their own city. They were shocked by the repetition in the North of many of the patterns of the South. We aren't so much "better" after all. They were hurt, and angry at "politicians" and at some fellow liberals — or people they had thought were liberals. "Why don't we just elect that fellow mayor," one said about a leader of the antibusing forces, "and show how bad we are."

The larger story, meanwhile, concerned the resistance to the busing by the mass of ordinary white folk. Their antagonism

against the minority that was pushing the proposals became
something fierce. This was not thought to be chiefly the Negro
minority. Rather it was a minority of comfortably well-off,
powerful, and articulate whites, generally regarded as not personally threatened or involved, who were strong proponents
of integrationist measures.

Each visible group among the proponents came in for its own
little attack, and it was instructive to see how all authority evap-
orated when the chips were down. Appeals to religious, scientific, and educational authority were about equally unavailing,
so far as I could see. The clergy (or, as one agitated lady critic
called them — and I think the added syllable does give a certain extra weight to the word — the "clergery") was heavily
attacked. It was pointed out that they have no children involved (New Haven is heavily Catholic). It was asserted that
there should be separation of Church and State. One lady who
made this last point also attacked the school board in the same
speech for having taken the prayer out of the schools.

The Catholic parish priests of New Haven made a unanimous
and temperate integrationist statement. This marked quite an
advance for what has been, with exceptions, a rather conservative body of clergymen. At least in the heat of the moment it
was not apparent that this statement gave rise to anything more
than efforts somehow to discredit it.

Psychiatrists, long lists of whom kept giving authoritative
testimony, were attacked as "out-of-town-do-gooders." It did
not help when one group of psychiatrists, admitting that many
of them lived in suburbs, explained rather grandly that they
were "in favor of justice everywhere." Various social scientists,
with their studies showing how much better pupils do in integrated schools, did not appear to have convinced anybody.
And the educators' claim that the whole plan was really intended to improve everyone's education was discounted completely.

The Board of Education had the worst of it, although venom

was spilled rather widely. Members of the board were bludgeoned night after night throughout the incredible series of meetings in the auditoriums of the schools of the city during the month of June. They should have won the admiration of the citizenry for their public spirit and patience, if nothing else, but I am afraid that they did not. The superintendent of schools, Lawrence Paquin, was the number one target. He has since accepted, and was then considering, the superintendency in Baltimore.

Officials of the city agencies, brought in by urban renewal, came in for an attack, and so did Community Progress, Inc. A speaker at one hearing demanded that everyone present who worked for CPI stand up. Among certain leaders of the opposition that organization came to be the chief symbol, or perhaps the chief agent, of the city's troubles. "The theorists have infiltrated our city!" as one of them put it. To be a theorist is a bad thing in New Haven, and not only with the local know-nothings. This is a favorite epithet of *New Haven Register* editorials, and even Mayor Lee has been heard to use it.

The size of the salaries of some public officials (actually not out of line but in some cases too low) seems to hold a piquant interest for some. One man, vigorously cheered, said, "I am prepared, and I am confident others are in agreement, to accept the proposal if the top salaried officials are willing to take a 50 percent cut in salary." A former alderman said, "My biggest regret as a member of the Board of Aldermen is when I voted to pay Mr. Paquin twenty-five thousand dollars a year."

There was a strong resistance to any participant in the argument who did not live in New Haven. In the hearings on the Equal Opportunities Ordinance back in May this had worked for the integrationists. The Chamber of Commerce and real estate group and their lawyers opposing that ordinance lived in the suburbs, without exception. Each one had to give his address before he testified and this became rather comical. The Negroes who testified in favor of the ordinance, of course, lived in the city to a man. As it happened, most of the other proponents did, too. The point became very clear.

On the school proposals, however, the situation seemed to be reversed. Many of the integrationists, except for the Negroes, lived *out* of town, whereas many of the opponents lived in New Haven. This obviously was far from being precisely accurate. Many white proponents underlined the fact that they lived in New Haven, and had children in the New Haven public schools, and were thus directly involved; the general impression to the contrary nevertheless persisted. One Protestant religious group that wanted to testify in favor of the proposals had a hard time finding any member who lived in town who could present their resolution. It was humanly rather instructive to watch notable social-action proponents who lived outside the city, or whose children were in private schools, as the point came home to them that on this issue their support was of no use — in fact probably would do more harm than good. Not all grasped this point.

The townspeople seized upon the (real or alleged) transiency of professionals in city government and in education and in the university as another ground for attack. These out-of-town educators, these Yale people, these CPI folk, are transients or tourists who have just come here, fasten their schemes on the city, and then move on. "Too many people who are in our city for the short time of two or three years of learning, teaching, or working are too willing to use our children and our tax dollars in an experiment that has failed in other cities," one woman said at the hearings. "Let the do-gooders and the university use their own families in the experiment . . . These people have no right to start a project, let it get out of control, and then leave the voters of New Haven to finish it. I for one will not let these window-shoppers use my children as guinea pigs while they move on to what they think are greener pastures . . ."

When something deeply resisted is proposed, primitive lines

of power and justice appear: Whose city is this, anyway? Old-line residents everywhere resent the intruders, the strangers, the "summer people," the newcomers, especially the "outside agitators." In New Haven, with its long history and then its wave of immigration, this can take curious forms. Although there are still faint traces of a DAR spirit in the vanishing tribe of Yankees, the politically significant feelings of proprietorship are those of much more recent claimants — an immigrant's nativism, as it were. I confess I myself was taken aback when a man of recent Italian extraction attacked Yale professors as being "pinko newcomers" who are trying to "take our city away from us — that we have governed ourselves for three hundred years." Let me hasten to explain that the only reason why this gave me pause was that use of "we" and "three hundred years."

But of course one should not even think of such things. None of us should acquire any civic credits or any debits because of any ancestry or any connections or any date of arrival. That ought to work both ways.

Most of all there was this sizzling hatred of Yale. Town-gown relations are particularly difficult in New Haven, where the town is exceptionally townish and gown exceptionally gownish. The systems of values and styles of life are widely different. Yale has been a rich boy's school in the recent past, and is not altogether over that yet; it has a now remote Congregationalist and New England Federalist heritage and a present Ivy League casual style and sophistication and whatever aristocratic pretensions this country allows. New Haven, on the other hand, is primarily populated by Catholic and Jewish working people of immigrant background.

More recently Yale has changed from a college to a high-powered university with graduate and professional schools, with students from all over the world, and with a large cluster of articulate intellectuals. Half of New Haven's population, on the contrary, did not go beyond the ninth grade. There is no longer a shock-absorbing college-educated non-Yale middle class. Although both the city administration and the Yale administration have worked hard in recent years to mitigate the town-gown antagonism, it is still there not far beneath the surface.

There are indeed some traces of the snobbery of class left in Yale, although much less than there must have been in years past. There is still a good deal of the snobbery of intellect, or rather perhaps of *education,* most of it of a rather unconscious We Happy Few variety. Yet there is much reverse snobbery on the part of townspeople: populistic common-mannish we-had-to-work-our-way attacks on the presumed privilege and presumed snobbery of all of Yale. This inverted prejudice is built partly out of the memory of real hurts and resentments but partly also out of the imputation of a snobbery that is believed to be there, whether it really is or not.

The busing crisis bursting forth in June 1964 was a complete contrast to the success with the Equal Opportunities Ordinance and the renewal program. It is the major recent political misfortune in this generally well governed city. Not everybody would say that. Some of the militant proponents might say, rather, "Well, you had to have that conflict anyway, in some form, someday, so it might as well have come in the way it did." Or they may criticize, as does Miss Shagaloff, the proposals instead of the furor — "Since you were going to have all that conflict anyway, why not ask for a really big change?" Or others would say, of the hearings and battles, "At least they show who the hypocrites are." (Is exposure of hypocrites a legitimate end of government?)

These are minority notes, though. Most citizens, I think, of whatever opinion on the merits and wherever they might locate "blame," would agree that the extended spiritual bloodletting over the busing was unfortunate. It brought out the old antagonisms in the city and developed some new ones, and strengthened them and spilled them over into the rest of the city's affairs, even those having nothing to do with buses or schools or race relations.

One difficulty with sudden changes in school districts is that great swatches of the white community can escape the net. The original New Haven school proposals had this notable line, "Integration is not possible without whites."

The gravest problem is that of the white suburbs. "The effect of the flight of the white middle class to the suburbs," said a report on New Haven's school problems issued a year after these events, "has been to dump the problems of poverty and racial minorities into the lap of the city."

"The high concentration of Negroes and the poor in the city," this report continued, "is in large part due to the public and private policies of the people who live in the suburbs . . . Suburban towns keep out the poor by rigid zoning policies. These policies reach an extreme in Woodbridge and Orange, where zoning laws have pushed up the median value of houses to well over $25,000 (U.S. census 1960). These communities have approved zoning laws which accept industrial or commercial firms, but which reject their lower or middle class employees as unsuitable for residency. This is having your cake and eating it too."

This report was issued by an integrationist organization called HOPE (Help Our Public Education) that came into being in the aftermath of the busing battle. About Negroes in the suburbs the report said, "The day-to-day work of excluding Negroes is done by the all white New Haven Real Estate Board with its multiple listing service." It is relevant to add that the all-white New Haven Real Estate Board throughout this period kept refusing membership to Negro realtors; membership on the board means access to shared, area-wide listings. "The real responsibility for this discrimination lies with the residents of New Haven's suburbs . . ." Woodbridge, North Haven, Hamden, Orange, and the others have money and in some cases good school systems, and remain essentially all-white while the central-city Negro population has grown rapidly; they have among them not a single public housing project.

The suburbs now offer a haven from integration. Schools are an important reason for the move to the suburbs, and abrupt and controverted action for racial balance in the city may increase the moving-out of whites. Many times angry parents threateningly made this point.

I read in the papers that Edward Logue, in Boston, suggested that each suburban school open up 10 percent of its student body to Negroes from the central city. He was quoted as having said, ". . . the suburbs can more readily absorb the cultural shock that would result from busing than can the city."

Then there are the 22 percent of New Haven's schoolchildren who are in parochial schools. The educational picture is markedly different from the universal public schooling to which a Westerner is accustomed. When you slice off layers of the upper crust for the suburbs and the private schools and then chop off this big chunk for the Catholic schools, you leave a remnant quite different in its social shape, location, and support from the school population in Laramie, Wyoming, or Hutchinson, Kansas.

Some parents switched their children from public to parochial school during the busing crisis. One knowledgeable Catholic woman said we were lucky the church for the parish in the Worthington Hooker area had no parochial school. Some former Hooker students, we know, had been admitted to parochial schools in other parishes. Rumors held that "all of Orange Street is talking about going to parochial schools."

In Boston the racial-imbalance fight has brought a direct challenge to the Catholic schools. Mrs. Louise Day Hicks, the elected chairman of the Boston School Committee, insisted that racial imbalance in the Boston public schools is not the responsibility of the School Committee and also is not harmful to education. A blue-ribbon advisory committee said the situation was harmful to both Negro and white children because it "prepares them inadequately for a multiracial community, nation, and world." Mrs. Hicks retorted that private and parochial schools are segregated by economic status and by religion and have an overwhelming predominance of white children. Noting the presence on the advisory committee of Cardinal Cushing, Archbishop of Boston, Mrs. Hicks said: "With keen interest many citizens will now observe the parochial school system of the archdiocese of Boston which educates more than 1,530,-000 boys and girls. Will this largest school system in Massachusetts now embark on a program of integration with the public schools, so that children of different races, colors, and religions will have the benefit of the 'integrated learning experience' which the blue ribbon advisory committee tells us is vital to quality education?"

Mrs. Hicks's suggestion that the Catholic schools integrate with the public schools is plainly one of those "you're another" polemical thrusts that are intended for a debating advantage only. Although I haven't been there, I believe I can sense something of the Boston atmosphere by extrapolation from New Haven — Mrs. Hicks's remark that much of Boston's problem stemmed from a "small band of racial agitators and a few college radicals" had a familiar ring to it. There do appear to be questions about the role of the Catholic schools, as of the suburban schools, where these constitute a large and available alternative to city schools that are trying suddenly to integrate themselves against great resistance.

And the same is true of private schools, although these include much smaller numbers. Only 2 percent of New Haven's schoolchildren attend these, but it is an important 2 percent because of the influence and standing of the parents, and the prestige of schools like Hopkins Grammar School. A few people, mostly liberals who would be on the integrationist side in the busing dispute, disapprove of these private schools on principle. The disapproval took on a much sharper edge under the summer's pressure. Opponents of the busing attacked private school people, too, not so much on grounds of public school principles as of the feeling people who were not directly involved should not be making the decisions. In their view, often vividly expressed, private school people were morally disenfranchised on this public school question. Under the weight of disapproval from both embattled parties, some sensitive people whose children are in private schools rather tiptoed through the city during those weeks. When someone on the board of a private school that was having financial difficulties observed that their enrollment should be assisted by the busing controversy in the New Haven public schools, the liberals among the trustees of that school were caught in rather an embarrassing squeeze.

I have four children, the youngest having been born in January of 1964. The older three had gone only to public schools, mostly to Worthington Hooker. As a matter of fact, my wife and I and — just to fill in the picture — both parents on both sides have gone to public schools. In Laramie or Hutchinson I wouldn't have known what to make of a private school person if I had seen one. I can remember a twinge of disappointment and confusion, after first coming to New Haven from the West, when I discovered that a professor whom I very much admired had his children in private schools.

In the spring of 1963, fifteen years later, now married and father of three, I found it possible to move our own oldest child, a girl then planning to enter seventh grade the following fall, over into a private school. It never occurred to me that I might soon be an alderman, or that there might soon thereafter be a fight over integration in the public schools. Both of these things, however, followed promptly on our decision. Some of the angrier constituents suggested that we had some insider's foreknowledge about the busing and cleverly had slipped our own daughter out of it. It indicates something of the flavor of those months to mention that both busers and antibusers pointedly suggested that we should move this daughter back from private to public school. We didn't follow their suggestion.

The opponents of busing had decided early in the fight that they would go to the courts to try to stop it. In June, before the public hearings, they held a meeting in a Catholic church in a ward next to the Fifteenth, and at that meeting they elected officers and collected money for the hiring of a lawyer. People who went to that meeting, incidentally, were proud of its decorum; repeatedly they would say things like "They accuse us of being emotional, but that was a calm, short, businesslike meeting — straight to the point. It was over in half an hour."

The court case dragged on confusingly and rather anticlimactically through the latter part of the summer, after the school board had announced its decision. The antibusers sought both permanently to have it held that the board had no power to change school districts for reasons of race and also temporarily for the board to be injoined from commencing the plan in the fall of 1964. The Superior Court judge in August denied the temporary injunction. One of the three counts held that the busing arrangement violated the purposes of the Sargent Plan for rebuilding New Haven's schools. Another held that the constitutional rights of children were violated if they had to attend more remote schools and to be transported by bus. The third and most serious count challenged the legal right of the school board to redistrict for reasons of race: "to change artificially the relative proportions of white and Negro children in various schools . . . The plaintiffs contend that such actions are outside the powers of the board and contrary to law." But the judge, citing the wide discretionary powers granted to the school board by Connecticut statutes and by

the New Haven Charter, rejected this contention. He also cited
a New Jersey case, arising from the integrating of a junior high
in Montclair. In this case a New Jersey court held that a school
board need not "close its eyes to racial imbalance in its schools
which, though fortuitous, presents much the same disadvantages as are presented in segregated schools." He cited also
a case arising from a pairing plan in the elementary schools of
Hempstead, Long Island, in which a New York court made
this complicated but important point: if the state statutory
provision that schools shall be open to children without discrimination as to race is held to prevent such a pairing (because children are denied admittance to a school near them that
does not contain their grade) then that state nondiscrimina-
tion provision becomes ironically a "Segregation statute, man-
dating continuation in schools of racial imbalance and making de jure what is now merely de facto."

There has been in fact a good deal of confusion about the
legal and the constitutional foundations of this problem. Americans overconstitutionalize questions of policy, especially in
this field. Constitutional debate is extended downward into
policy and upward into morals. Opponents of busing plans
have confusedly construed decisions that say that boards are
not constitutionally *required* to redistrict for racial balance as
meaning that they are not *allowed* to do so. They also have interpreted a paragraph in the United States Civil Rights Act of
1964 specifying that the law does not *require* measures to
end so-called de facto segregation in schools as *forbidding* such
measures.

These confusions were not helped toward clarity by the interpretations made by some people on the other side, who
seemed to say that the constitution and the Supreme Court's
decisions in segregation cases made busing mandatory. There
was a considerable tendency on the part of both groups to find
obligatory authority in the Constitution and the court cases,
and not to grant the area of discretion, of pragmatic adjust-

ment, and of moral and political judgment outside or beyond the strict obligations of law.

The school board's revised plan had been announced to a very attentive public on July 7, 1964. As part of its most controversial feature — the pairing of the seventh and eighth grades in the two junior high schools — it abolished the seventh and eighth grades at Hooker. These pupils henceforth would go, by bus, to Bassett and Sheridan Junior High Schools. As part of the other major feature pupils from other elementary schools within a cluster of schools, if parents requested it, would be bused into Hooker. Most of these new Hooker pupils would be Negro. The city waited with some anxiety for school to start in the fall of 1964.

Meanwhile, we had another fracas in the Fifteenth Ward.

5. Scattered Housing

"I don't know why they wanted me to come.
I'm just renting."

On the Thursday night in July when Senator Goldwater made his acceptance speech in San Francisco I left the Republicans on television in New Haven and walked once more to Worthington Hooker for yet another meeting — this time, the public hearing on the "scattered house," as it came to be called, on Willow Street. The emotional debris from the busing battle was still all around us, and I remember asking myself as I walked the block, Well, now, what is *this* evening going to be like?

I had known since May — before the busing outburst — that this was coming. In keeping with new national ideas for public housing, the New Haven Public Housing Authority had decided to try to scatter some units out into the residential areas of the city. One of the first of these, and the very first in a thoroughly middle-class white neighborhood, was to be a single family frame house at 277 Willow Street, in the Fifteenth Ward. I remembered that house from the campaign. A pleasant white-haired elderly couple, very cordial but surely Republican, had invited me inside, and I had given them an application for an absentee ballot.

Now the Congregational church in the neighborhood, the Church of the Redeemer, had inherited the house, and after some congregational soul searchings had decided to make it available to the Public Housing Authority. The Authority is required by law to hold a public hearing on any site for public housing. It had scheduled its hearing on the Willow Street house for June 25, but when that turned out to be the very night of the last of the furious gatherings on the busing question the Authority prudently postponed its hearing until July 16.

As I came into the Hooker basement on that night I saw the members of the Public Housing Authority — a priest, a Negro doctor, a woman, and an Episcopal minister — sitting in the front of the room, with a surprisingly sparse collection of citizens facing them in metal chairs. The chairman of the Authority, C. Newton Schenck, a civic-minded lawyer who lives on Everit Street not many blocks away in the Fifteenth Ward, was presiding. After the preliminary handshakings were over Mr. Schenck announced that he would allow a half hour for those in the room who favored the proposal and then a half hour for those who opposed it, and then yet another half hour for those in favor, and so on, until everyone who wished to speak had spoken — a pattern with which we were all by then quite familiar. Another angry set-to obviously was expected. Mr. Schenck then introduced Robert Wolfe, the executive director of the Housing Authority, who explained the purpose of scattering public housing and described the safeguards to the people in the area where the scattering was done.

I knew somewhat more about the purpose of the scattering than he then stated because I had earlier had a lunch with Mr. Schenck and Mr. Wolfe, at which we had discussed the matter. They explained the purpose of the proposed "scatteration": to avoid putting any more families in great concentrations like the Elm Haven project in the heart of the Negro section — a project in which almost 3 percent of the whole city's population now lives — and to put units in smaller clusters around the town.

Elm Haven had once been a model of desirable public housing, but it was far from that now. Our appraisals of these efforts at public good change rapidly in the swift flow of modern city life. In the early fifties, for example, we had regarded the Winchester School, a large new million-dollar plant, as quite remarkable, because it was then the best and newest school in the city and had been built smack in the middle of the Negro district. People in the area could scarcely believe that the city would spend all that money, and build that good a school, for *their* part of town. By the time of these controversies in the sixties, Winchester School had become just another example of a racially imbalanced "ghetto" school.

There is a similar story about Elm Haven. In a book called *New Haven Negroes: A Social History*, written by a Yale scholar named Robert Warner and published in 1940, there is a handsome photograph of Elm Haven, a low-income public housing project just then completed in the Dixwell area — new, shiny, functional, and presented as an appealing example of the better life that was coming at last for New Haven Negroes. Even in the first years of the fifties this Elm Haven project was shown to me as a sample of the humane marvels of public housing. By now, as the scattered-housing episode made evident, Elm Haven had come to have a negative meaning to many New Haven citizens — and such projects had come to present problems for social planners, too. A proposed hundred-unit project for a nearby town could be criticized because "you are building another Elm Haven." One point of the scattering was to move a family *out* of Elm Haven.

Some newer high-rise apartments, Elm Haven Extension, had been built in the fifties across the street from the original low buildings pictured in Mr. Warner's book. Into these tall buildings crowded newcomers to New Haven — mostly Negroes, many fresh from the rural South. The more established residents of the old project (also in large part Negroes) did not want to join with these new residents, and did not want to be identified with them. In effect, a social barrier grew up along the street that separates the two sections of the project. It was difficult, actually, to get the two parts of the project to work together. The New Haven Negroes were not eager to be identified with the newcomers, whose presence in large numbers damaged the picture of all Negroes in New Haven.

And the reputation of the public housing projects like Elm Haven drastically declined.

Back in 1952 and 1953, when my wife and child and I lived in McConaughy Terrace, a state-financed middle-income public housing project in the Westville section of New Haven, we felt ourselves to be twice blessed. It was the best apartment, and only modern kitchen, that we had had, and it was also fraught with social significance: our baby daughter played with a Negro boy. I can remember the pleased and rather unbelieving feeling I had when we moved into this neat, functional new apartment. A dozen years later, however, with the influx of the fifties and the passing of time, this project presents quite a different picture. Friends still living there, people of the utmost goodwill, have to say that there are — problems. The project is not highly regarded, either by the ordinary man looking for an apartment or by planners and reformers thinking of ways to meet social needs. The great faults of public housing, according to sympathetic critics, have been size, social separation, and forbidding design. The projects have too often been miniature cities of poverty and social disorganization cut off from the surrounding neighborhoods, multiplying difficulties by collecting them in one spot, and by providing an unappealing, institutional setting. As one friendly critic observed, public housing has not won the popular support through the years that Social Security, say, has won.

Very little new low-income public housing is being built; and very few units even of the housing that is built can house large families. During the year 1963 only 817 public housing apartments with five or more bedrooms became available in

the entire United States. Two six-bedroom apartments in Port-
land, Maine, are the only new units of that size built in the entire northeastern region (New York and New England) in recent years. It seems that unrealistic statutory limitations on
construction costs make it almost impossible to build public
housing units with six bedrooms — and yet these large units
would meet the most severe need.

The advanced thinkers about housing policy, though, don't
want those needed units built in the huge and isolated bunches
that have characterized much low-income public housing in
the past. Instead they have come to recommend "scatteration."

Mayor Lee was one early proponent of such a policy. "I was
on the Board of Aldermen when we started public housing," he
said later, talking about these housing matters, "and I voted for
it — but I had reservations about concentrating people in one
neighborhood. I didn't like the idea of Elm Haven Extension. I
admit I went along with it. Public housing like that isolates
people. You're a *project* family. Low-income public housing
almost caused more problems than it solved. We are out of the
business of that kind of concentration, like Elm Haven and
Farnum Courts. The largest project we have built recently is one
hundred and six units, and that's housing for the elderly next
door to luxury apartments."

"This new program shows more perception," the Mayor went
on, speaking of the dispersed and smaller projects, with rent
supplements. "The mayors of the country have fought for it
and believe in it. And you've got to hand it to Lyndon Johnson — this is his program. And the whole concept of scattered-site housing was developed in New Haven."

This last remark of Mayor Lee's referred to, among other
New Haven doings in the housing field, a demonstration project with twenty-six families and federal funds which had been
carried out in the city since 1962. It too involved scattered sites,
but the properties were only leased by the Housing Authority,
not purchased; this demonstration project made a trial of the

rent-supplement feature — tax funds filling in the poor person's
rent — that was then being considered for future national
housing legislation.

The intent of the scattering, in whichever way it is done,
is to break up the concentrations of the poor into smaller and
separated groups so that they do not make a single environment. By cutting the number one reduces the psychological
separation of all the "project families" from others. Distributing
the units throughout the city helps "class" integration as well
as racial integration. It minimized the impact of the projects
on the public schools. The logic and humanity of it are clear
enough. The politics of it, however, can be murder.

The Authority had proposed a site on Sherman Parkway for
the building of a new project at the same time that it proposed
to acquire the house on Willow Street. This Sherman Parkway
site, where six to twelve low-income units were to have been
built, was in a middle-class neighborhood where many Negroes lived, and they opposed it. "They are just as bad as anyone else," one disgusted supporter of public housing remarked.
The alderman from the ward, a Negro, testified against the
project, and he was joined by other residents, Negro and white.
Whites in our neighborhood cited that opposition by Negroes
to this project as justification for their own opposition.

Although the chances were thought to be strong, because of
the large proportion of Negroes in Elm Haven, that the Willow Street family would be Negro, still that was not certain.
The opponents were at great pains to insist that race had nothing to do with their opposition to the scattered house. The
woman who had first hesitantly called me about the project,
having got wind of it before I did back in early May, carefully
explained that the objection she and her friends had was not
to the family's being Negro but "it — it's the low" (low
income). I believe it is this way: the noncollege ex-plebe folk
who opposed the project wanted to interpret it strictly as a matter of class, income, and economics. Some were angry with me

for even mentioning the racial matter. *You* were the first one
to bring that up, they said. Middle-class college liberals were
also eager to separate the two but in the other way — to interpret such an issue as purely racial. If one should mention the
ills of poverty, the ghetto, and disorganized social life, they
would say, "Oh, but that's economics; we are talking about
race." On that matter they are clear. On the other, class-
economic matter they may not be so clear. "I'd be glad to have a
Negro family live next door to me." "How about a low-income
project family?" *Awkward pause.* "Well, that's different." And,
naturally, it *is* different. But the two are not so separable in
practice for workingclass and lower-income folk as they are for
the comfortable white middle class.

A mistake was made in conversations with the two professional families living on either side of the Willow Street
house. It was suggested to them that the family might be
white. This annoyed them considerably, because it implied
that they were racially prejudiced and that their prejudice
might be catered to. They agreed not to oppose the project, although they were not happy about it and would not testify in
its favor. Nevertheless, they were quite clear that their reservations did not have anything to do with the color of the family
that would be living in the house.

I knew the objections to the project that would be made by
some other families in the ward; I had had several long telephone conversations with constituents.

"What business has Mayor Lee and you people like that to
come around and tell us who we gonna have next door?"

"These people get everything free. We been paying taxes for
years to keep up the neighborhood. Why can't they live in
their own part?"

Now in the hearing in the Hooker basement a number of us
testified in favor of the project. I did so as the alderman in the

ward as well as homeowner in the neighborhood. My strategy was defensive, to try to answer arguments against the project while testifying for it. I listed the objections and questions that had been brought to my attention by constituents, and then gave answers to these questions. I thought I might thus both fulfill the double responsibilities of an elected official — to attend to the views of his constituents but also to represent his own best judgment — and additionally help the project along by mitigating opposition to it.

"Behavior of family?" With a private purchase you take your chances. In this case the Authority, which wants the project to succeed, will select the family from the large number well known to it with an eye to the success of the program. Some families have lived in its projects for as many as twenty years. Many families (how to say this properly?), many families in the project do not differ from the rest of us except, possibly, in income.

"Property values?" The property will be maintained better than it might otherwise be, since the Housing Authority will maintain it. The authority will have a stake in the property and its value, and in making this effort succeed.

As to "race." During the hearings on integrating the schools it was said many times by those resisting the school board's proposals that the proper way to bring about school integration was not by "busing" but by integrating neighborhoods. Here, then, if the family in this project should be Negro, which seemed a likelihood, is an opportunity to advance such neighborhood and "natural" integration. (I had thought when I heard the many statements in favor of *neighborhood* integration during the busing crisis that at least that ought to mean people would not resist the scattered-housing proposal when it came up. How wrong I was! They certainly did resist it, and some of the strongest resisters were exactly the people who earlier, in the abstract, had been recommending neighborhood integration — recommending it, that is, as an alternative to busing. Faced with a concrete proposal in their own street their reaction was another screaming negative.)

L. Thomas Appleby, then the city's Development Administrator, who was another resident of the Fifteenth Ward, made a defensive presentation similar to mine. He included an effective preliminary statement of the way he understood people might feel. Why should those of us who worked hard all our lives, saved our money, had no one help us, and finally were able to buy a house in this good neighborhood now allow the government to come along and plunk down some low-income multiproblem project family next door to us, subsidize their rent, and lower our property values?

He went on to answer this rhetorical question with responsible words about the needs and problems of the community as a whole. It was interesting to learn later that some people opposed to the project were grateful for this first part of his testimony, grateful that at least one of the city bigwigs understood their situation, even if he didn't come out on their side in the end.

Some of the others who testified in favor of the project did not, from my perhaps biased aldermanic point of view, do our common cause much good. One who lives on Prospect Hill, in the city's finest residential section, made some jokes about how as a Harvard man he lived in a nest of Yale men, three blocks from the nearest Harvard person. A bearded minister, who has voluntarily lived in slum parishes, said that his children liked Elm Haven so much that they kept wanting to move back there. A large-spirited citizen spoke about how important it is for us to live in mixed communities in order to get to know each other. I had tried to say that by the very principle of scatteration there would not soon be *additional* projects in our section, and another testifier, also not from the neighborhood, said we ought instead to want many more.

The half hour for those in favor of the project now ended

and, as we braced ourselves, Mr. Schenck asked for statements of those opposed. There was silence. Not a hand went up. Mr. Schenck, surprised, repeated his statement. Still silence. "I know there are people who are opposed," he said. Still no volunteers. Finally, when he had adjusted his statement now to ask whether there were any questions or comments, a few timid ventures were made. Two or three people raised questions, but rather diffidently. A considerable group sat in glum silence. Finally one woman bravely stood up and haltingly said that she knew there were many people in attendance who were opposed who just weren't speaking up. She looked around at her neighbors. They didn't say a word.

Why didn't they speak? Because, as many complained later, the proponents all had "prepared speeches," and because "they talk so good." If they, the opponents, had tried to talk, "it wouldn't have come out right; it wouldn't have sounded right."

A few negative remarks were made nevertheless. "Twenty-three years!" said the woman who spoke first, the wife of a driver on the Orange Street bus line. "We have all our savings for twenty-three years in our house. What are we going to do? What are we going to do?"

The hearing adjourned much earlier than we had expected. Some of the public housing supporters immediately concluded that there was to be no problem: "You've got it." But there were rumblings in private to suggest that things were not as harmonious as they had appeared.

As the meeting broke up a constituent, a Democrat who had been sitting behind me, asked pointedly and with controlled anger whether I intended to run again. He commented acidly that it must be hard to divide yourself between what you believe yourself and what the majority of your constituents want. He also spoke contemptuously of these "fuzzy-minded people" who say it would be "good for our kids" to have a project family live in the neighborhood.

While I was trying to discuss these large matters with him

word came of an altercation at the front of the room. It appeared that a young CPI employee had snapped a picture of a woman, despite her request that he not do so, and that she and her husband and the young man were having heated words. We finally got the young man to yield up his negatives to me, as an intermediary, since he and the couple refused to deal with each other. There was more tension in the room than had come out in the hearings.

One is struck by the way ordinary folk respond to a new proposal by reducing it to some one fact immediately connected to their own experience. The price the Authority would pay the church for the Willow Street house had been mentioned. A couple who had sat silently through all large issues of social policy made this one comment to me after it was over, "We didn't know there were any houses on this side of the ward that sold for as little as fifteen-seven!"

Several spontaneous discussion groups had already formed on the corner as I left, and kept going for a long time. I reached home in time to hear Senator Goldwater explaining on television that extremism in defense of liberty is no vice.

On the next Monday night the wife of the man who had wanted to know whether I intended to run again called me and asked in a formal manner for an interview. I named a time, and at the evening hour appointed she and her husband appeared at my house. A New York friend, the Reverend George Todd, once of the East Harlem Protestant Parish and now Director of Urban Work for the United Presbyterian Church, happened to have stopped in on his way back to New York that evening. He and I had been discussing the Harlem riots of the previous weekend (the night of Goldwater's acceptance speech and of the hearing in Hooker had also been the night an off-duty policeman shot a fifteen-year-old Negro boy on East 76th Street in New York, which event led to riots over the weekend).

When the constituents arrived I introduced Mr. Todd, who

then departed. "His boy goes to a public school in Harlem in which he is the only white boy in his class," I said, by way of making conversation. "*Really?*" they said.

The purpose of the interview, it developed, was to ask me as alderman to help the people who did not speak at the hearing to make known their feelings about the scattered house. It seemed that a great many people hadn't known about the hearing. Even those present had felt unprepared and overwhelmed by the "people who talk so good." More than four hundred residents of the area, I was told, had already signed a petition against the project. "I'll call Mr. Schenck," I said, and I did so right then. He replied that although he would not have another formal hearing he would meet informally with people who had something to say. Where? At my house, if you want, I said — a gesture I was to regret. To the interviewing constituent I explained what Mr. Schenck had said, and indicated that if she would invite two or three of the people who had spoken to her requesting such a meeting, I would invite the three or four people who had called me. I tried to be careful about the basis of the invitation because I knew how sensitive people were in the busing matter: we would invite just those who had specifically spoken to one of us.

On the night set for the meeting with Mr. Schenck my wife prepared to make tea and coffee and put nine tea cups on the table, a rather pathetic symbol of our misinterpretation of what was coming. The general spirit of the gathering may accurately be described, I believe, as To Hell with Tea, and there were more than nine people.

The first woman who came, all alone, remarked rather nervously, to fill the time as we waited, "I don't know why they wanted me to come. I'm just renting."

More came. By twos and threes, and by fours and fives, and alone and continually they poured into the house. Our few chairs were quickly filled, and such additional chairs as we could muster; the living room filled with standees, and our dining room table was shoved against the wall to provide more standing room, which was quickly filled, and the hall was filled, and we stood there, eighty-five of us, packed in tight, for an hour and a half's colloquy on the housing of the poor. Although it was July, fortunately it was not very hot, or we would have expired.

Mr. Schenck and Mr. Wolfe stood in the middle of this mass, in the archway that separates what once was the dining room from what once was the living room in our house. There was standing room only, and not much of that. The new Republican chairman of the ward, a man named Carpinella, regarded himself as the chairman and first spokesman of the group he had obviously organized. He seemed mostly impressed that "the same people" had testified for the busing plan and for the scattered house. "I have a list of them, and it's the same people, the same people," he said with considerable agitation, waving his list. I knew from extended telephone conversations with him that he felt this proved a kind of conspiracy on the part of Yale people, "pinkos," transients to work nefarious schemes upon the city. He was astounded and outraged, as he had explained to me, that as the alderman of the ward I would have testified *for* this dreadful project in our own neighborhood.

Then it appeared that Mr. Carpinella was not the only spokesman. The group had also brought with them — to my complete astonishment — a lawyer! The crowd sat nodding its vigorous agreement as this legal spokesman made their points for them. I had met the man, whose name is Di Benidetto, long ago when I had done part-time work of managing ineptly for two or three years a group of young adults at the New Haven YMCA. They were New Haveners of Italian extraction, still called by their old boys' club name, the Bearcats. Since Bearcat days I had read in the papers of Mr. Di Benidetto as a vocal Republican of the more conservative sort. Subsequently he and his parents were named by the Mayor, along with ten or eleven others, as "slumlords" guilty of repeated violations of the housing code. Also, he was to become an aspirant to the Republican mayoralty nomination to oppose Mayor Lee in 1965 — along with Mr. Carpinella.

Mr. Di Benidetto made as formal a presentation as he could under the unusual circumstances, standing backed against my living room radiator. He attacked the entire idea of scattered housing, "the most drastic extension of socialism I have ever seen." He argued that property rights were our most precious rights (this was just after the San Francisco convention, and much Goldwater rhetoric was in the air) and that "human rights are considered higher than property rights; this shows how far we've gone." He argued that the family put into the Willow Street house wouldn't be happy because the neighborhood is "never going to look well on that subsidized family." He also criticized the family's possible characteristics: "A mother and children may be counted as a 'family.' This should be clarified." He said that the mother might not practice "birth control or moral restraint" sufficient to keep the family from enlarging. His manner in saying all this was controlled and polite.

Mr. Schenck and Mr. Wolfe then defended public housing and scattered housing against all comers, and the evening became less polite. The *ad hominem* appears immediately in these things, and pointed questions were addressed to Mr. Schenck about whether he had ever *worked* and whether he had known what it was like to be poor. He defended public housing by invoking the name of Senator Taft, who co-sponsored the 1949 Housing Act, thus to baptize the program with Taft's conservatism. Attacks were made on alleged Negro behavior, on the sort of people who were said to live in Elm Haven — "they don't want to work" — and on the way they were said to keep up, or not keep up, their apartments. All of this with passion.

There is a great egotistical warp in almost any man's estimate of his own difficulties and accomplishments as over against those of other people. His own are mountainous, but he can look on another man's with a yawn. This warp is given an extra twist for groups, and yet another in contest for any important stake, like a home and a neighborhood and "property values." *We* worked; nobody gave *us* a penny; those project people are lazy; they don't know how to keep up their property; why should our tax money subsidize them, to live next door to us and pull our property down? "If we move someplace else now will you follow us there? You going to play cat and mouse with us?" This angrily from a young householder. The fierce hostility to "project families" and at least implicitly to Negroes filled my rooms like an evil vapor.

The Housing Authority, in addition to its usual prudence in the face of public opinion, had in this case a further obligation to the Church that had made the house available. The Authority had promised that it wouldn't proceed with the project if there were strong neighborhood opposition. A few days after the meeting I have described the Authority canceled its proposed project on Willow Street.

The Church eventually sold the property at 277 Willow Street to a Yale couple. The wife is a volunteer in one of the many new educational ventures the city is sponsoring. In her backyard now one can often see a group of her tutees — mostly young Negro children.

But the family that might have lived there is still in Elm Haven.

6. The Ethnic Resistance to Negro Rights

"For you, it is a contribution; for me it is a sacrifice."

WHEREVER THERE ARE large groups of white citizens of immigrant extraction one argument against the civil rights movement (or rather, against its moving "too fast") recurs incessantly. "Nobody helped us" . . . "We Italians had to work our own way up — why can't they?" A workingman of Irish background said to me after we adopted the Equal Opportunities Ordinance, "Equal opportunities, eh? They didn't have that when I was startin' out." In New Haven's struggles this argument must have been used, by conservative estimate, eighty-seven thousand times. One version of it I have come to think of as the Comparative Grandfathers theme. It begins, "Now, when *my* grandfather came over from the old country . . ." and it ends with some form of the idea that this most recent wave of immigrants, the Negro from the South, is receiving a special help that an earlier "my grandfather" wave — Italian, Jewish, Irish, Polish — did not receive. This argument is so pervasive and spontaneous as to represent an unmistakable reality of the popular feeling. It was one major theme in what came ubiquitously to be called, in the summer of 1964, the white backlash. It doubtless lay behind President Johnson's insistence, when he signed the Civil Rights Act of 1964, that the Act gives no special favors but only assures equality. And it helped to give emotional force to the idea of

"inverse discrimination" that was condemned in the Goldwater
Republican platform.

I want to make two points about this argument: first, it is
wrong; but — second — it is understandable. It is not necessarily morally reprehensible. Not everybody who advances it is
a racist. I think that *some* of the white resistance deserves
more empathy and understanding than militant civil rights
leaders are sometimes willing to grant (understandably on
their part, too).

I don't mean that the nobody-helped-us ethnic analogy is a
legitimate argument against the civil rights movement. Of
course it is not. As one tries to say to that workingman who said
he hadn't had "equal opportunities," the Irishman can lose his
brogue but the Negro can't change his color. The Irish-American can move up and out (a great-grandson becoming President) but the Negro is blocked by multiple rings of discrimination. As to the game of Comparative Grandfathers (whose had
it worse?), the Negro always wins that: his grandfather was
a slave. He was forcibly brought here, bought and sold; his
children never had a start. And, as one does not say in that
argument, there is something more lurking in the background,
that any reference to intermarriage and sex relations would
quickly make clear. There is still a terrible life-blighting, humiliating notion of the Negro as a fundamentally different
kind of being — in short, of race.

The marriage of one's daughter, always a matter of concern,
did not commonly reach the level of lynching parties with
other American minorities. A Negro woman in conversation at
a dinner remarked that perhaps the American Indian had the
worst treatment of all, but on reflection one has to say no. Will
Rogers bragged about his Indian blood, but Americans typi-
cally have not bragged about Negro blood. Even in the North
there are some self-starting racists who jump at you with their
terrible racial nonsense — "White and black must be kept separate; white women have a weakness in the head, white women

have a weakness in the head." Other minorities have not
faced the dark undercurrent of sexual-racial fears and stereotypes: white men cruising in the Corona (Negro) section of
Queens, accosting respectable middle-class Negro women, expecting them to be prostitutes; young Negro boys learning in
Harlem that there's a place down there where you can make a
few bucks; white males in the Southern town, and not only
there, who make a "sexual gain" out of the caste system.

The Negro, stereotyped, wrapped in myths, invisible, as the
novelists say, has then been blocked by racial discrimination
in housing, employment, education, health, and public accom-
modation and by the prejudice that discrimination helps to reinforce, which in turn causes more discrimination — in a brutal
circular social pattern that goes far beyond any white ethnic
groups experienced. Even if it were not so (as was argued many
times in New Haven's meetings), "two wrongs do not make a
right." But because it is built on the visible fact of racial appearance, and grows out of slavery, and was long written into
law in one great section of the country, and is structured into
the society in cruel patterns of unequal racial treatment, the
"wrong" to the Negro is fundamentally and qualitatively worse
than that meted out to the European immigrant, bad as the
latter often was.

Slavery crushed the Negro community, and left a deep im-
print on the Negro personality and family. Daniel P. Moynihan, then Assistant Secretary of Labor, was putting together
in the winter of 1964–1965 a government memorandum that
described the breakdown of the Negro family structure. A
main point was the humiliation of the Negro male: "When
Jim Crow made its appearance, toward the end of the nineteenth century, it was the Negro male who was most hu-
miliated thereby." This happened at a time when "a particular
type of exaggerated male boastfulness became almost a national style. Not for the Negro male. The 'sassy nigger' was
lynched."

No white immigrant group experienced anything as destructive as the battering of community structure, family, and personality by slavery and segregation, or the racial-sexual stereotype that set the Negro apart in unreason and fear. The white groups could be, and to great extent have been, assimilated, without unsettling social forms. The full assimilation of the Negro, on the other hand, requires the deep unsettling and reshaping of social arrangements through which we are now trying to work our way.

Moreover, the Negro "immigrant" from his "old country" (the South) arrives now in the Northern city at a much less advantageous time for unskilled, untutored people. Although the streets of New Haven were not exactly paved with the gold the southern Italian peasant dreamed of, yet the city did offer menial jobs and a chance. Now when the Southern Negro arrives, such jobs are gone or are going fast. The difference between the situation of the Negro and that of the white groups can be forcefully indicated by reference to the effects of time: for the white immigrant groups the generations more or less steadily advanced; for the Negro, however, starting without group resources and blocked by discrimination, that does not necessarily apply.

The depression was a dreadful period for Negroes. Disasters tend to fall doubly hard on the weakest group. Then during World War II great gains were made, but since then the position of the Negro — contrary to the notion many hold — has not shown unequivocal progress. There is a Negro share in the general economic progress, and there are great gains, especially in the last few years, by a small Negro upper and middle class. The overall picture, however, and the picture of the Negro's situation relative to the white world, which is what counts, is not so hopeful. There has been a sharp increase in Negro college graduates, high school graduates, millionaires, life insurance policies, savings accounts, government employees, ball players, heads of white churches, congressmen (when Gunnar

Myrdal wrote his *American Dilemma* there was one; now there are six), members of state legislatures, and in many many other indices of integration and of the advance of fortunate, mostly middle-class Negroes.

But another set of statistics shows a situation that may even be worsening: an increase, despite fair-housing efforts, in residential segregation in American cities; a continuing, perhaps even widening gap between the median incomes and the unemployment rates of white and Negro workers; an increase in the number of Negro children in all-Negro schools.

And the advance of more fortunate Negroes may itself add difficulties: a widening gap between the upper- and middle-class fraction and the mass of impoverished Negroes, and an illusion on the part of whites that there is greater progress than there really is.

For a fraction of well-located, well-trained young Negroes the future has suddenly become quite hopeful; jobs open up, corporation recruiters visit Negro campuses, communities welcome their token of integration ("Scarsdale wanted me, White Plains wanted me, Dobbs Ferry wanted me"). Some Negroes will advance more rapidly than they otherwise would because they are Negro. White people of ethnic background, not so well off themselves, notice this fact and complain about it, "Too much is being done for them." I tried to explain about the difficulties Negroes have in finding housing. "*They* didn't have much trouble" was the rather sour answer, referring to a Negro who had moved onto a desirable street. At one of the busing hearings a college and professionally educated bright young Negro from the Fifteenth Ward had his say — strong, effective, well said — right after rather inarticulate efforts on the antibusing side by some whites who also, as it happened, were from our ward. "If this is indicative of the present quality of New Haven education," the Negro said about the speeches he had heard, "then we have nowhere to go but up."

A businessman from the South told about sitting in his club

complaining to a friend that his son was not admitted to Yale;
the friend not only commiserated but explained that his son
too had been turned down. The Negro Steward waiting on
them said quietly, "My son is at Yale." The man telling
this story told it in annoyance. One hears it, however, with
pleasure: it is rather nice — the steward's son being at Yale.
But the many heartwarming American stories of such advances
of a top and (comparatively) fortunate group of Negroes do not
add up to uniform progress: too many Negroes don't benefit by
it.

*

Anyone who has been in the college or liberal or church
circles in which race relations have been the number one social
problem for at least twenty years could put together without
much trouble these answers that I have been giving. Obviously,
to him, the situation of the Negro is much more difficult than
that of the white immigrant. Such a person may be exasperated
— having worked it out so long ago and heard it all so many
times himself — to discover people who don't understand it.
To him this point seems overwhelmingly plain, and he is therefore tempted angrily to ascribe any noncomprehension to
absolute ill will and hatred and bigotry.

There can't be any other reason for opposing this busing plan,
he will say, except *racism*. I don't think he is right. The question whether one ought properly to call all antibusers racists
came to be an important one, in New York as well as
New Haven. At a gathering in the Museum of Modern Art during the fall of 1964, for example, Bayard Rustin used the word
"racism" to describe the people then demonstrating against the
school integration plan in Queens, and the audience applauded. Daniel P. Moynihan — who appears in this book, incidentally, in quite a variety of roles — was another member of the panel with Rustin, and he said angrily, "It's all very
pleasant for a nice middle class audience sitting in the audi-

torium of the Museum of Modern Art to call housewives in Queens racists — that's a stinking word."

There are many Northern white people who have not been raised on *The Races of Mankind,* Gunnar Myrdal, and the vicious-circle theory, and for whom the problem of the Negro, requiring civil rights Acts, open occupancy laws, school redistricting and busing, is not as obvious as the trained civil rights man thinks it to be. All it takes, I think, for these measures to appear to be favoritism is not racial prejudice but merely the absence of a positive civil rights commitment. That vicious-circle theory, after all, is not as easy for the ordinary white man to grasp as civil rights lecturers sometimes assume. In worlds in which a strong civil rights position is not an accepted social convention, it takes either an extraordinary compassion or else a certain ability to deal with abstractions in order to grasp it. One must be able to picture how a complicated social and psychological pattern works to produce the conditions one observes in Negro neighborhoods. That takes some learning. To reverse the meaning of the too often quoted song from *South Pacific,* "You have to be carefully taught." And the teaching is especially difficult to absorb when there is fear that the advances of Negroes threatens one personally.

At one point in New Haven's heated hearings the militant young leader of the local CORE ("We DEMAND, yes, DE-MAND . . .") said that bringing white kids into the Negro ghetto schools would have the added benefit of "showing the whites how Negroes live." Well, unfortunately, even if a school plan were adopted with this rather far-reaching intention, it might not have the desired results. For children from homes that are secure, intelligent, and compassionate, knowing more about how impoverished Negroes really live could increase sympathy or liberalism or guilt or determination to "do something." But what about the others? A fair-minded man, for one very common illustration, tried earnestly to persuade me that

my support for strong civil rights laws was wrong, by citing examples of conditions that he had encountered in making his
calls in slum Negro neighborhoods. He *knew*, or felt he knew,
"how Negroes live" — and that was the main reason he opposed these civil rights laws. He was against a school redistricting that would send his kids over to that school, and against
fair-housing efforts that would bring (as he fears) numbers of
those Negroes into the houses on his street. A civil rights advocate may explode at this and say that such a man is obviously
a bigot (a word that had quite a workout in our New Haven
discussions) and not fair-minded if he blames the conditions
of poverty-stricken people, without a chance or a hope, on race.
I quite agree that of course slum conditions do not come from
race but from poverty and hopelessness, and that the mass of
Negroes have been forced to be poor and hopeless, and that it
is doubly galling and unjust to have racial stereotypes built on
conditions thus forcibly created by racial discrimination. I
would suggest only that the ordinary white workingman is not
necessarily morally reprehensible for not having figured that
out. All we can say about him is that he is lacking in compassionate social imagination — but then, aren't we all?

And then there's money. Having more money means having
more options: moving to the suburbs or to a better part of town,
sending one's children to a private school, having tutors, trips,
or dancing classes. People without much money, with fewer
choices and less control over their situation, resent being stuck
with the bill for a historic national wrong. It is this point that
often gives the argument a passionate intensity. The backlasher often feels that it is he, and not the well-off white civil
rights advocate, who must bear the disadvantages of the cor-
rection of this national injustice to the Negro, an injustice that
he himself does not perceive too clearly, partly because a threat
to him personally interferes with his perception — "You

don't think it's right for a Negro to take Sam's job, do you, Bill?"

The great point is that he feels directly caught and involved. His feelings may in many cases be groundless or exaggerated, projected out of fear or prejudice far beyond the facts; yet there often is a kernel of truth in it. The sad and terrible fact that the Negro *en masse* is linked to ills of poverty should be the occasion for extraordinary efforts to break that link; for many an ordinary struggling white man, however (no ideologue or hero, he), that fact is rather the basis of a not altogether unrealistic personal fear. If schools are to be racially balanced, they reason, some white kids will have to go to the Negro ghetto schools. Whose children will be sent? Quite possibly his. The opponents said that the New Haven school proposals would take their child away from the neighborhood school and abruptly send him to a different and (at least they think) worse school in a worse part of town, away from the school, perhaps, that was the reason for buying a house in a particular district. When in response to this they are given general lectures in race relations, they turn with some ferocity on the proposal's white proponents, and they refer with passion to the real and recent struggles of their own ethnic groups.

To them it appeared that people who have the money and connections to get a good education for their own children suddenly then fasten on to other people, those who are caught and have no alternative, the necessity to send their children to a slum school. To put the general point rudely, but no more rudely than it was often put in New Haven's hearings, it seemed that comfortably well-off private school liberals, with good jobs and big houses in suburbs or in fancy parts of town, are bravely summoning the public school workingmen in two-family-house streets to face the moral crisis of our time. One woman told the old joke about the pig's comment to the chicken on the subject of the ham-and-eggs breakfast, "For you, it is a contribution; for me, it is a sacrifice."

In addition to the nastiness of this attack, it is undeniably in many individual cases quite inaccurate and unfair; it was difficult for wrought-up opponents of the school proposals, for example, to admit that there really were those — all honor to them — whose own children were immediately involved but who were nevertheless quietly and affirmatively supporting the proposals. In group terms, however, the opponents' angry attack has a touch of rough and primitive justice in it. The Yale and middle-class college-educated liberal communities do have, broadly speaking, a privileged sanctuary, and have not, broadly speaking, been exercised about disabilities to white ethnic groups. Mr. Moynihan wrote in *Beyond the Melting Pot*, rather revealingly, "The Irish were the one oppressed people on earth the American Protestants could never quite bring themselves wholeheartedly to sympathize with." Often the white proponents of civil rights proposals see only the distinction white and black, and the opponents of ethnic background see, rather, a series of groups — Irish, Polish, Jewish, Italian — in which the Negro is yet another one, now on the bottom, to whom apply the same counsels and possibilities as applied to the others: group solidarity and mutual help, upward mobility through hard work and education. "There are plenty of Negroes who have made something of themselves," an Italian lady said to me, all innocence at the fallacies implied in her use of this true statement. Again and again reference was made to having "them" make "their own schools" better, as an alternative to correcting racial imbalance. The error in this "self-improvement" point of view is large, but it is not surprising that the view should be held. To see why it is in error, requires some mixture of extraordinary compassion, personal security, and an ability to deal with abstract social ideas.

Even in the one white immigrant group that often does have these things, the Jewish community, there may be difficulties among those personally involved. The Jewish community has a liberal ethos on intergroup relations that the other white ethnic groups by and large do not. At the same time, though, it also has a deep and passionate devotion to education, going beyond that of the others, by and large. The original New Haven school proposals brought these themes in a predominantly Jewish section — Westville — into a sharp, emotional, and really rather poignant conflict.

The non-Negro groups differ among themselves, of course, and one could trace a slightly differing shape to the relation of each to the Negro, the Yankees, the others. One obvious feature of a city turmoil like this one is the way it draws in all the other conflicts and resentments in the town.

Among white groups the Jewish community has felt the sharpest and most recent prejudice. That cuts both ways. It may mean greater empathy, but also a tighter grip on what has been attained, a greater awareness of the barriers one's own group has overcome. The memory of one's grandfather's struggles, without civil rights laws, is more vivid. The Jews once lived in Oak Street, too, and had no rescue by urban renewal.

Much of New Haven's story throughout these months was the story of the anguish of its Jewish community.

I do not conclude that there should be any diminution of support for civil rights. On the contrary, these thoughts reinforce the secondary reasons for a rapid breaking down of discrimination: so that the average white man, who has his own difficulties, knows Negroes from his school and boys' club, and even more so that the mass of Negroes he encounters is not identical with the urban proletariat. The ordinary white man learns his lesson not from race relations lectures but from what he sees, taken — at best — at face value. It is important that the Negro not appear to him to be ineluctably linked to the ills of poverty and an ethnic group that hasn't, as the others have, "lifted itself." It is important that there be more and more middle- and upper-class, white-collar, business, and professional Negroes around to break his stereotypes.

But at the same time I think we should be wary of any exclusive and absolutist civil rights emphasis that is so single-mindedly concentrated on this one issue as to be inattentive to the broad social setting, and separated from measures of general economic and social improvement. We should avoid, I think, the attitude that wants absolutely to separate problems of race from problems of class, and is highly moralistic about race but conservative about social and economic welfare.

Direct governmental action to break racial discrimination is inescapably necessary, but unless it is set in the frame of generally improving conditions in employment and housing and education it will certainly become explosive and it may even someday become unfair. New Haven is going to work out its problem of racial imbalance in the schools, after some pain, because it has a progressive administration and is rebuilding half of the school system and will receive sizable funds from new state- and federal-aid programs; it can set the problem in the frame of a generally expanding and improving education for everyone. Without that frame the story would be different.

Most of all I think we should be cautious about the moral disapproval, and sometimes even the social disdain, with which this issue is filled.

Much depends, obviously, on what you are expected to believe in your world; most of us don't think these things out from scratch by ourselves. In many Northern college-educated and sophisticated circles a superficial antiracism, at least, is the norm. People in those circles attribute to themselves a moral superiority over the low-income white, who doesn't move in those circles and hasn't absorbed conventional brotherhood attitudes, that they really haven't earned. In fact, there is another and ironic turn to the screw: unenlightened racial attitudes may become yet another reason for Yankee and Yale white people to look down on the ex-immigrant white in a way that actually contradicts that superior enlightenment for which they give themselves credit.

"It's quite clear-cut," a cultivated type may say after one of the heated meetings. "It's the responsible people against the rednecks." A sweet, prosperous, liberal wife may be made "positively ill" by the speeches against the school proposals, which "are so illiterate." One civic leader, whose agitation under trying circumstances was understandable, burst out in private after a meeting, "They were just *poor white trash!*" There are many Southern echoes and Northern ironies. A good lady home from her summer place, now in the fall taking up this issue, referred haughtily to the "people who were being so difficult last summer." There may be an element of contempt in the picture of the ethnic backlasher as someone who has just made it himself and is insecure.

The ancestors of those who say these things did not in general exhibit the compassionate identification and environmental understanding for the white immigrants that their children display for the Negro. And now the failure of the sons of those immigrants to join in the compassion for the Negro becomes yet another count against them. I have heard Yalies and Yankees speak of "them" and "they" and "those people," referring to the antibusers of immigrant extraction, in a stereotyped and contemptuous way that would be swiftly labeled by some "stinking word" like "racism" if it were applied to the Negro.

And as to the repeated insistence that the whole thing is a moral issue, that is true enough too, in its way. It doesn't mean, though, that the full "moral" conviction attaching to the assertion of racial equality attaches also to every particular civil rights move, and it certainly doesn't mean that all of us who favor strong civil rights action are thereby morally superior to any of those who resist. It is much more complicated than that. It depends upon what our own situation and alternatives are, and in the working out of this thing we shall need more of Lincoln than of reconstructionist righteousness.

7. A Populist Conservatism

"There's nobody who represents a mediocre neighborhood."

THE PEOPLE who were being so difficult last summer kept insisting they were the majority. They felt they were being pressured for reasons they did not accept, by a minority with whom they did not identify and over whom they had no control. "A *minority* is pushing the *majority* around!" one man said to me, and that was a fairly common formulation. They kept calling for referenda, petitions, votes, the rule of the majority. "Put it to a vote!" they would cry. They mounted the campaign for an elected school board because the present appointed board had made "unpopular" decisions. They exhibited a kind of populistic conservatism, or antiprogressive majoritarianism — a people's party of the right.

There are row on row on row of once-workingclass now lower-middle-class families, and they appropriate to themselves the democratic symbols. They regard themselves as the "majority," and as the "people." They turn against the poor and Negroes as a nonconforming "unpopular" minority, on the one side; they attack, on the other side, the city officials and liberal spokesmen who present programs in behalf of the poor (low-income public housing) as being an undemocratic Elite: high-paid out-of-town administrators, Yale intellectuals, "theorists," "all the so-called do-gooders, these people that live up around the high-class areas."

"We taxpayers and parents who oppose are in the main simple working people . . ." The feeling that the Elite had the jump in organization over the simple working people was strong and extended to the suggestion, "It seems to me that we have been subjected or treated to a well-prepared group of people who obviously didn't write the speeches they were reading."

"I have been sitting here for the past hour and half listening to people from the Human Relations Council, intellectual giants, and most of the people in this room don't know half of what they said and are not particularly interested."

"Mr. Chairman, Mr. Paquin, or Dr. Paquin, Dr. Sachs, all you educated fellows, I'm not educated, but I'm raising a family, and I ask no one for nothing."

References to one's own large family, lack of education, and housing in something other than a "high-class area" would bring a stir of laughing, defiant identification from the crowd, as though to say, to all the intellectual giants and do-gooders and educated fellows, "We are the *real* people." One man was applauded when he said, "I've got eight children and expecting a ninth in September." Another was applauded when he said he lived "on the second floor, in the back."

One could have a certain sympathy for some of this — for the embarrassed diffidence and the feeling of powerlessness of the noncollege townspeople in a city in which there are many high-powered self-confident intellectuals. They had to argue against Yale professors and educators and clergy and psychiatrists and lawyers and social workers — people used to speaking and at home with the lingo, people who "talked so good." Although the opponents were a mixed bag, many of them were less well spoken, less well educated, and acutely conscious of that fact. They felt outside of government, unspoken for, unrepresented; they felt that their protests went unheard. Some of them were very angry when the alderman, for whom they had voted, and whom they had expected to speak up for them, seemed instead to be in the opposite camp. I can see in memory now an angry young constituent at a meet-

ing of my own, in the Hooker basement, calling out at me from
the rear of the hall that an alderman is supposed to represent
the *majority* in his ward. The petulant conviction that "they
(the school board or Housing Authority) won't listen to us"
and "their minds are already made up" and "nobody speaks
for us" and "it's all cut and dried" was instant and strong. The
other tactic for fighting back, besides "put it to a vote" was to
"get a lawyer" — somebody to speak for them.

There was pathos in this, and I could have sympathy up to a
point. That sympathy faded, however, when this self-sympa-
thizing populistic conservatism began to show a nasty and ungenerous attitude toward the poor and (less often overtly)
Negroes, and — as it did much more often — a definite hatred
toward the Yale group, Yankees, intellectuals, suburbanites,
administrators, liberals. This division in New Haven really overshadowed the ostensible racial argument.

Something like it was becoming visible in the 1964 presidential campaign. The petulant Goldwater supporters at San Francisco felt themselves pushed around by "minorities" and wrote
into the platform a condemnation of "inverse discrimination."
In the campaign itself, later on, Senator Goldwater was to make
remarks both against the "East" and the "Establishment" and
against the pressure of demanding "minorities." He praised the
long-suffering, hard-working "majority."

In the Johnsonian consensus, it seemed, there had come a
considerable shifting around. A large part of the responsible
press and of the high financial and business leadership moved
over to Johnson's side, joining the very large proportion of aca-
demicians and cultural leaders and mainline clergy that was already there. Civil rights issues were a major cause. They drove
an emotional wedge between responsible leaders and the feelings of large sections of ordinary white folk. And economic issues reshaped themselves somewhat. Many sophisticated businessmen were no longer outraged by Keynes or by deliberate
government deficits; liberal reformers no longer attacked the

business community or the free market very vigorously; Hubert Humphrey of the ADA talked comfortably about "reasonable profits" with New York businessmen, and a certain consensus appeared. But grumpy Goldwater supporters who hated welfare chiselers, taxes, and bureaucrats, and feared the civil rights movement, and didn't want low-income public housing on their streets were not in on that consensus. We seemed to have come to this rather unsettling fulfillment of the American dream, if that is what it was: a situation in which many a common man, backward-looking, property-holding, and wary, resisted the changes that the leaders of the community saw to be necessary and right.

Whatever the merit of these speculations for the whole country, they plainly did apply in many local battles having to do with Negroes and the poor. In a Detroit struggle over a "homeowners' rights" (anti-fair housing) ordinance in spring 1964, both Republican Governor Romney and Democratic Mayor Cavanaugh opposed the bill, but the voters passed it. That old tool of direct democracy, the referendum, was used to defeat local antidiscrimination ordinances in Berkeley, California, Tacoma and Seattle, Washington, and Cambridge, Missouri. In St. Joseph and Kansas City antidiscrimination ordinances survived referenda by very narrow margins. Governor Wallace of Alabama made forays into the North during the spring of 1964 which were resisted by impressive collections of political, labor, clerical, and journalistic leaders. Yet he was supported by a great many voters — in some cases a majority of the whites. And in the election that was to come in the fall of 1964, California opponents of fair housing (Proposition 14) would win by nearly 2 to 1.

One had the impression that leaders of both parties, leaders of big business and labor, leaders of all faiths, leaders of education, culture, and the press were struggling to bring along an all-too-large and recalcitrant public. These were now issues, in other words, that divided people not so much along lines of occupation, party, or ideology as along the line between responsible leaders on the one hand and some resistant popular feeling on the other.

Civil rights and antipoverty struggles take on this configuration because people in positions of responsibility by conviction or necessity must take a community-wide view, responding to claims of Negroes and the poor and to overall conceptions of justice. Many nonleadership people, in contrast, do not look beyond what they conceive — often in a wrong-headed and prejudiced way — to be their own immediate and parochial interest.

Since on these issues leaders are split off from followers, new, unknown, leaders are cast up: the spokesmen for the Parents and Taxpayers group in New York City; a Detroit candidate for councilman who drafted the homeowners ordinance; Joseph Einhorn of the Better Education Committee (antibusing) in New Haven. Senator Goldwater became something like this antileadership symbol in the nation.

When it came right down to it, of course, the anticivil rights feelings would not show themselves in much backlashing for Goldwater, except in the deep South. Instead they appeared in direct local attacks on civil rights measures. Probably that is the way the Northern white resentment will work out. It will not appear so much in votes against liberal candidates in general elections, where many issues are interwoven, as in specific local campaigns that isolate the civil rights target. Hundreds of thousands of Californians in 1964 would vote both for Johnson and for Proposition 14.

The majoritarianism of the "go slow" people is selective. Back when we were debating the Equal Opportunities Ordinance, which the majority obviously supported, the negative argument was quite different. It was full of legalism and constitutional principle. The opponents expressed a great sorrowful unwillingness to vote for the ordinance, in spite of majority support for it and their own deep sympathy for the Negro, because of strict constitutional scruples. When the school issue arose, however, and they felt the people with them, they changed their tune. "Do what the *majority* wants!" they cried.

Robert Weaver, then the federal government's top housing man and now the Cabinet member, said in his Godkin Lectures at Harvard the following year that there is a class war against the poor — "white, black, or any color" — going on in city after city across the country which is making difficulties for public housing and urban renewal. The question, Weaver said, is "Where shall we put the poor?" The answer from each neighborhood (as on Willow Street and Sherman Parkway in New Haven) apparently is "Not here."

One may see the minority part of this "first minority poor in history" take on a political meaning. The poor have lost even the potential advantage, and the democratic moral authority, of numbers. But, I said to myself in those days, democracy is not simply majority rule — any majority, in any group, on any question. Majority rule operates within certain ground rules; it is joined to another principle, of protected minority rights, or, rather, of rights of the human person and procedures of a free society. It is evident that one cannot subject human life and dignity itself to majority rule. In Dürrenmatt's play *The Visit* the majority in the town, eager to get the offered funds, votes to turn the innocent man over to the vengeful rich woman — to have his head chopped off. No majority vote by Germans in favor of the Nazi's "final solution" to the "Jewish problem" would have made it "democratic."

But the majority who think the poor are lazy and stupid and that Negroes are going "too fast" characteristically acts as though all questions in these fields are simply to be determined by a popular vote. They don't admit that there does arise, at some point, a claim of *rights*, of human equality and of human dignity, that goes to the foundation of a humane and just society and cannot be voted away by the fearful or complacent majority.

Also, we have these ground rules and procedures of freedom; actually, the majority is only to be respected when it develops within these: free speech, free assembly, freedom to organize against it, and the possibility that it will be overturned. No majority vote to suppress a newspaper or a speaker or an opposing party, or suspend elections, would be "democratic."

The majority commands respect only when it has carried its point in open discussion, under conditions that at least allow for deliberation and reasoned judgment, and for reversal. Otherwise the majority represents only power — the power of numbers. I was struck in our New Haven battles at the way voting was a substitute for talking. The power of this group was in numbers, in being the *majority*, not in reasons and arguments. In our PTA they insisted on having the special meeting; they showed up in strength, many of them scarcely ever before having come to a meeting; they were rudely impatient with the palaver. What they wanted was a vote, a vote on "this busing business," as their original motion had put it. When the vote was taken and they had "won" by 80 votes to 44, they were quite ready to break up the meeting. One of their leaders said later, when he declined an invitation to attend a discussion meeting, "We showed what we feel, and that's it." The democratic symbol of the majority was used *against* the democratic methods of deliberation and discussion.

I had not encountered before such a use of the weight of sheer numbers, of votes, of the majority, as a form of mindless power. Don't talk — vote!

The worst form of this majority business is reflected in the remark I quoted at the beginning of the chapter, "A *minority* is pushing a *majority* around!" Later reference to 85 percent of the population made unmistakable what was plain enough already, that the groups in question were racial. As a non-Negro

— a "white" person — I was included willy-nilly in this man's "majority," whatever my convictions might be.

I noticed similar references to the majority in local Church-State struggles over Christmas or official prayer in the schools. Again people would say angrily that a minority (strict separationists, and sometimes this had antisemitic overtones) was prevailing over a majority (believers, prayer-sayers, Christmas-celebrators). As with the racial version, these majoritarians simply assume that everyone in some numerically superior category is to be counted on their side, and that these numbers are to decide all questions.

In battles like these the American institutions of constitutionally protected human rights, and judicial review by the United States Supreme Court, which are our American way of institutionalizing the fundamental nonmajority aspect of democratic social philosophy, do not appear to be very well understood.

And then the "votes" of the "majority" have a claim to acquiescence only when they are taken in some continuing community more inclusive and more permanent than that of the parochial interests immediately affected by the one matter at hand. The political scientist E. E. Schattschneider writes in *The Semisovereign People* about the way parties to a conflict losing in one arena try to broaden the scope of the conflict to a larger one. By taking the matter out to the whole city, or the state, or the nation they may find allies and change the outcome. In these local struggles one feels exactly the reverse side of that point: the effort by the opponents of progressive local actions to narrow the relevant constituency down to those who are immediately (and usually negatively) affected. No one from the Greater New Haven area — only residents of the city, or only residents of the school district, or only parents of children in the school, or only parents of children in the seventh grade of the school, who actually would be bused right now, should be allowed to speak on the busing question. PTA meet-

ings featured angry attacks on speakers who have no children
in the relevant school. Testimony on a site for a public housing
unit should come, they seem to say, only from people in the
neighborhood, on the street, or even on the very block immediately adjacent to it. But obviously it can't work that way. This
consenting of the governed and voting of the people does *not*
mean, cannot mean, that every unit newly defined in a controversy may make itself into a voting, self-determining, and exclusive entity to "vote" away the problems of the larger world.

Mayors and city leaders are in for a most difficult time right
now, although also a stimulating and productive one. There are
the organized poor, plus CORE, sitting in one doorway of the
mayor's office, and the angry spokesmen from the petulant "majority" shouting at the other. It is important to listen to the latter, and to make them aware, if possible, that their arguments
are heard and their interests respected. But it cannot be that
their "votes" should carry the day.

In New Haven the "majority's" great demand became as I
have said, an elective school board.

It certainly is true that the school board makes weighty decisions. In the New Haven city budget for 1965, which the administration was preparing through that hot summer of 1964,
the department of education represented expenditures of more
than 11 millions in a budget of not quite 33 millions — over a
third, and much the largest single item. (In New Haven, unlike
many American cities, the department of education is formally
a part of the city government.) Decisions taken by the Board
of Education in 1964 were undeniably more important, and
also more controversial, than decisions taken that year by the
Board of Aldermen. These school board decisions dealt with
de facto segregation and school sites and teachers' salaries, and
the hiring and retiring and assigning of teachers, and school
prayer, and which of competing teachers' unions to negotiate
with, and finding a new superintendent. All reverberated loudly

in the city's politics, and most entailed some serious conflict of values and of interests.

And it is true that the board had made decisions a large number of the citizens would not support, were these decisions put to popular vote. New Haven had an unusual situation: a school board more progressive even than its teachers, and much more so than its public.

It is a fact, also, as the board's critics like Mr. Einhorn pointed out, that in almost all of the school districts of Connecticut, and in a majority of the school districts in the country, school boards are elected. Nevertheless, there were many of us who were not persuaded that New Haven should change to an elected board. However the arguments may come out in the abstract and in other times and places, a change to an elected board at that moment in New Haven would have been vengeance against the existing board over agitated issues like the busing and school prayer. School board elections would almost certainly have turned, although of course in a disguised way, on resistance to Negro demands — as in Mrs. Hicks's case in Boston.

I don't think "democracy" requires that school boards necessarily be elected. I had an argument about this one night with a Fifteenth Ward Republican who was a prominent member of the Einhorn Better Education Committee. He was wary, he said, about the experts' taking over and running things. He pointed to all the school districts in Connecticut that had elected boards, all but two in the state. He was shocked, he said, that the Mayor, the only elected member of the board (the Mayor is a member ex officio), almost never attended the meetings. How could the *majority* determine school policy? It was undemocratic!

Would one want all boards and commissions elected? Not to put ideas in anyone's head, but what about the Public Housing Authority? Certainly it too makes important and unpopular decisions. And so does the Board of Police Commissioners, which keeps turning down an alderman's request and instituting one-way streets where we don't want them in the Fifteenth Ward.

One may say that school policy is somehow different and more fundamental than these — but, if so, that cuts both ways. The nonmajoritarian parts of the good society are especially relevant in the field of education. If minorities are unequally treated in education it is especially damaging. Qualitative considerations are especially important in education.

Look, for instance, at another, older resentment against this school board. It used to be that every graduate of the old New Haven Normal School (later New Haven State Teachers College) could expect to be given a job in the New Haven school system. "Back then the New Haven schools would just hire the whole list of them," a knowledgeable New Havener reports. I remember during the aldermanic campaign standing first on one foot and then on the other on an angry teacher's porch while she poured out her story. A native New Havener, living all her life with her parents in New Haven, she couldn't get a job in the New Haven system! She had to drive all the way out to a distant town to teach. This made her furious. It's all that man Paquin, she said.

In this heavily ex-immigrant and workingman's city, to have a son or (more often) daughter go into public school teaching was very often the family's first step into the white-collar world, and a thing much desired. It was painful, and it was "unpopular," to end the tradition of having all such daughters hired into the New Haven system — but surely it was necessary, if one wished to improve the quality of the system.

The school board should of course be aware of popular feeling, and responsive to it. It may be that Mayor Lee could be criticized, as a sensitive Republican did, for having named no Republicans to the board. (The city charter requires that no more than four of the seven members of New Haven's Board of

Education, appointed by the mayor to staggered four-year terms, come from any one political party; nevertheless, that does not mean that the other three need come from the loyal ranks of the other party. They may be "independents.") And perhaps a wider variety of the citizens should serve on the board. A former alderman offered himself as a candidate for the board on the rather unusual ground that "there's nobody who represents a mediocre neighborhood."

Probably professional educators should not be as impervious to politics and public feeling as they sometimes have been. Professional educators tell us that education is one thing and politics another and they should be kept separate. Politics is dark, terrible, and messy. Education, on the other hand, is a profession, with a technical and expert content that cannot be grasped by laymen. A political scientist who once, as the director of a state "little Hoover" commission, asked why the state department of education should be organized differently from any other department of state government found that his innocent inquiry threw the commissioner of education into "a purple and highly articulate rage." The school system should be kept apart, so the story goes, from the main line of politics in the city and the state: state departments of education and city school systems should not be subject to the "political" powers but be set apart and independent and professional. Maybe so. But suppose innovation, imagination, and new policy are badly needed in our city school systems, and that the school bureaucracy is often inert and resistant?

Naturally, it is desirable to keep down, if one can, the factionalism within a school system — the internal politics; it is also wise to recognize that at least in a large system there will be some, nonetheless. Of course, it is desirable, too, to avoid favoritism in school appointments and advancements and the letting of contracts. This is politics in the low sense, and educators who have seen it intrude into the schools understandably want to keep it out.

Yet one wants not only the serious consideration by the top school people of the feelings, interests, and values in the populace; and the use by these school leaders of the "political" arts of listening, responding, persuading, building support both within the system and in the public at large, but also their alert attention to new educational needs. Perhaps one should call these things by other names, to keep away the curse of the association with politics in the bad sense — diplomacy, community leadership, the anticipation of future problems. Most important is the need to develop new school policy to meet new social conditions. School systems characteristically have not faced the problem of the influx of Negroes and of segregated schools until they were forced to. Democracy means inclusion and equality, not just majority will — and nowhere more importantly than in education.

From the point of view of the Mayor, he receives from the schools much blame and many problems, without having clearcut responsibility and control. The de facto segregation problem was such a hot potato politically that the Mayor was doubtless quite willing to keep his own hands off it. He was not happy about the way it was handled, though, and unhappy later when the school system seemed unresponsive to the turbulent unrest created in the city by the controversy of its making.

The fault may lie in the way we think about education and politics. Perhaps the Mayor has had too little to do with education in New Haven, for the honorable reason that he says he isn't an expert in that field; and perhaps the school administrators have had too little political skill and sensitivity, for the honorable reason that these never were felt to be a requirement of their work. But from now on, in the cities, this will surely have to change.

8. Election, 1964

"This Goldwater thing scares me."

I PICKED UP the newspaper each day with some uneasiness, through that summer of 1964. The riot in Harlem was followed by others in Bedford-Stuyvesant and in Rochester, and then in Jersey City, Elizabeth, and Paterson, and then in a suburb of Chicago, and finally at the end of August in North Philadelphia. New Haven citizens simmered over the busing and the newspapers were full of something they called backlash. In late July and early August the tension from these intermingled local and national events was at its height. It was a tangible reality, and there was hostility in the air at every social gathering. People seemed to repeat a gesture with the hand to the neck, saying, "We've had it up to here." After a particularly rough meeting one shocked liberal Democrat said, "These people are going to vote for *Goldwater.*" With the Mayor sick and the citizens furious with each other and headlines about riots, with Kennedy gone and Goldwater nominated, the atmosphere had changed a great deal from that of the night of victory eight months before.

But then the national scene, at least, began to look better. The polls began to show a strong public resistance to Goldwater. The most reassuring poll I read about was one conducted by a newspaper I knew, the *Hutchinson* (Kansas) *News*. To my astonishment it showed Johnson with a margin over Goldwater larger even than the margin in the same poll four years earlier, in the opposite party direction, of Nixon over Kennedy. If those Scouts whom I had known in the Southwest Kansas Council of the Boy Scouts of America were voting Democratic, we weren't in any trouble at all.

My wife and I watched the President's stagey nomination of his vice-presidential candidate, and the acceptance speeches, on the Applebys' television set. We were by then relatively calm. "TAMARRA," I said to Appleby, after listening for a long time to the presidential ideas stated in the presidential Texan, "TAMARRA IS YERRS."

And the opening of New Haven's schools was uneventful. At around seven-thirty on the mornings of that school year 1964–1965, a yellow school bus operated by the Chieppo Bus Company, under contract to the New Haven Board of Education, would stop at the corner of Livingston and Canner Streets in the Fifteenth Ward and in the Worthington Hooker grammar school district. The bus would pick up twenty-two schoolchildren, all but two of them white, who were on their way to their seventh-grade classes. I would see them out there on the corner, or, on rainy days, huddled on the Applebys' porch. The bus took them across a central piece of New Haven, a distance of about four miles, to the Susan Sheridan Junior High School. In any previous year these students would have attended the seventh grade at Worthington Hooker, which until the decision of the Board of Education in July 1964 had been an anomalous eight-graded school in the New Haven system of junior high schools. That decision, however, abolished the seventh and eighth grades in this school. The Hooker seventh-graders were now to go to Sheridan Junior High, along with all of the new seventh-graders from the old districts both of Sheridan itself and of Bassett Junior High School.

Sheridan Junior High School during 1964–1965 had only two grades: the "old" ninth grade, predominantly white, which consisted of the students who attended the school in previous years, and a giant new seventh grade, half Negro, which consisted not only of those who under the old arrangement would have attended Sheridan but also all those — a large percentage of them Negro — who would have attended Bassett, plus the small band from Hooker. The school as a whole was about 65 percent white. I was surprised to learn that the seventh grade was divided into *nineteen* ability groups for the academic subjects. Can the groupings really be drawn that fine? Need they be? These ability groups tended to have a distinct racial composition, the higher ones predominantly white, the lower ones predominantly Negro. The ability groupings determined the composition of most of a student's classes during the day, except in homeroom and shop. The two white seventh-grade boys whom I know who were bused to Sheridan from the Hooker district were very enthusiastic about it, and so were their parents. These boys were stimulated far beyond anything that had happened to them before, and beyond what Hooker, with very limited seventh-grade facilities, could have done. They were much in favor of the arrangement. It must be added, though, that they were in the top ability group, an all-white collection of good students.

At about a quarter to eight, meanwhile, another bus would stop at the corner of Canner and Orange Streets and again at the corner of Canner and Prospect Streets to pick up groups of eighth-graders — twenty-six in all. These, also former Hooker students, were now on their way to Bassett Junior High School on the other side of Prospect hill. There at Bassett these students formed part of an enlarged eighth grade, the counterpart of the enlarged seventh grade at Sheridan. Bassett had also its normal-sized and mostly Negro ninth grade. The school as a whole, with the eighth grade mixed (about 60 percent white) and the largely Negro "old" ninth grade, had 363 Negroes and 256 white students during 1964–1965. Bassett also had ability groupings, and there too the groups were mostly white at the top and mostly Negro at the bottom.

The racial symmetry of the ability groups was a point of criticism of the "balance plan" both by a few of those favoring it
("they've got a white third floor over there") and those opposing it. The principal of Bassett said that the effect of the ability
groups in reality is not as damaging to the purpose of integration as it may appear. The middle groups are mixed, he said,
and the students spend only three hours, or four subjects, of the
school day in classes divided by ability. The placing of a child
was done separately for each subject, so that he might be higher
in one than another. In art, music, home economics, industrial
arts, physical education, lunch hour, and homeroom there was
no ability grouping.

The initial situation in the two junior high schools differed.
Bassett had been heavily Negro, and had had a large new minority of white students brought into it. Sheridan had been
mostly white, and now had a large new minority of Negro students brought into it. Sheridan had had the best reputation
of the city's junior highs; Bassett, as a mostly Negro school,
had been looked down upon.

I asked a researcher who was studying the busing experience
whether the education of the Negro students who were in Bassett had been improved. Yes, he said — not, ironically, so much
by the association with the white kids brought into the school
as by the fact that now, as a result of the controversy, the school
system paid a great deal of attention to Bassett, with special
classes, able new teachers, new equipment. As for the white
students going to Bassett, they were almost certainly receiving
a better education in Bassett than they would have at Hooker,
and as good as they might have at Sheridan — although many
of their parents would angrily deny this.

Meanwhile, some teachers at Sheridan who had been accustomed to all-white, almost all college-preparatory bright students had a hard time adjusting to the influx of Negroes and of
less able students. One knowledgeable observer said that there
were teachers who had good reputations because they had al-

ways taught this top group but really hadn't had to work at teaching since "these students teach themselves." The busing influx and reassignment of teachers was for them a painful change.

Some of the new white students came into Bassett with an antagonistic attitude toward teachers, the Negro students, the whole enterprise. Their antagonism in certain cases doubtless was absorbed from parents (how could they help but absorb it?) and their attitude was "Just try to teach me something." There was some fear about fights. Jewish middle-class children taught at home not to fight were sent into a school with Negro children who were not necessarily "middle class" or taught any such thing at home. New "security guards" were added at Bassett. The principal said that discipline problems have been no worse than during other years.

At Sheridan the new Negro minority was in quite a different situation. Much of the new white minority at Bassett could be put right away into the top academic ability group, and could use its superiority in intelligence, or at any rate in educational performance, as a weapon for status. The new Negro minority at Sheridan was not in a position to do this, and for them it was rough.

At a quarter after eight yet two more school buses would arrive at the Worthington Hooker elementary school and some eighty lively fifth- and sixth-graders, all Negro except for three, would burst out onto the playground. I was there the first morning they arrived. Some of them no doubt were a bit apprehensive because of what they had heard about Hooker during the summer. One Negro mother, though very eager for a good education for her children, did not volunteer to send them to Hooker because she had heard the vocal opposition from the PTA and her children had had unpleasant experiences at Hooker's summer school.

It is always touching to see a youngster coming to his first

day at school. I was moved particularly, with that sudden gust
of feeling that hits you once in a while, by a short, sober Negro
boy with large eyes who clutched his big blue notebook to his
chest and looked around carefully to see where he was supposed
to go in this new school. Timidly he asked a white father who
was standing nearby with his son. It happened to be a man who
had expressed himself against the busing plan, and this man
gently tried to help him out. How many similar Negro children
there have been these last ten years! Venturing into hostile territory merely in order to go to school.

These students on the bus had gone in previous years to the
Ivy Street School, a largely Negro and overcrowded school.
Their parents had chosen to send them to Hooker, under a provision in the school board's final integration arrangements. They
were there, in other words, voluntarily, which was not the case
with the students in the junior highs.

My daughter Cynthia was in one of the Hooker classes into
which the new children — the "bus children" — were put;
her class had sixteen white children and ten Negroes. The only
anguish in the experience for her was separation from her close
friends, all of whom were spirited away to another class by the
new division required by the busing. After a brief weepiness
one night early in the school year, however, she bucked herself up by getting out her "President Kennedy letter." This letter was a response sent by the White House to a letter she decided to write to President Kennedy one afternoon after the
Birmingham bombing in 1963, when she was eight years old, a
letter in a third-grader's prose commending Mr. Kennedy for
all the good work he was doing for Negroes and asking why
white people are so mean to Negroes. Back from the White
House came a letter not from the President but from Lee C.
White, assistant special counsel to the President. Mr. White,
sitting down there in the White House answering mail, started
off this one well enough for a sentence or two. Very soon he
seems to have slipped, and to have dictated — or more likely

to have had his secretary pull out of the file of standard para-graphs — material rather beyond the third-grade range: "In view of the violent history of mankind, perhaps the questions should not be why prejudice and hatred continue to exist but how we have been as successful as we have in eliminating them from our society. By understanding the means by which prog-ress has been made, perhaps it will be possible to make more progress . . . the differences in the backgrounds of the various groups have often promoted insecurity and tension when they have been thrown together. But often by learning each other's habits and customs, fear of differences has been alleviated and people have learned to live and work together. Individuals have exercised the rights guaranteed by our Constitution and have accepted the accompanying results."

There was more like this. I am not sure that Mr. White had firmly in mind that his correspondent was eight. But Cynthia liked her President Kennedy letter anyway, and she kept it. Now in this moment of civil rights crisis she got it out and sat on the corner of her bed and reread it.

When I asked the research man studying the busing where it had most clearly succeeded I was rather surprised when he said that the real winners were those in the voluntary program in the elementary schools (the fifth and sixth grades). Hooker was one school he especially singled out, and he had in mind particularly the white children — in other words, Cindy Miller. Why this group? Because these children in the elementary schools were able to establish a better relationship of accept-ance, within the classroom and throughout the school, between whites and Negroes than the students in either junior high. They were younger, less tough, further from adolescence; and they did not make as much out of differences in educational per-formance. Although the Cindys recognize that by and large the Negroes do less well than the white students in the class, they do not make much of this fact. Grades and intellectual stand-

ing do not matter so much. Other features of life in the classroom and the playground are more important (Cindy is somewhat intimidated by the baseball prowess of the Negro girls),
and since the group is small and all of the classes are mixed the
students come to know each other as particular individuals in
the configuration of school life. Racial generalizations are sub-
ordinated. Also, the numbers of bused students are smaller in
the elementary schools. Hooker, which had the largest group of
Negroes bused in among the elementary schools had 89, and
these were distributed so as never to be a majority in any classroom. At Sheridan Junior High some 280 Negroes arrived each
morning — enough to constitute a bloc — and with the cliques
of a larger school and with the elaborate division into ability
groupings there is an amount of continuing psychological separation.

The junior high school program was involuntary. Many of
the parents were vigorously opposed to it and many of the students absorbed the parental attitudes. That program began in
an atmosphere of much greater opposition and tension than did
the voluntary elementary school program. The latter inadvertently may rather have profited by the diverting of opposition
to the more controversial junior high plan. It did not receive the
developed antagonism, and was therefore able to shake itself
down more easily into a viable operation.

The line of majority opposition, at least in the Hooker area,
probably fell between the involuntary busing of our children
out to the "Negro school," which most opposed, and the voluntary busing of the Negro children in to "our" school, which most
could accept. Many opponents of the busing plan during the
hearings said that though they opposed taking their children
off to another school they were willing to see Negro children
brought into "their" neighborhood school. This does not mean
that the year at Hooker went smoothly. A minority of the teachers were unhappy and upset, visibly so, and this communicated
itself to the children. There were those who referred to the "bus

children" or even the "Ivy children" as distinct from the Hooker regulars. One teacher found the Negroes to be the best students in her class, but that was unique; the more characteristic experience was the opposite, and there were problems of discipline.

Throughout the fall, at the end of the school day the buses left the schools shortly after 2:30 P.M., and the "bus children" were not able to participate in extracurricular activities that take place after school. Mayor Lee wrote a letter to the superintendent in late November — his first public word of any kind about the busing — asking that extra late buses be added to the schedule. The letter had scarcely left his desk before it was done.

There were some criticisms of the bus operation itself. Some Negro mothers from the Ivy school felt that four bus trips a day were too many, and arranged to have lunch provided at the school to obviate the noon trips.

An educator whose job connected him closely with the busing operation said that he now knew that it could be a success if: the physical act of busing itself is carefully done (not sixty children to a bus, which state law allows, but forty or thirty; complaints about the actual bus ride have dropped away after this change); the *number* of children brought in is not too large a fraction of the whole (better eight than the ten in Cindy's class of twenty-six); and the teacher responds to the situation creatively. Needless to say, the last is the most important point; it is almost the whole story. Some teachers, like the young teacher in Cindy's class, responded well. Other teachers found the whole thing added trouble, and students were quick to perceive a teacher's attitude.

A *Times* report on the pairing in New York City said the program seemed to be going well if the principal was on top of it; where the principal was overwhelmed there were problems. The principals varied in New Haven, too. There isn't any doubt that the attitudes and quality of the teachers and principals are centrally important. At the end of the 1964–1965 school year, later than usual, new assignments were announced, and new principals were assigned to Sheridan, Bassett, and Hooker for the next year.

Scars from the busing fracas were still visible in the New Haven body politic.

The group called the Better Education Committee, composed exclusively of Republican political figures, came into being as a result of the summer's events. It kept up a steady barrage of criticisms of the busing and of the schools in an effort toward making a case for an elected school board. The leader of this Republican committee was Joseph Einhorn. Later he and his committee turned fire on CPI, which the antibusing people blamed for the busing and which to them was a symbol of "outside theorists" upsetting the city's life.

But perhaps a New Haven citizen may be allowed one or two chauvinistic words: we didn't have any kind of boycott; we did institute and did carry out a much resented integration plan at the difficult junior high level, one involving a far larger part of the school population than, say, New York City's plan.

In New York City there had been a Negro school boycott in February 1964, in which 464,362 schoolchildren had stayed away from classes; then in the following fall there was a white boycott, in which 275,000 were absent when a pairing plan was instituted.

Miss June Shagaloff had begun the NAACP drive against de facto segregation in 1962. She lists a number of school systems that have been integrated successfully since then. It turns out, however, that they are of the size of Stamford, Connecticut; White Plains, New York; Oxnard, California, and Montclair, New Jersey. The cities she has found to be deficient, in contrast ("token or less than token"), include Chicago, Detroit, Cleveland, Buffalo, Los Angeles, and San Francisco.

Many cities have adopted "free choice transfer" or "open enrollment" programs like the voluntary cluster plan at the elementary school level in New Haven; Miss Shagaloff and the NAACP regard this as inadequate because "it puts the burden for desegregating the schools on the Negro parents rather than on the school board."

In New Haven's hectic July week of behind-the-scenes negotiations, one proposal that had strong support would have brought all the bused pupils from the overcrowded Negro schools out into the less crowded white ones, and none the other way. Obviously this would have been somewhat easier to swallow, because many white parents who resisted having their child sent away did not object to the importation of Negroes, and also because there was some feeling that integration was more easily achieved at the elementary rather than at the junior high level. This proposal was rejected because it "asks the Negroes to do something we aren't asking the whites to do."

The school boards in Hartford and Bridgeport both decided, after New Haven's experience, that though they acknowledged a responsibility to try to counteract racial imbalance they did not propose to do any busing. The Bridgeport board said that de facto segregation in schools is "socially undesirable and impedes full attainment of the goals of education" but that the board "does not intend to bus children," and that it will retain the concept of the neighborhood school. It said it will instead keep racial composition in mind in establishing school districts and selecting sites for new schools. The questions are whether it really will do that, and whether that is enough to achieve much integration. New Haven is reported to be the best integrated of the cities of the state, with Negroes living on 40 percent of the blocks of the city. Also, it is building anew or replacing 15 schools — 40 percent of the school system. Even so, the schools could not be fully integrated simply by placing sites strategically and by such redistricting as can be done without busing. In the heart of the Negro sections essentially segregated schools would remain.

In Hartford the superintendent of schools said that moving

pupils from their neighborhood schools "would almost certainly accelerate the pace at which white families would leave the city. The result, inevitably, would be a predominantly non-white school system." In New York City, administrators said the number of whites leaving the system was not as few as they had hoped, or as many as they had feared.

Miss Shagaloff says that cities use three levels of evasion. The worst is to deny — as in Boston and San Francisco — that the school board has any responsibility to correct a pattern of segregated schools. The next is to adopt only voluntary plans, like open enrollment. Yet another is to put emphasis on special programs for the "culturally deprived child." I confess I didn't understand what was wrong with this last one when she listed it, but later a section of Kenneth B. Clark's book *Dark Ghetto* explained it to me. Although gearing education to compensate for the cultural deprivation of low-income children sounds fine, it tends to put the burden on the environment and the book-less home rather than on teacher and the school, and thus to lower expectations. This last is what most concerns Dr. Clark, and it seems to me he is correct about the danger: there remains a very strong undercurrent in American society to treat the poor and especially the Negro poor as being capable of some-thing less than the performance of the middle class — if not innately, then by "cultural deprivation." Dr. Clark warns of this undercurrent, and wants to put the burden on the school to teach, to find the ways to teach, everybody and to expect in the end fully as much of a child from one background as an-other.

In New York City reports were similar to those in New Haven: the most significant change wrought by the balance plan was in the amount of attention and expenditure directed to the schools involved in it. New York's program for 1964–1965 was a pairing of eight elementary schools. This represented a minute percentage — 6/10 of 1 percent — of the total public school population of New York; perhaps I should note that New

Haven's program represented a much larger fraction of the city's pupils. Teachers in New York interviewed by the *New York Times* said things like "Last year I had a class of 35 pupils. This year I have 22. It makes a tremendous difference." . . . "Last year we had a four-hour school day . . . this year the children get five hours. Last year we had fewer and older books. Now we have all the books and materials we need." One Negro teacher commented, "I am sorry it took the pairing to give us the facilities and the books we need. The same conditions have existed for years. They should have been corrected long ago." A principal of one of the affected schools said, "Every school in this city, paired or not, should have the extra services we have been given."

The question, in New Haven as in New York, is whether these inner-city schools in reality can be given the smaller classes, better materials, good and experienced teachers and principals, and special attention that they need *without* having responsibility concentrated on them by a new program like the pairing. The irony of these programs seems to be that the chief benefit arises not in the direct effects of the new intermingling but in the indirect effect of the new school services and conditions that could have come into being — but probably wouldn't have — without the pairing.

Some say there are benefits to Negro noncollege pupils in being around the model of academically minded whites; others say that there isn't much to this point.

In both New Haven and New York there is a residual group of angry and resistant white parents, "sullen" is the word used by an alderman in New Haven. This group, fortunately, is reduced in size and in the virulence of their opposition.

Busing was a large issue in several places in the political campaign of 1964. In New Haven sometimes it seemed that the Republicans would campaign on that issue exclusively. New York City was having a dramatic busing battle featuring a white parents' boycott of the schools, and many other communities were having one form or another of the same struggle. Politicians running even for the highest national offices were declaring themselves on this local educational matter. The Republican candidate for the United States Congress in the Third District of Connecticut, which includes New Haven, made opposition to busing his major theme. His advertisements in the newspaper said, "Hear Bernie Burns speak out against busing!" and on election eve he paraded through some of the smarting wards of the city with a couple of symbolic school buses.

Republicans were not alone in making antibusing statements. Senator Thomas Dodd, the incumbent Democrat, declared himself while campaigning in New Haven to be opposed to busing (as did also, at a meeting of Fifteenth Ward Republicans in the basement of Worthington Hooker School, his Republican opponent John Davis Lodge). Over in New York the candidates for the United States Senate seat, Kenneth Keating and Robert Kennedy, who otherwise were trying to outdo each other in demonstrations of superior liberalism (where else in the country do candidates contend about which one the ADA liked better?), were both quick to declare against busing, at least in its long distance and compulsory aspects. Hubert Humphrey, the most unmistakably liberal of the candidates for the nation's highest offices in 1964, had quietly remarked early in the campaign that busing was not the right way to do the thing.

And the "conservatives," as they call themselves, made busing one of the more prominent and passionate new issues of the whole national presidential campaign. Toward the end of it, in Chicago and in Dover, Delaware, and in Pittsburgh and Cleveland and New York, Mr. Goldwater was using busing as his most pungent example of the evil deeds of liberals. It is, he said, "morally wrong," an example of "doctrinaire and misguided equalitarianism." "In New York," he said, "they are moving school children around in buses so they can establish what in some bureaucrat's mind is the proper mix of races, creeds, and colors." In his speech in Madison Square Garden he referred to the matter twice, condemning "forcibly busing your children from your chosen neighborhood school to some other one just to meet an arbitrary racial quota."

Miss Shagaloff is not sure that these politicians had done their homework, and suspects that some of them were declaring against things nobody had proposed. All that the NAACP asks, she says, are "meaningful" programs to end segregated schools. The resolution on the subject adopted by the NAACP at its convention in Washington in June 1964 specifically said that "the NAACP does not propose that Negro and white children be distributed from one end of a city to another, sometimes called "busing" or "cross-busing" to achieve a fixed proportion of white and Negro children in every now segregated white or Negro school." "But we firmly insist," the NAACP resolution went on, "upon the adoption of meaningful plans, which may or may not call for pupil transportation, to change the basic pattern of extensive and rigid segregation-in-fact."

The Democrats of New Haven and of the Fifteenth Ward were lackadaisical about the national elections of 1964; slow on new registrations (except for the civil rights groups registering Negroes); slow on absentee ballots, slow on ward meetings. They were lazy, I think, for this combination of reasons: complacency, because the polls showed Johnson and the Democrats running far ahead (75 percent of the vote, or more) of Goldwater and Company; lack of interest, because Kennedy was gone and Johnson evoked no comparable enthusiasm, and because Connecticut's reapportionment scrambles had chopped the state offices off the ticket and left no candidate nearer home than the congressman; and finally because, among Democrats, including party workers, one could find traces of what was then being everywhere described and discussed as backlash. "This Goldwater thing scares me," a Democrat would say, at some solemn moment in the discussion.

Although, of course, for traditional Republicans a Goldwater vote could signify something other than opposition to the civil rights movement, for independents and defecting Democrats in New Haven it plainly meant that one thing alone. So it was universally regarded. "I am afraid that people tell the pollsters they will vote for Johnson, but then when they get in that booth the bigotry will well up in them and they will pull that Goldwater lever."

The sad memory of Kennedy was obviously the deepest emotion among New Haven Democrats, and many Republicans, too, throughout 1964. There were poems of utter sentimentality, endless Kennedy books, placemarks with religious themes plus Kennedy quotations, pictures, framed reprints of his inaugural address, a film of his visit to Ireland, a world of memory items of which there are whole clubs of collectors. I remember a skeptical Negro taxi driver in Washington remarking to me in the spring of 1964 — out of the blue, as we drove by a group of sightseers bound for the Kennedy grave — "There's been more money made out of that man than anybody since John Dillinger."

When Hubert Humphrey appeared on the New Haven Green one evening in October 1964, campaigning for the Johnson-Humphrey ticket, he kept saying over and over at emotional high points that Lyndon Johnson had been *chosen* by John Fitzgerald *Kennedy*. When John M. Golden spoke to the Democratic town committee at their first meeting for that 1964 campaign, he recommended Lyndon Johnson by making one point: Johnson was carrying out *Kennedy's* program. On election day, 1964, when Johnson was running against Goldwater, the only politically relevant conversations among the women workers in the headquarters of the Fifteenth Ward, in the basement of the chairlady's house on Everit Street, had to do with Kennedys: the anniversary of the assassination was coming, and "they'll have to bring it all up again"; "he was so young-looking"; "that man had a beautiful face"; "a Boston paper ran a

Kennedy feature, did you see it?"; "that Jackie's going to be a great woman." The only candidate whose candidacy was discussed was Robert Kennedy, who was running for Senator in New York State. "Bobby has a rounded face, more of Jack's features." "If you'd close your eyes you'd think it was Jack." When Pat Cassidy came back from the polls in the Hooker basement, where on election day he is always the Democratic worker on the first machine, he told us about the lady who insisted that she wanted to vote (here in Connecticut) for Robert Kennedy.

The Republicans in the ward, more active than in recent memory, advertised their rally in the Worthington Hooker basement with these topics: scattered housing, busing, elected school board, and creeping socialism. No mention was made of Goldwater, and persons who attended reported that the meeting dealt almost entirely with local, racial matters.

On election day the Better Education Committee had signs and agents stationed just beyond the polls in both directions. The signs said "Sign here for an elective school board. Stop school bussing." The group collected more than 400 signatures at the Fifteenth Ward polls.

I noticed Henry Wallich, an economist at Yale and, as a Republican, a member of President Eisenhower's Council of Economic Advisers, who was efficiently reading his *New York Times* while standing in line to vote. "I wonder how he is going to vote," I said to myself. While driving people to the polls I encountered Mary Jane Taft, daughter-in-law of the late Senator Taft, who was that day much concerned about how her brother-in-law Bobby was doing in Ohio; she was also driving people to the polls — for the other side. She had Goldwater stickers on her Fiat and a big Goldwater button on her coat. "What did you expect?" she asked, with a grin. Later I noticed that the Republicans were using her house for ward headquarters.

The absentee ballot report in the middle of the day looked good: more than 2 to 1 in our ward, and downtown headquarters was telling with glee the report from the mostly Negro Nineteenth Ward: 50 Johnson, 0 Goldwater.

One woman whom I drove to the polls, a widow, presumably followed the instructions her teen-age daughter gave her, with a smile, when she left, "Remember — Johnson." But on the ride back she remained a little disturbed. "They tell me not to vote for the Democrats," she confessed, "because they are for this busing of our children."

The polls close at seven in national elections, and the opening of the machines was quick, as usual. The first machine sounded encouraging — even better than we had really expected. When I had the total of the three machines it was excellent, from our point of view: 1445 Johnson to 726 Goldwater. Kennedy had carried the ward by only 50 votes four years earlier, and the Republicans with Eisenhower had stampeded the Democrats in the two presidential elections before that. I was happy as I left the school. On the corner outside a Republican, angry at the busing and at other things, one who reads John Birch books like *None Dare Call It Treason*, burst out as I passed with "I hope you realize what you are doing, *finally*." This remark might be a little cryptic to anyone who lacked a key, but I think I grasp enough of the John Birch outlook to understand it.

The reports from the rest of the city were even better than those from the ward. Johnson carried New Haven by an altogether record-breaking 2 to 1 margin. In fact, when I saw the results from the city and from other wards I was not so sure but that ours had run somewhat behind and that there had been a minor impact of these controversies after all. The newspapers concluded, from the heavy Johnson votes in the affected Westville wards, that the busing had not had such an impact. Democrats in the Fifteenth Ward lagged behind the city — behind the state, for that matter. The adjacent Eighteenth Ward, similar except lacking in backlash, gave Johnson a better than 3 to

1 vote. I think that a handful of "white backlash" Democrats did switch in our ward.

There was one ray of hope for the Republicans, according to the Republican town chairman. The signatures on the petitions for an elective school board, he said, showed that the Republicans could do well in a *city* election in the future.

Meanwhile, Mayor Lee had returned to his office on the day after Labor Day 1964. City Hall employees gave him an impromptu party. Then three weeks later he fell and broke his ankle and had to stay home. When we saw him again he was hobbling on fancy aluminum crutches. He really wasn't fully in charge again until after the Goldwater election and Thanksgiving Day had passed. The agitated matters from the summer had by that time begun to diminish in importance, although they didn't go away. The Mayor resumed his central place. New Haven politics and government resumed their normal recent shape, with the renewal of the city as the feature attraction and ribbon-cuttings or ground-breakings every fortnight.

I want to make a pause here — now, at last — going back some in time, to discuss that renewal and also to describe Mayor Lee. He and his programs loom large enough in New Haven affairs to require a section all to themselves.

 Part II

The Renewing of a City

9. New Haven's Rebuilding

"If we hadn't got Macy's it would have been just awful."

I HAD TO CHOOSE, one night back in June 1964, whether to attend the Board of Aldermen, and vote approval on New Haven's Church Street "front block" redevelopment project, or the Worthington Hooker PTA, and vote on the busing. I chose the latter. We aldermen had already had both a hearing and a special meeting on the redevelopment project, so the final vote was a formality. The two occasions, though, symbolized the sharply contrasting themes in the city's affairs that came to their climax at exactly the same time.

The city had a dinner a fortnight later at the Ambassador Restaurant to celebrate the completion of the plans for the front block, the centerpiece of New Haven's renewal. The Mayor, looking faded, did come and preside and introduce the star performers in New Haven's renewal, one by one, with a joke for each. The dinner came on Wednesday of the week of public hearings on busing. The next night, at the final one of those hearings, a Republican alderman commented pointedly that the Mayor seemed well enough to go to a dinner celebrating urban renewal, even if he was too sick to have anything to do with the busing problem.

I felt often in those months, as at that dinner, as if I lived in two quite different political worlds. One consisted of aldermen, ward maneuvering, old ethnic antagonisms, and all the controversies of the summer. The other consisted of the renewal people, of the Development Administrator's modern office, of the bright pictures of new buildings, new plans, and new ideas.

The man who held these two worlds together was the Mayor. When in the fall of 1964 he had recovered and returned to work, I talked to him about the wrangle over segregation in the schools. He said the whole subject should be put in perspective. There's a lot more happening in New Haven than that, he said. I knew he was right.

I certainly never expected when I first began to live in a rather dingy New Haven back in 1947 that I would ever hear it referred to as the Athens of America; and yet in 1964 I heard a television announcer say this, at the half of a Yale-Princeton basketball game, while the screen showed pictures of the city's new architecture.

I did not expect, either, that I would ever hear the city of New Haven called the West Point of Urban Renewal, or the West Point of anything, for that matter, but New Haven under Lee had become a training ground for talent in the city-administering fields: Edward Logue, New Haven's first Development Administrator, was now chief renewer in Boston, and L. Thomas Appleby, New Haven's second Development Administrator, soon was to become the same at the other end of the Eastern urban corridor, in Washington, D.C. Other alumni were scattered across the country.

I left New Haven in 1953, just as Mayor Lee took over; I returned in 1958 to find the city dug up and changed. While living elsewhere I had bought a copy of *Harper's* for October 1957 and read an article entitled "Lee of New Haven and His Political Jackpot." It called Lee "the first city mayor in the country to make urban renewal the cornerstone of his political career." But when I got back to the city I learned that New Haven's renewal was by no means clinched in 1957, nor in 1958. It had moved forward more or less steadily during the planning stages and during the first (Oak Street) project.

The Church Street project, located in the center of the city on the Green, was perhaps the most important of New Haven's ten projects. This effort ground to a halt in the late fifties — at about the time Mayor Lee was featured in that article and was deciding not to run for the Senate, and was attaining a national reputation and being studied by the researchers for Professor Robert Dahl's book *Who Governs?*

Although notable renewal in other areas of the city was accomplished or well under way, the citizenry tended to equate all of it with that one big project in the center of the city, and that project came to have a long history of difficulties. The idea right along had been to rebuild some blocks near the Green with a new department store and a new hotel, both of which New Haven long had needed, together with a new office building and new shops and garages. The Connecticut Turnpike and the Oak Street Connector would provide easy access, and the Temple Street Garage easy parking. All this was essential to attract shoppers back from the suburban shopping centers and to resuscitate the heart of the city. Actually putting the combination together required a very long hassle, and involved a court case with a jewelry store that wouldn't move, and endless negotiations with possible hotel operators and stores.

The whole thing might have flopped. The magazine articles about Lee in 1957 and 1958 commended his courage, and indicated the reasons for the reluctance of mayors and politicians elsewhere thoroughly to identify themselves, as he did, with a massive urban renewal program. Eviction notices are sent to voters, there are endless perplexities and tortuous negotiations, and there is the possibility of a large and very visible failure. It was implicitly assumed, however, that Lee and New Haven were over the hump — but that really wasn't so. Even after fame and early success, the central downtown project could have become a ghastly mistake. There was a stalling, awkward pause on that front after 1958 (although much was still going on elsewhere), and many disappointments and cliff-hanging decisions. The provision by the federal agencies of the funds to acquire the land in these projects does not mean that the next steps are assured — that a developer will be found who in turn will be able to put together the combinations of builders and buyers and renters to make a success of it.

The fortunes of the central city's renewal effort reflected themselves neatly in the size of Lee's political victories. His margins in 1955 and again in 1957 were very large by New Haven standards. These victories reflected the enthusiasm aroused by the first project, on Oak Street, and by the plans for the big central project, and led to the writings about his "political jackpot." In 1959, however, when those plans had not materialized, Lee's margin fell off, and then in 1961 it fell again. An important reason for these political dips was the huge hole in the middle of the city.

One of Lee's public relations ideas in the earlier period had been to instruct the city's taxi drivers about the city's plans, in order that they might be "ambassadors" to visitors from out of town. In 1959 and 1960, nonetheless, the New Haven taxi drivers whom one encountered were not ambassadoring very well. Instead, they were cursing a torn-up city. Republicans today can go back and gather an embarrassing set of statements by the Mayor, from the mid-fifties on, promising that by this date or that the "front block" or "middle block" project would be started — by which date it was not.

But after 1961 the main projects began to go smoothly again (the neighborhood projects had meanwhile been moving steadily forward). One big break came when Lee persuaded Macy's to open a branch in New Haven. I remember that one of Lee's administrators seemed to be holding his breath through the days of negotiations; "If we hadn't got Macy's it would have been just awful," he admitted with a sigh of relief when it was over. In September 1964 the New Haven Macy's had its opening ceremonies with Governor John Dempsey of Connecticut and Kingman Brewster of Yale and David Yunich of Macy's among those on the platform, and with many favorable references to New Haven's mayor.

The year 1964 saw the climax, or perhaps the penultimate chapter, of the ten-year renewal effort by the Lee administration: Macy's was built and opened alongside the new building for Malley's, and the front block complex was finally put together and construction on it begun. Lee and company had more projects being planned — notably a new federal-state-city government center on the eastern side of the Green and the Church Street South housing projects. With the nailing down of the central-city blocks, though, the success of the whole effort basically was secured. As the Mayor once said — and it seems that Democrats have trouble with this word, since President Johnson once mentioned the need for a "memorial" to God in Washington — when the front block is there beside Macy's it will be "a memorial to the Democratic Party."

The building of New Haven's memorials had not been the work of Lee alone or of the city government alone, of course, despite the inference one might draw from some of the promotional materials. Secretary of Labor W. Willard Wirtz, the speaker at an annual banquet of the New Haven's Citizens' Action Commission, chided the banqueters about one omission from their colorful brochure. "I read all the way through it looking for some mention of the federal government," he said, "and finally I found a very small one under a picture on page eighteen." The federal government already had given New Haven more than $35 million in urban renewal grants, and had promised to deliver $30 million more; it had also let fall upon the city a gentle rain of checks for other purposes — to wrestle with juvenile delinquency ($800,000 in 1963, $750,000 in 1964), to make war on poverty ($430,000 and $150,000 among the first antipoverty grants announced by Mr. Shriver, with subsequent additions), and to carry out many other educational and social and planning purposes.

It certainly has not been true in this case that the great federal power in Washington has been a threat to the struggling homely unit of local government; quite the contrary. New Haven's recent local government has not found in the federal government, for all its complicated laws and intricate bureaucracy and sometimes rather wooden general requirements, any usurper or competitor or interfering alien power. Rather, it has been an absolutely indispensable source of succor. Washington provided the money. Without these federal grants, renewal on the scale that New Haven has undertaken would have been out of the question.

Lee had the good fortune to become mayor just as the possibilities of urban renewal, "the first new idea in social legislation since the New Deal," as he described it himself, were taking form.

It has also not been true in New Haven that "social gains" have undercut the power of the partisan machine and political boss — power that rested, so the story goes, on favors the bosses could do for the needy immigrant masses. Nor have welfare programs undone their own foundation by Republicanizing great sections of the previously Democratic urban mass. Mayor Lee's regime in New Haven shows that these notions do not exhaust the possibilities. His administration, growing out of the partisan machinery of city Democrats, has used the social legislation of the national government to realize ambitions for the city and at the same time to advance the fortunes of a politician and of his party. Washington has not been a rival but a major source of support to the New Haven city government. The social legislation has not been a competing source of "favors" to individuals but a continuing source of great public projects for which the city, the party, and the Mayor could take credit.

Mayor Lee indicts previous city governments, in fact, for failing to make use of their opportunities along these lines: the mayor in the thirties (a Democrat, by the way) did not get PWA buildings in New Haven, as administrations in other cities (for one, La Guardia's) did ("that was 90-10 money" — the city had to put up only 10 percent of the funds). Part of the reason Lee's regime has had to do so much, spend as much, tax and borrow as much as it has is that previous city governments, for at least a quarter of a century, did little or nothing. "We are doing things that should have been done twenty-five years ago — fifty years ago," Lee says. "Murphy was sort of like Jasper McLevy, down in Bridgeport," adds one local politician, about New Haven's mayor from 1931 to 1945; "McLevy would say, 'God sends the snow; let God remove the snow.'" Lee's administration not only gave God more help in getting the snow off the streets, and improved the other expected and routine city services, it also added a whole new dimension of rebuilding the city. And for that, the help of the federal government has been indispensable.

It is quite true, though, that the passage of some large-spirited, city-helping national legislation down in Washington does not of itself accomplish the great ends set forth in the preambles. There must also be local leaders who take up the possibilities they offer, and work them out in the particular conditions of a particular city. "Those Washington fellows pass a housing bill or a mass transit bill or an antipoverty bill," says Mayor Lee, "and then they pass on to foreign policy or something. We have to pick up the thing and stick with it and make it work. We have to implement it. We are always finding problems that the legislators didn't know existed. They talk about 'redevelopment,' but we have to face what it means for displaced businessmen."

Lee and his people must persuade, beguile, cajole, or prod a long series of bureaucracies to make something like the right decisions about New Haven, and successfully bring the city along to add its part, and then combine the result of all these decisions into a planned remaking of the city.

The great trick in urban renewal appears to be to have people working for the city who know how to forage in its behalf out in the nation's bureaucratic jungles. It is not enough that the federal government pass city-helping laws; there must also then be hunters for the city who can make their way through all the Titles I and Titles II to find the meat.

Professor Dahl wrote in *Who Governs?* that Ralph Taylor, who came in 1955 to be the first director of New Haven's Redevelopment Agency, ". . . had one great asset . . . the mayor necessarily lacked; he was considered a professional by his peers throughout the country, many of whom he knew well. As the New Haven program began to attract attention, respect for the Director soared among his professional colleagues, including those in the federal agencies. Thus he took on more and more of the task of negotiating with the "feds"; he knew how to cut through the interminable delays characteristic of bureaucratic agencies, and he exploited statutes and rules to gain concessions for New Haven. . . . The city was able to move far partly because its agents moved fast; at a time when most cities were still debating whether to apply for federal funds, New Haven had already secured a disproportionate share of what was available."

Edward Logue, the most important of all the Lee developers and planners, who joined with Taylor in the formative decisions for New Haven's renewal, had been a chief assistant to Chester Bowles during Bowles's brief term as Governor of Connecticut. The most abrasive and controversial of the Lee people, and something of a Harry Hopkins-like lightening rod for the opposition, Logue went on in 1961, to his more severe problems in Boston. L. Thomas Appleby, Logue's successor as Development Administrator (which means deputy mayor for all the planning, renewal, housing, and future-oriented sections of the city government), had worked in the Housing and Home Finance Agency in Washington, had grown up in Washington as the son of a notable New Dealer, and knew the ropes. By this time New Haven had become famous in the city planner's world, and had no trouble attracting top people.

These operations take place in an intricate bureaucratic interweave, with decisions in one office rebounding in other offices. I rather expected the Mayor and his palace guard to have a great deal to do with other governments, but I hadn't realized how much an active mayor copes also with all the private worlds. "I have bought more obsolete churches and synagogues than anybody in the country," Lee once said.

One day the New Haven administrators are going down to Washington or New York to see the "feds"; another day they are going up to Wethersfield, Connecticut, to talk to the State Highway Commission; and another day they are talking to the East Haven people about the collaboration for the new regional incinerator. But at least as often they are meeting with the Catholic Archdiocese in Hartford or Paul Ylvsaker of the Ford Foundation or David Yunich of Macy's. I would not have guessed how much negotiating there is with all the engines of the business world: with Sargent's Hardware Company, to keep them in New Haven and to persuade them to build in the Long Wharf renewal project; with Gant and Company, the makers of shirts, to persuade them to build there too; with the Holiday Inn people, to persuade them to build a motel (a project announced by Lee during the 1963 mayoralty campaign); with Malley's department store, and with Sero Shirts, and with A. C. Gilbert's, and with Olin Mathieson, and with the United Illuminating Company, and with the local Fusco-Amatruda Construction Company to work out their part in the front-block plan — with local and with national business in all its guises.

Why has New Haven been able to bring off as much "renewal" as it has done? In the first place, obviously, New Haven is a manageable size. That certainly helps. My own quite unprofessional feeling is that as mayor of New York City one would start the day by reading the morning papers, and then put one's head on the desk to have a good cry. In the second place, New Haven had a vacuum of power and a fairly obvious need, and except perhaps for the newspaper, no strong base of opposition. Lee was putting into effect plans, or dreams, that a wide variety of New Haven residents had entertained for years.

Mayor Lee's renewal program, moreover, was able to receive broad support from Republicans, conservatives, and business-men, as well as from elements more accustomed to supporting a liberal Democratic mayor. It received this broad support in part because of skillful politics and a fortunate history. New Haven's renewal started under Republican Mayor William Celentano, Lee's predecessor, and thus came to him with a bipartisan, community-wide aura about it. Lee successfully built this up and promoted it through the Citizens' Action Commission — a broad and representative group of bankers, telephone company employees, teamster's officials, and house-wives, with lots of businessmen in it. Plans for redevelopment were presented to the CAC for its blessing before they were an-nounced to the general public. New city planning books praise the CAC, as well as the idea of a development administrator, as innovations that helped make New Haven's program work.

The crew of administrators whom Lee brought into the city — Logue, Taylor, Appleby, and others — have been es-sential to the program's success; they had the connections and the knowledge to make the thing work. One of these administra-tors, however, discounts this last as not being peculiar to New Haven: "The talent is there, for any city that has the political set-up to make use of it." So you may say it comes back in the end to the Mayor.

10. Mayor Lee

"Wholesale and retail."

W HEN IN 1949 I set out on my first venture in political doorbell-ringing, the New Haven party hack who gave me instructions explicitly stated that "issues" were a waste of time. The
whole point of the election, he said, was that the incumbent
Republican Mayor Celentano was an Italian (I was to skip
voters with Italian names) and that young Dick Lee, the
Democratic challenger, was a good New Haven Irish boy. It
was rather disheartening advice. Sixteen years and six Lee
terms later, the city election would be fought on different
grounds: New Haven versions of great national issues like
urban renewal, housing, employment, education, integration,
poverty.

I didn't know anything about Lee when I dutifully campaigned for him that first time; by the time I joined the Board
of Aldermen I knew much more, but not at first hand. In the fall
and winter of 1964–1965, though, I came to see a great deal of
Lee, both in public action and in private. I found him a striking mixture. While he was a shining national example in the
modern world of urban renewal, complicated housing programs, and new devices for warring against poverty, he was
also a city politician. George Washington Plunkitt of Tammany Hall could have approved of much of his work. "Have I
got any wakes to go to this afternoon?" he would ask his secre-

tary, after completing calls to a congressman in Washington and the Ford Foundation in New York.

It helps a politician to represent some combination of identities, so that one set of voters and another can each have some section of his Larger Being to support. La Guardia was helped by being a one-man melting pot, and President Kennedy by being both Irish and Harvard. Lyndon Johnson is a great plastic Texas figure, a one-man consensus, liberal and conservative, Southern and Western, rural but now urban, one who like Walt Whitman "contains multitudes." Lee's political success in New Haven rested on two such combinations. He combined the old-line party politics of the city with the most modern urban planning. And — more important in the first step of politics — he had the great political good fortune to reflect exactly his city's basic ingredients, a workingclass New Haven with immigrant memories, plus Yale.

Lee lived every day, in a way that seemed to me unusual, with the people and the physical surroundings (such of the physical surroundings as he had left standing) of all the layers of his life, from his birth in a second-floor flat on Starr Street to the day when his friend the President of the United States John F. Kennedy leaned over to him, felt the lapel of his suit, and asked, "Feinstein's?" (Lee, an Ivy League dresser, had introduced Mr. Kennedy to the Yale-based firm of Fenn and Feinstein.)

His father was a factory worker. Lee lived most of his life in the lower-income district, now largely Negro, in which he was born. During the busing battle he stopped one conversation by saying that his own daughter had been raised in the backyard of Bassett Junior High. He was, for practical political purposes, Irish. He was a Roman Catholic; every victorious Democratic candidate for mayor since 1899 has been an Irish Catholic. When you campaigned for him, voters would tell you affectionately that they had known Dick Lee since he was a boy, or that they had seen him Sunday at Mass, or that they knew his family, or that he had delivered groceries to them, or that they had been present at the Knights of Columbus breakfast when the priest did not show up on time and Mayor Lee himself gave the prayer. I encountered on many porches of the Fifteenth Ward samples of the affection in which Lee was held, stretching back through all the phases of life — "Anybody on Dick Lee's team is good enough for me." One lady explained to me that she was a Republican and always voted Republican and would vote Republican again this time, as she always did. Then, as I turned to leave she added, "But I hope Dick Lee wins."

At the same time that Lee had this political gold mine of associations with the townsfolk he also had solid connections with Yale — a difficult combination, in a city with a large latent supply of town-gown antagonism. Dick Lee, the home-town Irish boy, had also been the public relations director for Yale during the ten years prior to his becoming Mayor. Robert Dahl wrote in *Who Governs?* that the Mayor ". . . was one of the few members of Mory's, Yale's undergraduate eating club, who had never attended Yale; and he was perhaps the only associate fellow in any of Yale's ten residential colleges who had never attended a college or university of any kind. He was on a first name basis with a large proportion of the Yale establishment from the president and deans to the headwaiter at the faculty club." Lee also knows the guards, groundskeepers, and especially the trainers and the coaches. Whitney Griswold, the late president of Yale, was an old friend of Lee's. When Griswold was a young instructor in history Lee had tried to persuade him to run for alderman.

Once, in the middle of a discussion, Mr. Lee asked, "Do you think it hurt King's chances for the presidency?" I looked at him in blank confusion. We had been talking about an incident involving Governor Wallace of Alabama, to whom Lee had sent a telegram of unwelcome when a Yale undergraduate group invited him to speak. The date the college boys had picked was the evening before New Haven's 1963 city election, and Lee was in the middle of his campaign for re-election. I thought Mr. Lee's remark might have something to do with one of those mildly racial jokes that were current at the time, about Martin Luther King, President Kennedy, and so on (for example, the one that ends "No, I am awfully sorry, Dr. King, but it's always been called the *White* House"). It turned out, however, that the King in question was Kingman Brewster — strictly Mr. Brewster to me — who was then acting president and is now president of Yale.

One day in his study Lee pointed to a photograph on his mantel and said affectionately, "You know who that is? That's Carl Lohman, who was secretary of Yale, and my boss. I learned as much from him as from any man." Lee had undoubtedly learned more from Yale than many who pay tuition to go there.

Lee is not built on the imposing lines of the portly saloon-keeping alderman of generations past. He has had the experience, which must be nearly unique among Irish city politicians, of having his doctor suggest that he drink more beer in order to put on weight. He is a slight, short figure, and normally weighs one hundred and forty pounds; during his illness he was down to one-twenty-four. Proportionately he has a large head — in my experience the largest politician's head relative to the rest of the politician with the single exception of Harold Stassen (this is a physical description only and is not intended to have any symbolic overtones). Lee has a lined, mobile face and an open, engaging expression. One can get something of his physical effect by picturing the young James Cagney, with a large head and a big smile. Most important, Lee has a husky, loud, and distinctive voice and a quick tongue. Therefore, despite his size, he has no trouble making the place where he sits the head of the table.

He had a Scottish grandmother named Campbell and some English ancestors too, but these politically inappropriate forebears are discreetly kept in the shadow; for the purposes of New Haven politics, as I have said, he is Irish. And the Democratic Party out of which he has come has been, like the party in most cities — especially of the East — Irish-dominated.

I think the Irish-American genius for politics is a contribution to the shaping of the nation which has not received as good a press as it deserves. Neither the middle classes and hinterlands — with their small-town Protestant myths — nor the intelligentsia — with their excessively ideological politics — are well equipped to appreciate it.

When such students of these matters as Daniel Patrick Moynihan, co-author of *Beyond the Melting Pot*, and William V. Shannon in *The American Irish* explain why the Irish came to be so ubiquitously the political leaders of American cities, they say that not only were the Irish here first and had the advantage of knowing the language, but they also had a distinctive knack for politics. The Irish peasant's loyalty to one small corner of society, and his respect for rank, and his realism, and his experience in the Irish Nationalist Movement made him ideal material for precinct work in the American city. Mr. Shannon says also ". . . for the Irish, politics was a functioning system of power and not an exercise in moral judgment. While E. L. Godkin and Henry Adams despaired of the American experiment, the Irish took over city hall."

Mayor Lee reflects, in a modern generation's way, all of that heritage. His opponents would certainly not deny that he is an able politician, though they might want to inflect the word in their own way. What this chiefly means, I think, is that he has an accurate sense of power relations and of the probable attitudes of great groups of people. Also it means a certain adroit flexibility and complexity in response to these phenomena. To the single-minded men of principle this often appears to be opportunism and expediency, and is part of what give politics and politicians a bad name. To Irish realists and practical politicians, however, such maneuvering with the currents is of the essence of their craft. "Always remember in politics," Lee says, quoting a maxim he claims he learned from John F. Kennedy, "that your friends today may be your enemies tomorrow, and your enemies today may be your friends tomorrow."

Another Irish Democratic trait is organizational ability, or at least organizational loyalty; when one tries to do some co-ordinated political thing with the fissiparous tendencies of other groups one appreciates the Irish loyalty to the precinct captain, and the Organization. Another is the realistic, or even cynical, awareness of the difference between words and forms on the one hand and human actualities on the other: "Ah, Mr. President, what's the Constitution between friends." I remember that the first time I met Lee, in the late forties before he was mayor, he strode around his office at the Yale News Bureau explaining the deficiencies of most canvassing of voters in the wards. "You know what these guys do? They don't really ring the doorbells. They look at the house and they look at the name and they say, 'Foley, yeah, he's a Democrat,' and they go on to the next house. That's if they go out at all, which mostly they don't."

Mr. Shannon makes another point at quite a different level about the possibilities of quick success in politics for able young sons of immigrants whose road elsewhere was blocked. "James Curley was a congressman at thirty-six and mayor of Boston at thirty-nine; Joseph Tumulty became President Wilson's chief aide at thirty-three; Alfred E. Smith and James J. Walker were floor leaders in the New York legislature while still in their thirties." Richard C. Lee was an alderman shortly after he could vote, a candidate for mayor at thirty-three, mayor of New Haven at thirty-seven.

Surely one important component of the Irish success in American politics has to do with certain celebrated personal traits: gregariousness, and talkativeness, and a quick fellow feeling for human emotions — the verbal facility and humor and passion and color and eloquence and empathy that have made the great Irish actors and writers. To be a success in politics, generally speaking, you have to love going to meetings, and talking, and arguing, and keeping up with people. The articulateness is not sufficiently appreciated, in a country that is too much taken with the yup-nope, strong silent man of the Gary Cooper type. The gregariousness may also be under-rated by a people who picture a lone man on his horse against the sky. Unlike other Americans (tight-lipped Yankee individualists, for one type, thinking ahead to the bank balances of tomorrow), the Irish have not undervalued the open, expressive, communal life. Surely all this has much to do with their political success.

Richard C. Lee, if he may be counted as Irish, fully represents all these traits and virtues. He represents them, actually, more clearly than did his friend John Kennedy. President Kennedy, for all his Irish heritage and wardheeling grandfathers, and in spite of Robert Frost's advice to the contrary, with respect at least to the characteristics just mentioned appears to me to have been more Harvard than Irish. He was shy, at least at the beginning of his career, reserved, "cool," very restrained in his expression of emotion, discriminating in taste, disinclined to dramatics, detached, intellectual, witty, self-deprecating, careful and selective about what he said — never corny, rambling, vain, or verbose. Certainly he loved and responded fully to the intellectual puzzle and the moral challenge of the intricate matter of public policy in his time. One may doubt that he loved to the same degree the accompanying sheer burly, time-consuming, corny human politics. He came to like campaigning, we are told, but he would probably never have been as skillful in persuading all-too-human congressmen to do what he wanted them to do as his successor has proved himself to be.

Mayor Lee is quite different in this regard from John F. Kennedy. He is a talker, a joker, a shaker of hands and a teller of stories and an actor of roles. One of his aides said that he didn't understand the importance of that constant yacketa-yacketa-

yacketa of the Mayor's until he missed it in the busing battle.
Political scientists put it somewhat differently, when they speak
of leadership as being "the center of a communications net-
work." Lee talks to people constantly, trying out ideas on
them, and listening then to find out what people are thinking
and saying. He is a very entertaining and interesting fellow, full
of lively stories, which he tells with gusto. A conference with
the Mayor is likely to be composed of a hard core of swiftly
transacted business surrounded by a great colorful covering of
stories, jokes, items of gossip about whatever is on his mind,
and playlets with the Mayor playing all the roles. One day
when Lee was riding by, waving and smiling at children at
Conte School, a little girl stuck out her tongue at the Cadillac
and the Mayor. "I am a Republican," she announced. "You look
like one," the Mayor answered.

One style of political leadership deals in silence and mystery,
creating a certain distance between the leader and his followers and a Gaullist penumbra of awe around him. Lee's style is
the complete opposite of that and consists, rather, of gab, can-
dor, directness, informality, and total articulation.

Lee occasionally wrote speeches for college dignitaries during his Yale days, hires good speech writers today, and works
hard himself on his formal speeches; he often tries for touches
of Stevensonian political rhetoric. His natural abilities, however, are in spontaneous speech, and his nearest analogue on
the national scene is not Governor Stevenson but Hubert
Humphrey. Like the Vice-President he is a tirelessly talkative
expositor of public policy. He is also like what one hears about
Al Smith in his days as Governor: he is able to make the dry
facts of government not only clear but even interesting. "He
can sell you anything, you know; he can make you buy the
Brooklyn Bridge," said a former alderman who did not always support Lee. Lee's campaign propaganda called him a
"salesman for New Haven." At several decisive points in the

history of renewal in New Haven — the negotiations with the State Highway Commission over the Oak Street Connector in the early years, and those with Macy's in recent years, for a few — it has been Lee personally who has brought the talks to success.

"Wholesale and retail," Lee said, coming back into his office with two traffic tickets in his hand. "The late Senator Brien McMahon once said to me, 'We try to make it wholesale, but we never pass up a chance to make it on the retail.'" This adeptness at the retail side of politics, doing favors, remembering names, greeting everybody with a big smile and a joke, is one of the features that connect Lee with the great tradition of city politics symbolized by Plunkitt, and distinguish him from the cold-blooded reformers whom the Plunkitts have always despised. But Lee's wholesale politics — the rebuilding of almost the entire city — goes beyond anything Plunkitt and his ilk had ever dreamed of.

Glazer and Moynihan wrote of the experience in New York City, in perhaps a too disparaging summary: "The Irish were immensely successful in politics. They ran the city. But the very parochialism and bureaucracy that enabled them to succeed in politics prevented them from doing much with government. In all those sixty or seventy years in which they could have done almost anything they wanted in politics, they did very little. Of all those candidates and all those campaigns, what remains? . . . In a sense the Irish did not know what to do with power once they got it . . . the Irish just didn't know what to do with the opportunity. They never thought of politics as an instrument of social change — their kind of politics involved the processes of a society that was not changing." Whether or not that states the thing quite fairly, it is a useful backdrop against which to characterize, by direct contrast, Mayor Lee. He *knew* what to do with the opportunity. He knew what to do with power in government as well as in politics, and he made politics most emphatically an instrument of social change. He did that in an unlikely place, the long-time preserve of the American Irish, City Hall.

Lee and some other mayors like him represent, I think, what Lincoln Steffens and Jacob Riis were looking for sixty years ago, mostly in vain — a city leader who combines the political skills of the bosses with the humane purposes of their arch-opponents the reformers. Perhaps it was not possible sixty years ago for there to be such a hybrid animal. Riis thought he had found what he wanted in Theodore Roosevelt — "a valiant fighter against the slum" — but Roosevelt was only Police Commissioner, not Mayor, and he quickly went on from the city to higher things. Since then both the political machines of the cities and the ideas of the reformers have undergone changes, and so have the social foundations on which both are built. It has now become possible, and none too soon, for American urban society to cast up a leader like Lee, at least under the peculiar conditions of New Haven, Connecticut.

In October 1964, when Hubert Humphrey made his campaign visit to the New Haven Green, Mayor Lee presided over the rally. Humphrey was introduced by his fellow Senator, Thomas Dodd. A onetime Lee administrator who has since gone on to another place turned to me as Dodd was speaking and said, "It shows you that you have to take the tide of fortune at its flood. Dick should be here tonight as *Senator*, making that introduction." President Kennedy, at a dinner during his Yale commencement visit in 1962, took a similar line. He told Lee that the Mayor had made a mistake in not trying for the Senate in 1958. Mr. Kennedy said that you have to take your chances when you have them in this business, and go for the highest thing available, and not look back. The late President Griswold of Yale said in response to this that many citizens of New Haven are happy that Mayor Lee did not go to the Senate, but stayed to finish the job in New Haven.

Lee himself is ambivalent, in retrospect, about his decision in 1958. He has been known to grumble some at local liberal Democrats who confidentially advised him back then to stay put as Mayor. "They thought they'd have Chester Bowles as Senator and me going on forever as Mayor and things would be fine for them." He stopped himself. "No, to be fair," he said, "I wouldn't have done it anyway. I liked the idea at first, but then I got to thinking about all the questions a Senator is supposed to talk about — foreign policy and all of that — and I didn't think I should do it. I don't like to talk about subjects unless I really *know* about them."

One view is that New Haven has somewhat exploited Lee, a young politician who might have been expected to go "higher." Another view is that the greater satisfactions for him, as well as benefits for the city, lie with the course he has followed. "He can look around the city and see all things that he has done — the physical rebuilding," said a Washington hand who now lives in New Haven. "That's better than rattling around as a freshman Senator."

One day in the winter of 1965 I went with the Mayor on a visit to the Scranton neighborhood. He came out the back entrance of the Quinnipiac Club on Church Street, limped over to his car (he was still nursing his broken ankle), and greeted his driver and me. "Okay, Scranton School," he told the policeman who was driving for him, after he had settled into the car. "Well, I've been trying to sell the New Haven library to the bench and the bar and the legislators of the state of Connecticut," he then remarked with reference to the luncheon from which he had just come. "That's what I am, you know. The real estate agent for the city of New Haven. That's about what this job has come to be." I knew from the newspapers something of what this was all about. Lee and his planners were working to arrange for new government buildings — federal, state, and city — on the block facing New Haven's

Green on the east side; when that was arranged a bit of musical chairs with other buildings would be set in motion. The library would move into the present post office, since a new post office would be a part of the new federal building, and the present library building could then be sold to the state for a courthouse. Together with the present courthouse and a new police building it would form a cluster of court and police offices on a block facing the Green on the north side. "That's going to be the justice block," I said. "Yes," said Lee. "I told those lawyers and judges and legislators that we'd have justice all in one block, but that doesn't say anything about the *quality* of justice. All I can do is to provide the physical facilities."

As we drove along Tower Parkway toward the school I asked him about a quite different matter, the appointment of the members of the Equal Opportunities Commission. "Bill Celentano has agreed to be chairman," Lee said. I mentally chewed on this large piece of news for a minute and found it to be good. Celentano was Mayor from 1945 until 1953, preceding Lee. Celentano defeated Lee in 1949 and in 1951, the second time by the city-wide margin of exactly two votes. In 1953, then, Lee in turn defeated Celentano. In almost every election since then there have been preliminary rumors that Celentano might be the Republican's candidate against him again, but in every case Celentano has turned back at the end of the diving board and not taken the plunge. "I said to him," said Lee, " 'Bill, you know you aren't ever going to run again as long as I'm Mayor, and there are lots of new people in town who don't know you at all, and this is your chance to get back into public life and do a public service.' " Part of the significance of the appointment of Celentano was that he probably remained the city's most eminent Republican and his appointment gave the antidiscrimination effort a bipartisan cast. Perhaps equally important, Celentano was a much respected member of New Haven's very large Italian-American community, a major center of unhappiness over recent New Haven integrationist measures.

As we were driving through the Dwight neighborhood, one of the newer renewal areas just west of Yale, Lee pointed to an empty lot. "We're going to have a co-op housing project here," he said. "We hope to have the project run all the way to the corner, but I don't know whether we are going to get it." "Two-twenty-one-d-three?" I asked. The Mayor said yes.

We passed a sign that read "Legion Avenue Shopping — Open Sundays," and shortly thereafter we pulled up in front of the Jesse J. Scranton School, a completely undistinguished two-story red-brick school built in 1905. "Pick us up in about half an hour," Lee said to Mike. "I'll bet this is a section of town you've never been in," he said to me, as we got out of the car. Legion Avenue is a rather unprepossessing street of kosher markets, bakeries, and pants shops. The Scranton School, a block away at Scranton and Orchard, is set down on a street with narrow frame houses crowded close together, a shoe repair shop, a synagogue, and a closed and empty shop or two.

As soon as we had come into the school building Lee began pointing out what had been done to it. "We took out all those old lockers and had these boxes and hooks put in," he said. Without ceremony he went into a classroom, where a score of first-graders, more than half of them Negro, were playing a game. "Oh!" said the teacher, somewhat startled. Then she smiled. "Look who's here! Children, do you know who this is?" Most of the first-graders didn't, but the fifth- and sixth-graders, whom Lee visited later, all did. "We saw you on TV" . . . "You're Mr. Mayor" . . . "You're Mayor Lee." The principal of the school caught up with us and showed Dick the building's needs and defects as we went from classroom to classroom. The President of the Scranton PTA joined us, coming with the principal to show the Mayor the school. She explained to me that the PTA and a group of merchants from

Legion Avenue were beginning to talk about what their neighborhood should do — whether they wanted to become a redevelopment area like Wooster Square and Newhallville, or
what. At present they just wanted the school fixed up, and Lee,
who as mayor is also chairman of the Board of Finance, was
looking it over. "We've been neglecting Scranton," he said
between visits to classes on the second floor, "because we didn't
know whether the state would put Highway Thirty-four right
through here or not."

Lee hobbled down to the basement, the rest of us tagging
along, to a prekindergarten class and a mothers meeting. The
CPI classes for prekindergarten children require that the mothers come once a week for a discussion. To the gathering of six
young mothers, all Negro, he gave an impromptu lecture. "We
have to teach the men that their responsibility doesn't end
when they've fathered a child, or when they put the check on
the kitchen table," he said. The women laughed and nodded
hearty agreement. "It's not a Negro problem; it's not an Italian-American or Irish-American problem; it's a problem for
all of us. My own son David went to prekindergarten classes
and got a lot out of it."

In the hall again, Lee said to the PTA president, "You scout
for me," and she checked the girls' washroom. "All clear," she
said. Lee went in and looked it over. "See?" she said, pointing
to some deficient washbasins surrounded by peeling paint.
"Yes," Lee said, "we'll have to do something about that. The
rest of this looks all right." Then to me he added, pointing at
the more than adequate pink tile, "I did this. I remember
when we put this in." Back in the hall again he went over some
further points. "You have oil heat," he said. "I remember when
we shifted Scranton from coal to oil."

Later Lee took me out for a drive around the Hill and
showed me Welch School, a four-story monstrosity built in
1883 which he used as an object lesson in the long neglect of
New Haven's needs (some of the schools Lee has replaced

had been used for recruits in the Civil War); and the new Hill High School, now under construction, a lesson of another kind. This high school was designed by the Eero Saarinen firm. "How many cities would get architects of that caliber to do a high school?" the Mayor asked. He pointed to the buildings that would come down and the sites for new ones in the approach to the city from the turnpike. He had Mike drive us into the tunnel under Macy's up to the point at which the tunnel then stopped, emptying abruptly into the dirt of the work on the new front block complex. Standing at the mouth of the tunnel, pointing at the construction going forward on the front block, Lee said with satisfaction, "When those buildings are here, nobody can argue with *them.*"

The issues of busing, especially, and of integrated neighborhoods did not disappear.

At his first meeting with the aldermen after his return from illness, the Mayor talked at length about these matters. "We'll have to do it by our two-twenty-one-d-three approach," he said. He meant that the integration would primarily have to come through the building of the many new nonprofit co-op housing projects New Haven had under way, all integrated and one in the center of the Dixwell area.

As to the possible political repercussions of the busing, which were not overlooked, the Mayor kept telling us to put things in perspective. "Remember you're not running for the school board," he said.

In public Lee continued to be silent about the issue until late November, when he gave out a statement. He had been receiving complaints from parents, he began, and now he was making recommendations to meet those complaints in a long letter to the superintendent of schools. He explained at the same time that he was not an expert on education and that he had always left educational decisions to the people in the field; his only job with respect to the schools is to raise the money for them, as chief fiscal officer of the city. However, in this case he felt compelled to make these recommendations, mainly about the junior high schools, and to request that they be followed up soon: late buses, so students could stay after school; more homework; a check on an inadequate supply of textbooks; and better remedial education. "A grandstand play," muttered one critic.

Should Lee have spoken out earlier? Some critics of the plan felt he should have opposed it; some Republicans taunted him for not speaking out during the summer. Some liberals felt that he should have thrown his full weight in public behind the balance plan from the start. There is a small group on the left and liberal side who think Lee is overrated, and isn't all that progressive; his silence on busing is one item in their case. As it worked out, Lee's November comments could be taken either as critical of the board and superintendent or as a helpful effort to make the plan work.

In his state-of-the-city message in February 1965 he noted that the summer's controversy had concerned only 313 children out of the 21,000 in the New Haven school system, the number that were being bused involuntarily to achieve "more equitable racial balance." He said, "I would stress this point and stress it now. This program will end in June of 1966 — just fifteen school months from now — because in September of 1966 the Hill High School and six other new schools will be open."

From the start, the Bassett-Sheridan pairing had been arranged for only the two years until June 1966. Did the Mayor's statement simply reiterate that already established fact? Or did it mean also that any kind of busing for "racial balance" was not to happen thereafter?

Although the summer's antagonisms gradually subsided during the school year, they did not vanish. There were enough left in the following spring to provide the Worthington Hooker PTA with another power struggle over the unbelievable issue of who should be the members of the nominating committee for next year's officers? Usually you have to twist somebody's arm to be on the nominating committee, which in turn has to twist arms to obtain nominees. The factions on this great question divided exactly along the lines of the busing ruckus of the previous summer. Perhaps I should observe that some of the liberals were quite as eager to fight the fight again as were their opponents the antibusers. A battle like this one is almost entirely personal and symbolic, the bearer of antagonisms quite independent of the question at hand; it does not matter much to anyone who become the officers of the PTA, except symbolically and negatively: we don't want those other fellows to win.

Here is an illustration of the irrationality and suspicion that were still to be found. Just after the PTA meeting that featured the vote on this nominating committee matter, the angry rumor was passed around that a member of the school board, a law school professor known for his integrationist views, had brought in a group of Negroes and paid their memberships so they could vote for the liberal candidates. (The busing program finally adopted had brought a group of new Negro parents into the hitherto all-white Hooker PTA; some of them participated fully and immediately in the school's life.) How could this absurd rumor have begun? Well, it seems that the professor had come late to the meeting and, standing at the membership-buying desk, had loaned the necessary fifty cents to a moneyless friend — white, incidentally — who had come with him. Behind the two of them in line stood a number of Negro women, who also bought memberships. A suspicious antibuser saw this scene — and drew instant conclusions.

This PTA meeting came on Wednesday of the week of the marches in Selma, Alabama. On the preceding Sunday the marchers had been beaten; on the following Sunday they commenced the successful march to Montgomery. On the night previous to the meeting, Tuesday, there had been the abor-

tive attempt at a march when the marchers confronted the
troopers and then turned back. Among those who had flown
down to Selma for that day, at the call of Martin Luther King,
was the associate chaplain at Yale and director of Dwight Hall,
Yale's Christian Association. He arrived back in New Haven
from Selma at five o'clock Wednesday morning, and then came
late to the Hooker PTA meeting in the evening to cast his vote
in the election of a nominating committee.

Meanwhile, in the winter after the Goldwater election, the
Republican group called the Better Education Committee had
handed in its petition for a referendum on an elected school
board. The City Clerk, a Democrat elected on the slate with
Mayor Lee, found among the 7000 names on the petition
enough technical irregularities to disqualify it. When that petition had been thrown out, however, and before the BEC could
gather another one, there came a surprise. Mayor Lee formally
requested that the Board of Aldermen set up a charter commission to consider the question of an appointed versus an
elected school board! He also asked that the commission consider several related questions, the most important being
whether the board should be given its own independent taxing
powers. Throughout the fall and winter the Mayor, who does
his thinking out loud in continuing conversations, had in private often said, almost aggressively, "All right, let them take
the whole responsibility — taxing power, and everything." If
there was to be an elected school board, he said, then let that
board find the money, too. Let them face an angry delegation
of teachers and find the funds for raises. The Mayor was not
necessarily against an elected school board; he was against
adopting the change as vengeance against the board he had
appointed. If the change were to be made, then he would suggest that the new board take the whole package, including the
miseries of financing.

His request for a charter commission on the matter, coming in the late spring of 1965, had its obvious political side. Supporters chortled privately about its being a master stroke. It took the rankling school board issue out of the mayoralty campaign that was coming in the fall. At the same time, Mayor Lee did feel that this was a serious question that New Haven needed to examine on its merits.

On a June night in 1965 — exactly a year after the first Hooker busing battle — the Board of Aldermen considered the Mayor's proposal for a charter commission. The committee on legislation had reported it favorably by a 3–2 vote. The minority pair, both Democrats and one a Negro, had argued that no change in the school board need be considered, and that considering such a change implied criticism of the present board, and that the whole matter was political in a bad sense on both the BEC's part and the Mayor's.

We had our argument, as usual, in the caucus rather than on the floor. Some aldermen argued flatly the political benefits of getting this thing out of the fall elections; others argued that in addition the question needed to be dealt with on its merits by a commission.

Setting up a charter commission requires a vote of 22 aldermen, so the City Clerk's office had telephoned us all to make sure we would be present. Even so, the vote was close. Six were absent, and one alderman said that with him "it was an emotional matter" and that he couldn't support the commission. He attributed a rather nasty fight over Christmas celebrations in the Hamden schools, in which there were strong antisemitic undercurrents, to their having an elected school board. The two dissenters from the legislation committee continued to dissent. Nevertheless, as the votes went along the rows everyone else, including the three Republicans, voted for the commission, and it carried with 24 votes. The charter commission was endorsed, and it had a full year in which to report — until the summer of 1966 and after the 1965 election was well out of the way.

Two years is too short a term for a mayor; he just gets turned around from one election and has to start thinking about the next. Mayor Lee was already warming his motors for the 1965 election.

11. The Great Society

*"All our citizens must have the ability
to walk through those gates . . ."*

Down in Washington, meanwhile, 1965 was proving to be
an extraordinary political year. Congress was enacting major
social legislation, which was something I have never quite believed it could do.

I am a member of that in-between generation who has
neither the experience of the New Deal nor the naïve hopeful-
ness of youth, and therefore expects nothing from the Congress of the United States. I was too young to have followed the
New Deal. Just as I was old enough to shift from baseball to
politics, Franklin Roosevelt was shifting from domestic to foreign affairs, and then Nebraska voters were replacing George
Norris with Kenneth Wherry. (Senator Wherry is especially remembered for his references to "the Anti-Sherman Trust
Act" and "Indigo-China.") I was a liberal throughout my college days and after. I was in favor not only — as I have said
— of an FEPC but also of national health insurance (as we
called it then) and of federal aid to education, and of conservation of natural resources (a Missouri Valley Authority, for
example), and of public housing and expanded unemployment
insurance, and of all sorts of aids to the poor and every good
and humane thing that was recommended by the New York
liberal newspaper *PM* as it made its way to me in Nebraska,
and recommended by the ADA, of which I was a rather
lonely member out there on the Great Plains. But it did not

occur to me in those days that any of these things would ever, actually, be passed into law by Congress.

The election of 1938 slowed the New Deal, and war stopped it. Bright postwar hopes were dimmed by the meat shortage election of 1946. The Fair Deal was interrupted by the Korean War, and through the fifties Congress was mostly to be deplored, even after McCarthy was gone. About the best Congress could do in the line of new social legislation throughout that decade was to pass a multibillion-dollar highway bill, making six-lane speedways for racing ninety miles an hour into Las Vegas. One developed a whole lecture about why Congress couldn't do anything: the House Rules Committee; the seniority system; Southern one-party states sending back year after year the reactionary chairmen of committees; malapportionment; cumbersome procedures; the Conservative Republican-Southern Democratic coalition. Congress, one explained, was built for inaction, and especially on domestic social legislation.

Imagine then, the pleasant surprise that began to grow in members of my generation first in 1964 and then especially in 1965 as measure after measure we half believed could never become law went whipping through Congress. In 1964 Johnson ("Let us continya") brought through the Kennedy tax cut and the Kennedy civil rights bill, commenced the "war on poverty," and put through a collection of conservation measures.

Then came 1965. Federal aid to elementary and secondary education, federal aid to higher education, Medicare, programs to combat air and water pollution, restrictions on highway billboards, a rent-supplement program, a rent-certificate program, an arts and humanities bill, a Teachers' Corps, a teachers' fellowship program, a mass transit bill (perhaps even someday a railroad from Boston to Washington!), a voting rights bill, "heart-cancer-stroke" research, an urban affairs department, an end to the national-quota system in immigration: item after item that we had sought in vain for years, plus new ones, passed Congress and were signed into law.

Of course I have exaggerated slightly the poverty of congressional accomplishment in the years between 1938 and the Johnsonian harvest. Sitting in a Washington restaurant one night an urban renewal man was enthusiastically saying that the Housing and Urban Development Act of 1965 (the Act that was to come forth in August, after vicissitudes, from the presidential proposal delivered to Congress in March) "is the greatest piece of legislation for housing and for cities since the law that started public housing in 1937." A more circumspect friend said, "What about the 1949 Act, which started urban renewal?" A few things did happen in the Congresses of those intervening years.

But not many. Take aid to education, as the most important example of all. Since World War II the efforts to enact federal aid to education have made one of the saddest stories of legislative frustration in American history. Robert Bendiner wrote a book about the *Obstacle Course on Capitol Hill,* and aid to education was his bloodcurdling example. There was no education bill in 1949, when Cardinal Spellman clashed with Mrs. Roosevelt; no bill throughout the nineteen-fifties, merely frustrating try after frustrating try, with both political parties and a majority of the public favoring federal aid; and no bill in 1961, with President Kennedy in the White House and the issue of religious schools on everybody's mind.

After that 1961 battle, as a matter of fact, many proponents threw up their hands. The rifts in society, particularly over Roman Catholic schools, seemed to be so wide that no bill could pass in the foreseeable future. But four years later, a school-aid bill sailed through Congress. A White House assistant who worked on it described it as "incredibly easy." What happened?

The most tangible and immediate reason for this surprising legislative success is the rather perverse one that the Republicans in 1964 made a grave mistake. They nominated an ideological symbol, and the heavy defeat of this Bryan-of-the-

Right brought down many of his party who would otherwise
have won. Connecticut, for example, which as I have said has
recently had rather closely balanced parties, elected six Democrats for its six seats in Congress. Goldwater's gift to the Democrats in the House of Representatives of the Eighty-ninth Congress was almost forty seats, and that meant that there was
for the first time since 1938 a working liberal majority in the
House. The Southern Democratic-Republican coalition, which
had more or less prevailed throughout my adult life, did not
run things anymore. These bills at last had the votes.

That was not the whole story. Sitting in a borrowed
bathing suit beside a swimming pool in Washington (a long way
from Goatville) I repeated to a presidential assistant the argument, given by some liberals cool on Johnson, that the President didn't deserve much credit. The votes were there in
Congress. The assistant loyally and I think also truthfully said
that was quite wrong: if you knew what it is like down here, if
you knew how many snags and bogs and personality quirks
there are — how many different ways a bill can be stopped or
fouled up — you wouldn't say that. It took *this* President to
make this legislative record. Specifically on federal aid to education, it took the firm commitment of the President to education as the number one priority.

The Elementary and Secondary Education Act of 1965,
signed into law in that April, was the biggest among the many
accomplishments of Congress in that year. "That's the Act
that can really help the people who need it," said a CPI worker
back in New Haven. "More than the Civil Rights Act. More than
the Economic Opportunity Act." It can do so, he added, *if* the
big money, in Title I, goes where it is supposed to go — to the
schools of the poor. Some states are already turning the act
into "general aid" — giving the money to the middle-class
schools that put on the pressure. But here in Connecticut,
he said, we really intend to give that money to the schools
that are supposed to get it — those in areas of poverty.

In addition there was new *state* money for urban schools, and that indicates another reason for the change in the political climate: reapportionment. Connecticut's state legislature was being reapportioned in a very complicated struggle, involving the courts and the threatened use of a Yale computer and much jockeying for partisan advantage. The Republicans successfully used the reapportionment fight to avoid having to run state legislative candidates on the Goldwater ticket of 1964. The whole spectacle had not been very edifying but the underlying change was an important and salutory one — in the long run as important for education, Negroes, and the urban poor as anything that happened during the year. It meant that the state government could no longer be deaf to the needs of the cities. Both state political parties pledged themselves to programs of special aid to schools in the poor areas — which was quite a reversal, especially for the Republicans. The Connecticut legislature then passed a $10 million bill to aid schools in areas of poverty. With the state money plus the federal money, New Haven's school system was to have a million and a half in *new* funds for the schools of the poor, in the year 1965–1966.

A city educator, talking to me about the anxieties in Hooker over the busing, said "Remember, the money follows the bused kids." The national and state education money, plus CPI, plus the large city rebuilding of schools, put New Haven's school integration in a setting with expanding possibilities.

The reapportioned legislature should yield more benefits for cities in years to come. That fact indicates another important source of the political change, the United States Supreme Court. The Court followed its 1962 decision to intervene in these matters with a 1964 decision that gave the formula one man, one vote; that shifted the very foundations of power in state government.

The Supreme Court is another institution that has been a

surprise. In fact one might work out a pattern of reversal, that the American governmental institutions originally intended to represent the conservative or nondemocratic principles of government — the Presidency and the Supreme Court — have come instead to be the chief centers of progressive action. Congress, reversing expectations, has been more conservative than the Presidency. Within Congress the Senate, intended to be the more aristocratic body, has recently been less conservative, and the House, expected to be closer to the people and their desire for change and equality, has been the more conservative. And a similar reversal of roles between the federal government and the states is of course a major feature of our political history.

When I first formed ideas about it, in the late thirties, the Supreme Court was "nine old men" striking down New Deal legislation — a fundamentalist roadblock to social progress. Since 1954, in contrast, it has become something else altogether, and the antagonistic slogans came from the other side: "Impeach Earl Warren." Not only in the segregation decisions but in matters of reapportionment and civil liberties the Court helped both to educate the country and to open up political possibilities. "Morally the most impressive of our original institutions," Edmund Wilson said of this court.

The election of Kennedy in 1960, and first the leadership and now the memory of the youthful President had much to do with the change, too. So, ironically, does the assassination, which punctured developing hatred and sectional resistance, and gave to youth and idealism a new hero and martyr. It also ended a Washington stalemate; remember how back in 1963 we talked about a deadlocked democracy and an impossible Congress and whether parliamentary government could cope with the technological age?

Behind change in institutions and power arrangements there is also a change in the atmosphere. One can see this if one contrasts the fifties with the sixties. Professors back then complained about "apathy" and a lack of social idealism in their students; today some professors fear their students are irresponsibly radical. We worried, back then, with traces of middle-class self-pity, about the organization man, the gray flannel suit, the split-level or ranch-house suburban development, "conformity," "togetherness," the "affluent society." We talked then, if we were at all aware of the problems of social justice, about mere "pockets" of poverty. Religious groups were not in "dialogue"; and a Roman Catholic-Protestant impasse was the major block to aid-to-education — a block that appeared impossible to break. We rather complacently assumed, after the Supreme Court decision in 1954, that the problem of racial discrimination was on its way to being solved.

In the sixties there has come a dramatic revival of social idealism and of serious public purpose. This has been somewhat obscured by the understandable concentration on foreign affairs and omnipresent awareness of the nuclear confrontation under which it has taken place. The new mood has also been somewhat hidden because many new leaders, not wanting to feed another time of complacency, have emphasized the critical side — what we are still not doing, what is wrong with American society — rather than stressing what has been and is being done. But the change in atmosphere is large and the list of accomplishments is long. There is a whole sweep of programs to bring civil rights and to end poverty, and these are by no means confined to government. We are breaking through the impasse over parochial schools, almost without noticing it. There are Peace Corps, both foreign and domestic. There is a great change in the social literature that is widely read — Michael Harrington's *The Other America* and James Baldwin's *The Fire Next Time* instead of *The Lonely Crowd*. From 1955 to 1965 there has been a reversal in student attitudes toward social ideals and public service. This shows, perhaps, how life keeps renewing itself as it goes along, or how much resilience there is in American ideals. New generations grasp them afresh.

What caused this? The civil rights movement, above all. The "Negro revolt" has had many beneficial effects beyond those to the Negro himself — benefits it has brought to the nation as a whole. Historian C. Vann Woodward wrote in the *New York Times* that supporters claim the civil rights movement has "acted as a powerful social catalyst. It has touched off the campaign against poverty, inspired attacks on urban decay, delinquency, and unemployment and provoked a reassessment of our whole public school system." The impact of the Negro movement *has* been large. The left part of it, such as members of the student Nonviolent Co-ordinating Committee (SNCC), would not agree with the favorable picture drawn here about current American politics. Many denounce Johnson, laugh at or angrily attack the poverty program, find legislation too slow, the "establishment" middle-class, politics full of compromise. One may disagree with them about all this and at the same time believe that their movement — the larger movement, of which they are one wing — has helped to make the creative period in American domestic politics they do not acknowledge we are in.

Francis Keppel, then the United States Commissioner of Education, was quoted as saying, "Thank God for the civil rights movement!" Even in our New Haven busing battle, a civic disaster, one could see something of what Mr. Keppel had in mind. There certainly was a citizen turnout and interest in "education," such as it was, that went beyond anything previously seen. Also, some people made extravagant protestations of willingness to pour money into the inner-city (Negro) schools. A new interest in the quality of education appeared, and even some new comprehension of the need for better ways to finance urban education than the property tax.

The most important change the civil rights movement may bring is to shift the focus of attention. A major difference between the fifties and the sixties lies in the agenda of topics for public policy, and the civil rights movement has played a predominant part in the change. In doing so it may bring benefits beyond its own intentions to the community as a whole. Perhaps there can be a reversal and also an enlargement of the special aspect of the movement, making it positive and inclusive. There is much that the power of the civil rights movement, and the moral authority of the Negro leadership, and the potential political strength of the Negro community can do for the nation as a whole and for the disadvantaged of all races.

One can distinguish these three elements in the situation of the American Negro, compared to situations of other disadvantaged persons:

First, those disadvantages that he shares with the poor of all races — poor housing, unemployment, social disorganization. President Johnson, at Howard University in June 1965, said that "Negroes are trapped, as many whites are trapped, in inherited gateless poverty."

Second, those additional disabilities that accrue particularly to him, as a result of racial discrimination, of "ancient brutality, past injustice, and present prejudice." "Negro poverty," said the President, "is not white poverty." Because there is this second set of problems there must be, in addition to social legislation applicable to everyone, specific antidiscrimination laws and efforts, to overcome this specific barrier.

But third — a lesser point beside the others, to be sure, but a real one — the Negro's clear identity as the victim of injustice, and his distinct claim upon the national conscience. There is a whole collection of interracial ideas and organizations devoted to overcoming the injustice done to him. And he has numbers, gathering in larger and larger concentrations in the center of our great cities. He has great potential political power. In New Haven the hope that the city will retain progressive government rests in large part on the Negro voters. There are some advantages in the Negro's distinct disadvantage, not only to him but also to the nation.

Furthermore, Negro leaders have acquired moral authority. In the Sunday School in which my wife teaches, the name Martin Luther had an odd, truncated sound to the little latter-day Protestants in her class. The great religious leader whom *they* knew about, from his personal visits and from many, many references by preachers and Sunday School teachers, as well as from newspapers and television, was Martin Luther *King*.

One hopes that a new kind of Negro leader is emerging, the type who knows, respects, and uses politics. One wishes the Negro community had the precinct captains the Irish had.

This seems to be what is happening with the "advancement of colored people": the first barrier, legal segregation, has been technically overcome; the second barrier, racial discrimination, is being overcome, so far as law and all sorts of corporate action can do it; we are coming now to the third barrier — society-made economic and educational disadvantage. But at each step one moves farther from a peculiarly Negro problem. Slavery and legal segregation in the South were absolutely so; discrimination is markedly worse for the Negro but it is by no means his experience alone; and disadvantage from social and economic structure is the lot of many others besides the Negro. As we move to this third level many others besides the Negro are included.

The Negro, as the real victim of what Mr. Johnson called "the one huge wrong of the American nation," is also the chief symbolic victim of all the wrongs of the society. The campaign to overcome the injustice done him must help to bring many changes in both thought and policy of the country — changes that apply to Negroes and non-Negroes.

To many a do-goodish lady from North Haven or Woodbridge (in marked contrast to many lower-middle-class "explebes" of New Haven) the Negro is indeed a special object of charity and concern. He has a claim on the conscience of the Yankee woman of the Harriet Beecher Stowe tradition that no non-Negro can match. A great many ladies volunteer to work in antipoverty ventures; they tutor and they assist teachers and they help in literacy classes and "enrichment" classes. Their response would not be the same were all the clients white.

And the civil rights movement today has a moral elevation and political strength beyond that of any movement for social and economic legislation. The enactments of the Civil Rights Act of 1964 and the Voting Rights bill of 1965, if you think about it, were extraordinary events. The 1964 civil rights bill was made *stronger* by Congress than the bill orginally proposed by the Administration — which not too long before its proposing had not been inclined to send up a bill at all. There was a tremendous support from nonpolitical sources. Take the clergy, for instance. A clergyman is now almost expected to be a strong civil rights partisan, and troops of clergymen visited the Congress in behalf of the Civil Rights Act. ("Oh, the clergy," said Senator Dirksen, striking his brow.) Or take students. They are an important source of the "Movement," doing voter registration in Mississippi, tutoring in New Haven, and having speakers on racial matters every week. The numbers who pay attention to civil rights, and the depth of their passion and commitment, go quite beyond that attending any other issue.

There is a widespread white middle- and upper-class support for civil rights beyond the support given to other liberal measures. There are conservatives, middle-of-the-roaders, businessmen, and other respectable folk, newsmagazines and cautious newspapers, not at all liberal on, say, economic or social philosophy, who nevertheless are integrationists. Their one commitment on the unequivocally humanitarian side, so to speak, is sympathy for the Negro and opposition to racial discrimination.

The effects of all this reach well beyond the Negro community and the conscious objectives of the "Movement." The plainest illustrations of such larger benefits are new items of legislation and social policy, a revived social idealism among specific sets of citizens (Yale students and clergymen), new foci of attention in public affairs, and a shift in the political atmosphere. All of these the civil rights movement helped to bring about. One may be able to go further, and say that there has also been a desirable effect reaching all the way down to the ground floor, to the country's social philosophy and set of values.

I was tempted, at least, to conclude that this last was true when I read the civil rights speeches of President Johnson. On March 15, after the events in Selma, Alabama, he made a historic speech. As "a man whose roots go deeply into Southern soil," he adopted as his own — in a deeply moving moment — the motto of the civil rights movement, "We shall overcome." That was only one of the most notable of his altogether notable series of speeches on this subject. Still more striking in its philosophy was the commencement address at Howard University in June, to which I have referred. This first modern Southern President carried presidential commitment to the civil rights movement to a new level. ". . . it is not enough just to open the gates of opportunity," he said. "All our citizens must have the ability to walk through those gates, and this is the next and more profound stage of the civil rights movement." In doing so he also expressed an advanced environmental understanding far in front of anything characteristic of the American past. From his *New York Times* report one could almost see the reporter's jaw drop: "Mr. Johnson talked tonight not of legal but of sociological problems, not of what could be done to enforce rights but of what could be done to change the social patterns of decades. Seldom has his office been used for such a broad-gauged social purpose."

Americans have characteristically interpreted "freedom," our prime social value, too much in abstract and legal terms that take little account of real differences in the social arrangements heavily affecting a man's exercise of freedom. Freedom *from* interference has been what we have meant in the past, primarily from interference by government. But now the President

of the United States had said, ". . . freedom is not enough.
You do not wipe away the scars of centuries by saying now
you're free . . ." He picked up the figure often used by Whitney Young, Jr., of the Urban League — "You do not take a
person, who for years has been hobbled by chains and liberate,
bring him up to the starting line of a race and then say, you're
free to compete with the others . . ." Many others besides
Negroes have been hobbled, in other ways than racial discrimination.

The phrase "equal opportunity" runs throughout the civil
rights field, and the idea of equality of opportunity is a fundamental item in the American creed. Mr. Johnson went beyond
it: ". . . equal opportunity is essential, but not enough. Men
and women of all races are born with the same range of abilities. But ability is not just the product of birth; ability is
stretched or stunted by the family that you live with and the
neighborhood you live in, by the school you go to, and the poverty or richness of your surroundings. It is the product of 100
unseen forces playing upon the little infant, the child, and finally the man."

It is to take away nothing of the importance of such environmental understanding to the Negro to say that every word of
it applies also to non-Negroes, and that it may open humane
possibilities for our politics that I hadn't thought even Presidents could perceive.

12. City Hall

*"I think how I will rearrange
the furniture when I am Mayor!"*

O N MAY 17, 1965, the eleventh anniversary of the Supreme Court's decision on school segregation, I went to a testimonial dinner given by the city of New Haven, and held in the Yale Commons, in honor of Constance Baker Motley, who was then the new president of the Borough of Manhattan. (She has since been appointed a Federal Judge, the first Negro woman to be one, by President Johnson.) The chairman of the dinner was the mayor of Mrs. Motley's native city, New Haven, and the principal speaker was the mayor of the city to which she has moved, the Honorable Robert F. Wagner of New York. The nature of the occasion and the company led to jokes about mayors. Mr. Wagner told the story about the man walking the city streets complaining about smog, smells, traffic, pollution, crime, and slums. "Why don't you tell the Mayor?" he was asked. "Tell the Mayor!" he replied. "I *am* the Mayor."

In Mrs. Motley's response to her home-town's testimonial she then included — along with an effective civil rights speech — a joshing remark of her own directed especially to Mayor Wagner. "I sit there at those ceremonial dinners in Gracie Mansion," she said, "and I think how I will rearrange the furniture when I am Mayor!" When Mayor Lee got up to speak again after Mrs. Motley, a formidable woman, had sat down, he turned to his friend Bob Wagner and said, "Boy! Am I glad she moved from New Haven to New York!"

A fortnight later Mr. Wagner announced that he wouldn't run again. Although his stated reasons were personal, Wagner faced a more serious political threat to his arrangements of the furniture than the speculative future aims of Mrs. Motley: this dinner came a week after Republican Congressman John Lindsay had announced that he would run for mayor of New York.

The willingness of Mrs. Motley and Mr. Lindsay to enter the municipal morass may indicate a new visibility for city politics. Mrs. Motley, whose father had been a chef at the Yale secret society Skull and Bones, went directly from law school to the NAACP Legal and Educational Fund, and participated in the major civil rights cases. Her move into politics as a New York state Senator and then into city politics as Borough President may suggest a new awareness of the importance of city government on the part of some in the civil rights movement; policemen and sheriffs and superintendents of schools and school board members, among other important actors in the drama of civil rights, are subject to local politics.

Congressman Lindsay's decision has significance for municipal affairs, too. That spring a friend of Lindsay's, also a liberal Republican congressman, made this point while visiting Yale during the first flurry about a possible Lindsay candidacy. Someone like Lindsay, he said, might just take municipal government and concentrate on this; there's all that worry, he said, which Goldwater touched on when he talked about "law and order in the streets."

And one could find a good deal more meat in the subject than the law-and-order theme, important as that is. The governments of cities now stand at the center of the most interesting and important part of domestic politics, but citizens, and even some politicians, don't yet quite realize this. Certainly our old concepts — about "bosses" and "reform" and "good government forces" and "corruption" — don't fit what is now happening.

Richard Lee, a graduate from Hillhouse High School a few years before Mrs. Motley, shows the kind of double agent a mayor now can be: the agent of his city in Washington, the state capital, and the national bureaucracies in the one direction; the representative of national politics to his own city in the other direction. He can be a creative kind of executive-mediator who takes the possibilities provided in national programs and shapes them into a reality that fits his town.

A mayor can cut laterally across the fields of government and of city life, and try to bring some interconnection among them. Much of a city, like everything else, is organized now by fields and specialities, with their national hierarchies. Superintendents of schols stay only three to five years, and development administrators or traffic and parking directors move on to bigger places and higher salaries just as college professors do. They live not in the local spot they happen to be inhabiting at the moment but in the nationwide world of their specialty. A mayor, in contrast, can actually live in a city, fit together its parts, knock together its heads, put together a mixture of the specialists and their programs for his city.

A mayor nowadays, according to Mayor John C. Houlihan of Oakland, California, is not confronted merely with problems of garbage collection; he must deal with all sorts of "sociological" issues. Mayor Houlihan made this statement (or perhaps this complaint) at the spring 1965 meeting of the United States Conference of Mayors, a meeting much agitated by one sample of the new sociological matters mayors have to confront — the organizing of the poor by antipoverty programs. This organizing often seems, at least to the mayors, to be directed *against* city departments and City Hall. But while mayors are trying to cope with such large, new, interesting difficulties, much of the layman's language about city politics seems to remain about what it has been for fifty years and more.

For the most part, if you think about it, the office of mayor has not had a very sturdy or favorable place in the imagination of Americans. Quite possibly, with our frontier and cowboy myths, we have a more positive picture of the Sheriff than we do of the Mayor.

There are contradictions in this neglect of City Hall. We probably have as celebrational an attitude toward the nation's form of government and of political life, pictured in the abstract — democracy, the constitution, government of the people, for the people, by the people — as any folk has ever had. This is combined, however, with a superficial and cynical attitude toward politics and government in the concrete. Also, we place a decided value on "grass roots" and on government "close to the people"; sentimental and exaggerated forms of this feeling for governments that are small and close to home are one of the chief impediments to our grappling satisfactorily with the tangle of modern life. And yet despite this celebration of democracy and this sentiment for the town meeting, American ideas do not include favorable pictures of the actual and present local units of democratic government, at least in an urban setting. Quite the contrary. City politics and City Hall and the mayor and the board of aldermen are anything but glamorous symbols.

Although Americans believe in local government, they do not really affirm the city, though most of them now live in one. And although they believe in "democracy" they do not believe in "politics," and they are not aware that this is contradictory.

And then, in truth, mayors have not been very interesting — certainly not mayors of medium-sized cities. They have not had much power. There have not been many stimulating ideas about what a mayor could do. Mayors in such places used often to be part-time officeholders, insurance men, funeral directors, lawyers, for whom the office offered a certain advertisement. One of Lee's campaign themes against Mr. Celentano was that New Haven needed a "full-time mayor." What was the mayor like in Lee's own childhood? "He was a man named David E. Fitzgerald, just a fellow you saw on ceremonial occasions so far as

I could tell. He gave out prizes." Hardly a figure to catch a boy's imagination.

How many historical mayors can the ordinary intelligent American name? And of those, how many are positive figures? La Guardia, but he is a very special case, especially suitable to musical comedy. Mayor Lee, incidentally, has in the sunny study of his McKinley Street home a collection of books about La Guardia, and also about John F. Kennedy. Curley of Boston is known, but negatively, and Jimmy Walker of New York, also, mostly for his extracurricular activities. The "reform" mayors of cities in the Progressive era — like "Golden Rule" Jones of Cleveland and Brand Whitlock of Toledo — are nearly forgotten. Grover Cleveland is the last mayor of a major city, Calvin Coolidge of any city to make it as far as the Presidency. All of these men have been mayor only briefly before rising to a higher office.

Although city politics and city government have changed a great deal they are still thought of by some laymen in just the categories that Steffens was struggling to outgrow, "corruption" that needs "reform." He broadened the picture to include the businessmen who passed the bribe, but the imagery was still that of the good guys (or rather, for Steffens, the one lone good guy) "cleaning out" the bad guys. The center of the story was a tussle to get city government into the right hands; what the right hands then did with it was not thought about much. Popular myths have still one lingering set of ideas about cleaning up a city — Peoria, or Crescent City, or Hot Springs — which means raiding the joints, smashing the slot machines, closing down the red-light district, and another, sometimes interconnected set of ideas about throwing the rascals out. This means putting together a reform ticket for a crusade that overthrows the boss and his machine, exposes the way they have been boodling, bribing, and selling city transit franchises, puts several aldermen and — perhaps — a businessman or two in jail, and thus brings honesty and efficiency at last to the city. The traditional outcome of this, alas, has been that the reform impulse fades after one term or two, and the bosses come back.

The backsliding impermanence of this reform impulse should have made clear that one cannot permanently remake a city's politics without believing in politics and sticking with it. One cannot give government a new direction just by negating the old; one must believe in a government's governing, and have positive purposes for it to fulfill. At least the more superficial followers of the old reform had only negative purposes, since politics and government were not their genuine and continuing interest. Plunkitt of Tammany Hall said they were only mornin' glories, fading as the day wore on because they weren't trained up to politics. And the "honest and efficient" government may be empty and boring; there is nothing for it to do but to sit there being efficient.

Characteristically, the rogue who was boss was a good deal more interesting person than the faceless good men of reform. It is amusing to read of Steffens struggling to support Seth Low, the "good" mayor of New York City, even while admitting that he did not find him a very attractive man, and struggling to oppose Boss Richard Croker whom in fact he rather liked.

There can now be far more to city government than the corruption-honesty question. The Lee administration, handling giant millions unknown to other regimes, has nevertheless been surprisingly free of money corruption — from feathered nests and hands in the till. That negative virtue is hardly its main point.

Lee has sometimes been called a "reform" mayor, but he is not exactly a reform mayor in the tradition of this ancient picture. What preceded him was not "corrupt." New Haven's problem was not corruption but stagnation. New Haven had not had the rich and colorful scandals that Waterbury, say, enjoyed in the thirties.

Mayor Lee is unlike reform mayors also in that he did not come into power by gathering a new group of crusading amateurs outside politics to overthrow entrenched party hacks. Instead, he was and is supported by his party's leaders. At first he was the protégé of John Golden, the long-time New Haven Democratic leader, to whom some of his opponents might have applied in the days of his greatest power the term "boss." Golden spotted Lee as a young alderman and brought him along.

And Lee is no mornin' glory amateur. He has been engaged in politics since before he could vote. In contrast to the outsiders and amateurs of reform, when Dick Lee became mayor he "hit the ground running," as he himself once said. He had been around City Hall all his adult life, as police reporter, alderman, and minority leader on the Board of Aldermen. And it is to be hoped that Lee is unlike some earlier reformers, too, in that his work will last. Certainly the rebuilt city will last. He has been mayor long enough, twelve years at the end of 1965, to have brought a major work to completion. He has set a standard of expectations about New Haven's mayors that will not soon fade. The Republicans, to win, would have to put forward an extraordinary candidate, and the Democratic gossip about successors to Lee must now use him as the measure — an exacting standard quite beyond what one would formerly have applied to the office of mayor.

In the outlook of middle-class, college-educated Americans on city government, insofar as they have one, about the only question beyond "corruption" has to do with the form the government shall take: strong mayor-council, weak mayor-council, city manager, and so on. Textbooks tell about the rise of the city manager system, about Galveston and Des Moines and others. From the day of Steffens and Riis until the very recent past, reformers have thought that municipal politics ought to be cut off from national party politics. Many of the New Haven persons who used to believe that and to nod favorably at meetings of the National Municipal League when the great virtues of nonpartisan and city manager government were recommended are now strong supporters of Lee. Nonpartisanship is not necessarily desirable, at least for a larger city, where there are real differences of value and interest and real problems of organization. The parties, like politics and government, may deserve a better reputation than generally they have had.

The whole question of the form of city government may be overemphasized. Richard Lee, as alderman, mayoralty candidate, and mayor, has been through five fights for charter reform, every one of which lost. He now throws up his hands and says there are more important matters to attend to. The last fight, in 1958, was a fierce struggle to strengthen the office of mayor, reduce the size of the Board of Aldermen, and otherwise straighten out the city government's constitution. Mayor Lee strongly supported the charter reform; the party leaders, including those of his Democratic party like John Golden, quietly opposed it. The League of Women Voters, after internal agonies, decided the proposed reform was not pure enough, and did not support it. The battle was the most intense of any in Mayor Lee's tenure so far as the politicians were concerned. The charter reform lost, and Mayor Lee gave up on that end of things. "It fills me with a frenzy of indifference," he said recently during another, lesser effort at changing the charter. All that he has accomplished in his years as mayor has been done under what is technically, in a textbook sense, a "weak" mayor system. But he has been anything but a weak mayor.

The "reform" idea, a large and vague one in American political history, is particularly ambiguous with reference to city politics. Almost contradictory purposes of government can be comprehended under the word (budget-cutting "efficiency" versus needed social services: which is "reform"?). The components of humanitarian social action and of positive government have been overshadowed by the "corruption" question and by efforts to change the mechanics of government. Especially have they been overshadowed by efforts to change the

city's power arrangements, in general away from political parties and professional politicians to some other group regarded
as more pure in heart. No doubt in some cities at some times reform in these senses has been necessary and desirable. However, there is, or should now be, more to city politics than that.

What New Haven needed was a much larger and more energetic role for its government than reform in any of these old-
fashioned senses offered.

A mayor can now be a miniature President — the central
source of initiative and strength, and the focus of attention, for
the community of which he is the executive. A nonpolitical administrator like a city manager, or a merely ceremonial mayor
who is without real power, or even a nonpartisan executive cannot fill this role as effectively as an elected, political, powerful,
partisan mayor. If he is a good one, that is. Party organization
connects him with a great organized slice of the masses, and
they with him. The conflicts of party politics offer perpetual
criticism, and force him continually to pay attention to public
interests, opinions, and values. Also — this is a more significant
feature than is sometimes realized — they give drama, interest,
and excitement to community affairs. It is by no means a minor
aspect of Dick Lee's mayoralty that he is an interesting fellow
and that nobody is bored by city government as he carries it
out.

Obviously one of the great assets of a President is his com-
mand of public attention and the means of communication. On
his much smaller stage a strong mayor can have something like
that, too. A spotlight is focused on him; he in turn can focus it
on the neglected needs of the city. And he now has new resources to deal with those needs. He not only must cope with
that depressing list of crimes, blights, snarls, addictions, and
pollutions that come under the heading "urban problems," but
he also has powerful new instruments available to him to do so
and perhaps to do something more positive at the same time.

These new instruments are chiefly the result of federal legislation: urban renewal; a great maze of housing legislation, by no means confined now to "conventional" public housing; the anti-poverty program, especially including the community-action program with its "umbrella" agency in each city; all the educational money; juvenile delinquency funds; mass transit grants, and an open-spaces program, and library money, and much more. The Great Society is largely to be a City Society, and the leaders of it, mayors.

At the first meeting of the board that I attended a Republican alderman attacked Mayor Lee because there was unemployment in New Haven. I do not think it would have occurred to anyone to do that under Mayor J. W. Murphy. As I write, CORE is attacking Mayor Lee, after he named eleven "slumlords," as being himself the "12th slumlord," because CORE has found some people relocated into substandard housing owned by the city (the houses are scheduled for demolition, but often that takes a long time). I am sure no one would have thought of doing *that* under Mayor Murphy, either, or even under Mayor Celentano in the late forties.

There has been a sharp rise in the New Haven citizen's expectations about his mayor and his city government. This comes partly from country-wide developments; mayors and city governments everywhere find that citizens expect them to do much more than they used to do. Partly also this comes from the large picture of the city's doings encouraged by Mayor Lee. A lively administration with its works and words continually in the papers may receive not less but more pressure than an inert and reactionary one, because hopes and expectations expand faster than performance possibly can.

Lee's mayoralty demonstrates that there are larger aims of city government than had been envisioned by the old-line chewed cigars, and also that more politics are required to attain those objectives than had been mastered by the goo-goos.

For that matter, it shows also that there are larger ends than these traditional good-government forces had ordinarily thought of.

The criticism of the limited and antipolitical outlook of middle-class "good government" people is now quite common, in academic and higher journalistic circles as well as among professional politicians, who presumably have always known, or rather sensed, its faults. In many of these, although not yet in the middle-class public at large, the word "politics" has been cleaned off and invested with a certain fresh dignity. And the merely administrative honesty-and-efficiency view of local government has come under attack — rightly, in my view. I think, however, the notion of the "political" that is set over against it needs to be given somewhat different substance than some are inclined to give to it.

Congressman Lindsay, a Republican running for office in a heavily Democratic city, quoted La Guardia's remarks that "there is no Republican or Democratic way to pave the streets." It is understandable that both Lindsay and La Guardia — lonesome Republicans in the vast New York City sea of Democrats — would thus try to play down the strictly partisan aspect of local government. That statement, nevertheless, is often quoted in other circumstances and with a larger and dubious meaning: that there is no policy problem but only an administrative problem in local government. Before Lee became mayor there were good-government people who would apply the slogan to New Haven, and with that larger meaning. How wrong they were! There *are* questions of policy with respect to paving the streets. Should the streets be paved or the money saved? Or spent on something else? Which streets? In which district? (A great symbol of new Negro voting power in the Southern town is the day the streets in the Negro section are paved.) Local government in a city of any size is not mere routine or a merely "technical" or "administrative" matter, manageable by "business" methods. It is a conflict of interests — and of values. Policy, we may say, is a line of action connecting the facts of a situation to some large set of values. It is the evaluative aspect that distinguishes "policy" from administration and technique.

Where the objective is simple, unequivocal, noncontroversial, tangible, and attainable by means that themselves raise no further problems, technical work raises no difficulties. Then there is no Republican or Democratic, no liberal or conservative way to pave streets. The only question is, how best to do what all agree should be done. In serious politics, though, the ends to be served admit of no such description.

Politics, the activity of directing or shaping the society, is addressed to ends that are not simple and tangible. Though one may give a single term for the ends — justice or the common good or the public interest — the meaning and content of such a term is complex, slippery, difficult, and changing. Moreover, its application is not agreed upon; it is of the essence of politics that men differ and contend with respect to it. Their notion of what is good is connected to their interests and to their particular situation, although it cannot be reduced to that alone, as some seem to reduce it.

The ends of politics, moreover, are not neatly separable from questions about means. The judgment about the concrete content of the ends of politics depends upon an interpretation of a specific situation, which in turn is contended about. One might argue that politics is pre-eminently an activity that cannot be reduced to technique. Perhaps more than any other aspect of life, it involves multiple objectives that have an intangible and qualitative aspect and about which men do not agree.

A merely administrative view of city government is rightly set aside by many recent academics in favor of a political understanding. But what does that "political" mean? The management of conflict, it is said. Well, that is certainly a major part of it. The variety of groups whose interests conflict need to be recognized in a way that a narrow technical-administrative outlook may not do.

The nonpolitical and technical view of city government tends to be a class-oriented view, its critics say; the "best people" and "business methods" it favors tend to reflect the dominant middle and upper class, and the absence of parties and of party competition tends to keep the mass of citizens from having the organization and the engagement that brings their interests effectively into play in the city's affairs. Nonpartisan, nonpolitical city government tends to be government by the downtown business community and the newspaper, Republican in the North without being so labeled. A political setup not only may bring the recognition of a wider set of divergent interests; it may also respond to a wider set of values, and of ends that the government may pursue.

The notable thing about Dick Lee beyond his bringing new groups and interests into the picture of New Haven politics is that he realized larger purposes than had been pursued by city government before him. The physical redevelopment that many had wanted became a reality because he set his sights as mayor very high, and had the political skill to hit the mark.

Mr. Lee's doings as mayor fall conveniently into three levels. The first concerns improving the established run of city services like police and fire and snow removal and leaf removal and garbage collection. Fire stations have been rebuilt with award-winning architecture. The city has a new fireboat named the Sally Lee, a new dog pound, improved street-marking, $15 million worth of rebuilt sewers, a new assessor system, a new emergency communication system, a radio-controlled stoplight system. One could make quite a list, much longer than this. Salaries of policemen, firemen, and especially of teachers have been raised. All of this, nonetheless, might have been the work of an able city manager. All of this is simply to do well what everybody expects city government to do.

At the second level — urban renewal and the city-wide planning that goes with it — something is added that goes beyond what the old-fashioned City Hall had been expected to do.

The Lee administration plans and rebuilds the city. Urban renewal has its critics, but New Haven shows it can be both humane and successful. In the spring of 1965 the Lee administration announced yet another series of plans and buildings: a national Knights of Columbus headquarters building; the government center on the Green; and the $15 million housing complex called Church Street South.

The third level is an even more significant expansion of the purposes of city government, the "war on poverty." New Haven's situation has been different on several points from that of cities like Chicago and Cleveland and Syracuse, where there has been serious conflict between City Hall and either the agency or some spokesmen for the poor. New Haven's started earlier — in 1962, well before the federal antipoverty program. It was originally financed with Ford Foundation funds rather than government money, and it was brought into being by the initiative of City Hall rather than by national legislation.

Technically, Community Progress, Inc., is a quasiprivate agency that is not a part of city government. Actually, however, it is closely related to the Mayor, without whose administration it would never have come into being. Under the community-action section (Title II) of the Economic Opportunity (antipoverty) Act of 1964, the section that encourages one umbrella agency to attack poverty in a city and draws heavily on New Haven's experience, the local community commits itself to eliminating poverty. That's a long way beyond what even the most ambitious mayors considered their job to be in the past.

13. Urban Renewal and Housing

"You have shoved out the poor to make homes for the rich."

A FRIEND OF MINE who teaches at Amherst looked around at the very impressive rebuilding of the center of New Haven one day in that spring of 1965 and, after the manner of professors, was not impressed. "Where are the Negroes who used to live here?" he asked me, as we were driving to the railroad station. "That's what this 'urban renewal' means, you know; they push the poor people out and put up these luxury apartments and fancy stores and office buildings. 'Urban renewal means Negro removal.'" He echoed the most pungent criticism of urban renewal now often made by its friends — or perhaps I should say by liberals.

There are criticisms also from the right, of course, about government interference with freedom and subsidies for "uneconomic" uses of land. I do not have much trouble with the objections from that side. Like some others I became convinced a long time ago that a great many human needs are not going to be served by a free market left entirely to itself. The criticism that hurts is the other one, the criticism from friends, from liberals — many of whom now have a certain disenchantment or at least confusion over urban renewal.

Why, they ask, should taxpayers (in effect) subsidize the building of fancy apartment buildings like University Towers, which has a swimming pool and rents in the higher bracket, and Madison Towers and Crown Towers? The answer is in their being valuable properties that help to make a beautiful city and markedly increase the city's tax base; also, we want the people who live in those apartments, with their money for spending and their potential abilities, to stay in the city. We need them.

The liberal critic probably finds this answer just confirms his worst fears. He says, "You have shoved out the poor to make homes for the rich. You may help the city's finances, but what happened meanwhile to the people who used to live on Oak Street?" There are two answers that supporters of urban renewal in New Haven, like L. Thomas Appleby, give to this. One is defensive, designed to show that those people are better housed now than they ever were on Oak Street. Another is more positive. Without urban renewal, they say, the problems of the destitute residents of Oak Street would not have become the specific, visible community responsibility that they have become. And something like urban renewal is a weapon the community needs to meet that responsibility.

The defensive arguments deal in two sets of statistics: those on relocation and those on the enforcement of housing codes. The first set shows that the overwhelming majority of people displaced by urban renewal — the removed Negroes — have moved to better housing. The second set shows that urban renewal has not simply been shoving the slum around from one place to another; there isn't as much substandard housing in New Haven as there was when Oak Street existed.

Are the people who lived on Oak Street and in other renewal areas now paying a higher rent than before? (That is another point in the attack on "Negro removal.") Yes, they are on the average paying slightly higher rents. Many relocated families — 151 of the 886 from Oak Street — have moved into public housing, where they have priority and where rents are 21.8 percent of the family's gross income. Many relocated families are on welfare, so that the change one way or another in rent does not affect their own family budget; their rent is part of their grant. What about the others? I looked at a study of the

100 families then most recently relocated into private housing in New Haven. It showed that they paid 16.8 percent of their income for rent before relocation, 20.3 percent afterward. Thus their rents on the average did go up somewhat, but they are getting better housing and the 20.3 percent they are now paying is below the 21.8 percent the public housing laws regard as standard.

That is the average. What about individual cases? I looked over the case-by-case summary of these 100 families — their income, the rents they paid before and after relocation — and found that the extremes have been pulled in. The worst case before relocation (worst, that is, in percent of income paid for rent) is that of a woman with a large family who made $365 a month and paid $151 a month for rent, 40.3 percent of her income. She is now, after being relocated, paying $120 a month, 32.9 percent of her income — and she is still the "worst" case. Most of the *increased* rent is being paid by those who were paying rather low rents before relocation. The percentages come down from 40 percent but up from 15 percent, and more of them now cluster around 20 percent. Obviously these figures don't tell you about all the misery, but they do indicate that, on balance, relocation from urban renewal in New Haven has not added to the misery.

Is there a long wait and much scrambling around to find a place? Not, I am told, if the relocation agency can help it. The agency's fourteen workers go to great lengths to help a relocated family find a house they want, even if the family turns down the first five offers, and even to the point in one celebrated instance of playing cupid so that a couple could meet public housing standards.

Do the families move to another slum? Or to a Negro ghetto? The New Haven Family Relocation Office has a wall chart showing where all relocated families from each project have gone. The Negroes cluster only in the public housing projects.

Otherwise throughout the city the racial distribution is very mixed.

These claims that urban renewal does *not* make worse housing for the poor are convincing to me, so far as New Haven is concerned. Nearly 30 percent of the housing units in New Haven were substandard in the early fifties, before the city's urban renewal programs began. Now less than 15 percent are, and this is rapidly improving. The overwhelming majority of the 5000 families relocated from New Haven's projects — 95 percent from the early Oak Street, Church Street, and Wooster Square projects and 99 percent from the more recent Dixwell and Hill High School — have been placed in "standard" (not "substandard," not "slum") housing. In the nation as a whole, federal statistics indicate that 9 out of 10 families relocated from renewal areas have moved to standard housing.

Moving itself is a nuisance, and sometimes more than a nuisance, although statistics indicate that 1 American in 5 moves every year. Being forced to move is particularly painful. Nevertheless, people are forced to move by a wide range of public programs. Highway construction, for one — especially for the new Interstate 91 going north to Hartford — has knocked down as many houses in New Haven as the city's very extensive urban renewal. Why isn't there the same criticism for the highway's displacement of people that has been leveled at urban renewal? People also are displaced by private construction. In none of these other cases is the family treated as well as by urban renewal, which has careful procedures in relocation, to find "decent, safe, and sanitary" housing for displaced families.

This brings us to the positive argument for redevelopment's effect on the urban poor: it has brought them to the community's attention, and at its best it has provided new neighborhoods and a new set of possibilities in addition to new houses. Experience with family relocation in New Haven and other cities was one of the principal wellsprings of the national antipoverty program. Renewal and relocation uncovered problems of the urban poor that had been kept out of sight for decades, and made these problems a public responsibility. In New Haven the connection was direct. Community Progress, Inc., came directly out of the effort to cope with the relocation problems that accompanied urban renewal — problems that quickly go beyond solely finding housing and involve comprehensive social services.

The "antipoverty" mixture of education and employment efforts is valuable but alone it will not lick the problem of the ghetto and the slum. Something like urban renewal is needed too.

To go back to the question of "Negro removal": Is that "removal," if you think about it, necessarily bad? It depends upon what is done with the removed people and with the cleared land. Urban renewal actually has greater potential for eliminating ghettos and segregated living than any other program yet devised — if a city uses it in the right way. Without the active slum clearance of urban renewal it is not really possible to break up the worst of the ghettos. It may be possible with strong fair-housing efforts to move a small and select number of Negro families, mostly middle-class, out into the white suburbs, but the great masses of Negroes will stay right where they are now, in the center of the cities. Having the middle-class Negro move out, incidentally, is a rather mixed blessing, since these are leaders who are needed in the center of the city where problems are concentrated.

Civil rights laws alone are certainly not going to alter the racial patterns in the Harlems of the land. The Negro masses are not going to move out, and it is absurd to expect white families to move in. The only way to obtain widespread integrated living in the blighted centers of the great cities is by clearance — knocking the worst slums down and starting over.

Then comes the question. What is built on the cleared land? And what is the mixture of elements — industrial, commercial, residential — in the city's overall plan? And what are the rents in the residential projects? Although it is perhaps unwise to engage in specific invidious intercity comparisons, it has to be said that cities vary widely in their answers to these questions. What that Amherst friend and other liberals like him ought to do is not to condemn all urban renewal but to discriminate. New Haven's ancient Connecticut rival Hartford has a magnificent project in the heart of the city called Constitution Plaza. Connecticut as a whole can be proud of it as a great accomplishment. All of the redevelopment in Hartford, however, is on those 25 acres; in New Haven it is spread over 1000 acres. It is true that luxury apartments, the telephone building, and the Oak Street Connector were put in the place of Oak Street's firetraps, but in other renewal areas throughout the city new low-rent housing projects are a major feature: housing for the elderly in Wooster Square, Newhallville, Dwight, and Dixwell, and co-op housing projects in the same neighborhoods. One of the cooperative housing ventures that was just then in the spring of 1965 being finished and shown to prospects is directly in the middle of the Dixwell area. Like all of these projects, it is integrated. To buy a unit, a family has to have $325 to put down, and must be able to pay from $91 to $129 a month, depending on the number of rooms. That does, it is true, put these units out of reach for the very poor; those who can pay it, though, not only have their rent, utilities, and property tax paid but are building up equity. A young former resident of Dixwell walked eyes-wide and marveling around this project, the Florence Virtue Homes, and remarked, "I never thought I'd see anything like this built *here*."

Too many people, in New Haven and nationally, equate all of urban renewal with new business buildings downtown. There is — or there can be — much more to it than that in the planned rebuilding of the housing and the community facilities of deteriorating neighborhoods. Suppose that sixty years ago, when Jacob Riis, despairing and angry, walked Theodore Roosevelt night after night through the miserable conditions of Five Points and the Bends, they had had available a program like this one, a public agency that could come in, plan, and rebuild the thing.

Two other criticisms of urban renewal may make an appearance — criticisms that often are connected with the "Negro removal" accusation, and come from the same socially conscious people. One relates to planning-with-the-people and democracy, and is illustrated by the comment of a national church's urban work executive who remarked, "New Haven's urban renewal is one of the worst in the country. Too few people are involved in the decisions." The other has to do with excessive bulldozing and is represented by Jane Jacobs and by those whom Mitchell Sviridoff, director of New Haven's antipoverty program, calls "slum romantics." The remark of a New Haven literary man illustrates this second one: "I used to be in favor of urban renewal. But then I talked to artist friends of mine who couldn't any longer find top-floor studios and cheap cold-water flats . . ." If you put all these criticisms together they make quite a poignant and negative bundle: happy slum dwellers enjoying the varied and interesting life in their cold-water flats are shoved out of their congenial neighborhoods, without having any voice or part in the decision, by a few powerful bureaucrats; their homes are destroyed, and after a long and messy delay, badly designed office buildings and luxury apartments may be erected on the cleared land where their homes were. It is a stirring indictment, but it is not really accurate.

There is a tendency in such a complex program as urban renewal for pungent and colorful criticisms to get lodged in the public mind quite independent of the proportions of things. Each of the criticisms taken separately has now only a small piece of the truth; combined, they make a picture that is quite mistaken. Each represents a fault that has appeared in some cities and some projects, especially at an earlier stage in the short fifteen years of urban renewal history. Although there have been occasions on which developers have been too quick with the bulldozer, destroying some aesthetically and histor-ically valuable buildings and some viable, functioning lower-income communities, that is not the main story. Since 1954 there has been a continually growing emphasis on neighborhood con-servation, on selective "pocket" renewal, and on the rehabilita-tion of existing sructures. I am impressed that the best of the renewal administrators keep learning and improving their pro-gram, taking account of the criticisms that have been made.

And the charge that "too few people are involved in the de-cisions" is partly wrong and partly wrongheaded. In the late fifties "citizen's participation" and "planning with the people" became a major theme in the urban renewal world. A case in point is New Haven's Wooster Square project, which was de-veloped in more than a hundred meetings with the people in the area. The same thing was going on in 1965 in Dixwell and Newhallville areas and is beginning in the section called the Hill. That's part of the answer; the critics are not right on the facts. But the other part, harder to state, is that they may have some soggy premises. Not all planning-with-the-people is as dandy and democratic as it sounds. For one thing, which peo-ple? A narrowly circumscribed neighborhood can tell you what it wants positively, and also negatively — for a not unfamiliar example, exclusion of Negroes, no low-income public housing, no site for a public high school. That's what the people in the area themselves want but it is a bit difficult to work with on a community-wide basis. Both the urban renewal projects and CPI were to be criticized by the "new left" people at Yale, for not "involving the people." I think there *is* an intriguing set of new problems here, with both renewal and the poverty programs setting up their own little political structures. But I don't think the leftists with their attack on the "power structure" understand the problem fully.

As to the varied and attractive aspects of unbulldozed city life: they may apply to Greenwich Village, but not to the worst blocks of East Harlem or to Oak Street. Surely it is perverse to romanticize the worst of our cities' slums. For one major part of our urban-problem slum clearance (urban renewal) is essential, and nothing but slum clearance will do the job.

There is progression in the American effort to grapple with the city and the slum. Public housing was the great thing in the late thirties, urban renewal in the fifties, antipoverty now. Each of these has at first been oversold in enthusiastic propaganda; against each of the first two there has then come a negative reaction, an overreaction really, when it was discovered that the program was not a cure-all. We may predict that the same thing will happen with the war on poverty. It is important to counteract this recurring problem by not looking on these programs as panaceas in the first place, and then by not overreacting, overdoing the criticisms, in the second.

Low-income public housing projects, built in the late thirties and the forties with such hope and promise, now are said to have become legalized slums or fireproof slums. At the very least it is desirable for slums to have become fireproof, but it is evident that much more has been accomplished by public housing than this. Decent housing that simply was not available and not likely to be provided by the free market (low-income housing, I mean) has been provided for thousands of families. That is no small accomplishment in the continuing story of the human effort to make a decent life.

It is true that public housing has not accomplished the larger objectives its supporters hoped it would and city reformers throughout the long battle against "the tenement" had looked for. It did not eliminate slum life and slum behavior. In fact, in some cities the pins in the city map that indicate social disor-

ganization — delinquency, crime, dope addiction, and the rest
— tend to cluster in a rather embarrassing way in the low-income public housing projects. Although there is a reason for
this situation, it does show that merely providing decent, safe,
and sanitary housing, under public control, is not enough to
win the "battle against the slum."

Faced with that fact the liberal and onetime public housing
enthusiast has a choice: he can turn aside in disgruntled confusion (which too many do), or he can push on to find out what
more and what better needs to be done. Urban renewal, which
grew in part out of the background of public housing, is now
in the stage that public housing was a few years ago: dawning
disillusionment. And liberal onetime supporters now have
that same choice, to turn sour or to push through to some clarity about the fundamental concept. Admittedly there are
many failures and deficiencies in urban renewal as it has
worked out in practice. It is a complicated program with a long
and hazardous distance between cup and lip, and it is new.
What is represented fundamentally, nonetheless, is the expanded role for public purposes and planning that liberals long
have wanted. That conservatives should resist is understandable. Liberals, however, rather than parroting certain now standard criticisms, should work to make urban renewal the effective tool it can be for purposes in which they believe.

The great question is housing. Do the renewal plans provide
for enough housing units, especially for the poor?

Housing of the poor, as the critics say, should be the first
criterion, outranking all others. It is supposed to be, according
to the statement of purpose in the original legislation. The
Housing Act of 1949 declared its intent to "remedy the serious
housing shortage," to eliminate "substandard and other inadequate housing through clearance of slums and blighted areas,"
and to realize "as soon as feasible the goal of a decent house
and suitable living environment for every American fam-

ily . . ." The other purposes to which urban renewal has been put have less justification in the legislation — but proponents of those other purposes may have more power in the cities.

Urban renewal is a potent instrument. Like all powerful instruments it can be misused and doubtless has been. The question finally comes down to the political forces in the city. When used properly, as in New Haven, redevelopment can be a good thing — for the poor and the city as a whole.

What are the housing programs that New Haven has used? First, housing for the elderly. In discussions leading to the Wooster Square project the residents of the area insisted at the outset that they did not want public housing projects of any type, luxury, middle, or low-income. When they began to plan for housing for the elderly, however, the people kept saying they wanted more of that — so much so that in the end ing more housing for the elderly. Now there is a two-building, they even accepted a high-rise project as a last resort to obtain-six-story project for the elderly on Wooster Square.

There are also projects in Newhallville, and in the Dixwell area; and a new 106-unit high-rise apartment, designed by Paul Rudolph, near the center of the city. "I wish I had two thousand units of housing for the elderly," says Robert Wolfe of the Housing Authority. "It's terrific." The reasons for its acceptability are not hard to find; the elderly, generally speaking, are good neighbors. And citizens may sympathize and identify with the elderly. "That could be you or me," one man said.

Old people make up an important part of the poor. There are 25,000 people above sixty in New Haven, one sixth of the total population. Just over half of these own their homes. Many of the remaining half have housing difficulties; in the 1960 census, 1250 households headed by an elderly person were living in substandard housing, 200 of these in homes they owned. The New Haven authority has now built or started to build 333 units of housing for the elderly. In the new Church Street South complex there are to be 300 more. If you subtract that

633 from the 1960 number — well, as a city official said, it's not perfect, but we're getting close.

The most important of the programs in New Haven has come to be the 221(d)3 nonprofit co-op housing. The Mayor, as I have said, testified in Washington in behalf of that section of the Kennedy housing bill of 1961, which was one of the pieces of legislation Mr. Kennedy was able to extract from that Congress. New Haven built the first 221(d)3 project in this country, and now has built or planned eleven more. A nonprofit sponsor, composed of a church, a human relations council, the Junior Chamber of Commerce, and aided by government subsidized loans, *sells* the units to families who meet income standards.

The family pays $380 or $390 dollars down, plus $89 to $120 a month, to purchase a unit. It is likely that they may sell for a profit some years hence; meanwhile they are building up equity. The first project, now fully occupied and already added to, is Liberty Square, 36 units with splotches of bright colors behind Mike's Putnam Restaurant in the heavily Italian section on the Hill by the railroad station. As I write, a Negro is president of the tenants' council in that predominantly white and Italian project.

The most notable of the several projects of 221(d)3 housing in New Haven is the Florence Virtue Homes. The sponsor is the Dixwell Congregational Church. The city administration was determined that this project should be integrated, and went to great lengths to make it so, finally including direct appeals by the Mayor to deans of the several schools of Yale. It happens that New Haven's Negro Dixwell neighborhood lies close to the western edge of Yale University, so that the Florence Virtue project can be at once in the middle of the Dixwell area and within walking distance of Yale. The new development of which it is a part has been given a public-relations name: University Park Dixwell. All through the winter of

1964–1965 I kept hearing the reports on the number of white families applying for apartments. There was no problem about Negro families, more of whom applied, with fewer questions and doubts; "Yes, you still win if you are white," one white critic said disgustedly. The determination that the project shall be integrated necessarily has meant that Negroes who could have used the housing were kept out while whites were being sought. When the project opened in the spring of 1965 it was 55 percent Negro, 45 percent white, a large number of the whites being graduate students and instructors at Yale. Perhaps that makes for rather an odd community — young Yalies plus older Negroes — but it is an important start.

Critics say this 221(d)3 program does not provide for the poorest families. I went on a tour conducted by the New Haven CORE, which maintains that for all its progress New Haven hasn't solved this most difficult of housing problems, families with low incomes and many members. CORE did not add, although city officials tell you this when you take the names to them, that many of the most difficult of these cases are also "multiproblem" families — prostitution, delinquency, dope, jail record — which makes finding housing for them difficult. The large poor family, however, especially if Negro, need not have these negative characteristics in order to find housing an acute problem. The 221(d)3 units like Florence Virtue are out of reach financially for the really poor, and although the projects have met with a generally favorable response some residents of the area, and CORE people, are critical on that account. But new projects for the city, and additional programs for the nation, were then being planned that would help to meet that point.

In the spring of 1965 Mayor Lee made another of his dramatic announcements of new projects for the city: a $15 million housing complex called Church Street South, planned by Ludwig Mies van der Rohe. This project will include many different kinds of housing, 700 to 800 units mixed together: public and private, low income and higher income, housing for the elderly and housing for young families. The housing for the elderly will include about 50 units of "congregate" housing, in which the residents eat together in a central dining room.

The complicated maze of national housing legislation that has developed since 1937 has tended — inadvertently — to reinforce social separations: low-income public housing here, middle-income there, private insured-mortgage lower-middle income in this development, high-priced private housing in that suburb. This Church Street South complex is an effort to counteract these separations.

The Church Street South collection of projects is not the only one in New Haven that involves a mixture of types of housing. All the renewal areas do that. The new University Park Dixwell section will have not only the Florence Virtue Homes but later on also some higher-priced private apartments. Church Street South is the most ambitious intermixing so far. A regional housing man at one of New Haven's innumerable groundbreaking ceremonies asked about Church Street South because of the "new social concept."

In Church Street South there will be playfields, open space, a site for the New Haven Boys' Club, a new elementary school, parking spaces, shops, restaurants; the whole thing will be within easy walking distance of downtown New Haven. The site is right across from the railroad station, where among other unprepossessing things an incredibly decrepit hotel called the Hotel Garde used to stand. (I made the mistake of staying there once, for an unbelievable Edgar Allan Poe-Charles Addams night.) This section, which was my first and discouraging glimpse of New Haven when I came out of the railroad station in the fall of 1947, certainly did not look then like an area someday to be redesigned by Mies van der Rohe. Included in this complex are at least 50 units of low-rent apartments, specifically providing apartments for large families, to be erected according to the announcement "on a scattered-site basis."

Another notable project is the one St. Paul's Episcopal Church is sponsoring in the Wooster Square section, a set of apartments which will have low and moderate rental units under one roof. This is done, according to the pastor, "to bridge economic levels as an answer to the ethical problems of stratification and separation on a wholly artificial basis." "Recent problems in finding sites for scattered housing at low rental demonstrates the problem," he added.

In Chapter 5, when describing the scattered-house incident in the Fifteenth Ward, I referred to a demonstration project then under way in which the New Haven Public Housing Authority *leased* private dwellings and supplemented rents. The project was to run for three years, 1962 to 1965, and was supported by a grant from Washington. It was devised in part to deal with the difficulties in securing adequate public housing. The Public Housing Authority would find appropriate housing in the private market — not that this is easy — and pay the difference between the going rent and the public housing percentage (21.8 percent) of the family's income.

A report on this effort in 1965 said that one part of its success had been neighborhood acceptance. The 26 families in the demonstration had not met opposition and in many cases had established a happy relationship. One reason for this may be found in a footnote in the report which states that no public hearing is required for this type of project. Many neighbors don't know anything about the program or who is paying the rent of the people next door; the people assisted are not publicly stamped and labeled "project families" or "low income," and the fears and stereotypes are not given an occasion to be defined.

This program is a matter of national controversy, going back to the first days of public housing. The idea then was supported by real estate interests and conservatives, who preferred that the government not build houses but, rather, support the rent of people renting in the private market. Some public housing folk still resist the idea because of this history, and because they fear it means government subsidy of slum landlords, and because it is a program that may be competitive with conventional public housing. Supporters of the program, on the other hand, say that they can pick the properties so the less responsible landlords are not included and that this is a swift and not too expensive way to provide the housing families need.

The success of the New Haven demonstration no doubt helped to bring about the provision for a national program of the same kind in the Housing and Urban Development Act of 1965. Actually, there are in that Act *two* programs in which rents are subsidized. One, which came to be called the "rent certificate" program, is like the New Haven demonstration program. A housing authority signs a lease for a privately owned property. The other, the "rent supplement" program, provides this subsidy to the rent of the poor for projects set up under other auspices, including, in one experimental part of the program, private nonprofit agencies like churches and human relations councils that build new projects with a subsidized low-interest (3 percent) government loan, just as in the 221(d)3 program — Florence Virtue, to give one illustration. In both cases the rent payments may be subsidized, so that they may now be available to the lowest-income group.

The Housing and Urban Development Act of 1965, while winding its way through the United States Congress in the spring and summer of 1965, was changed. The Administration had proposed that the controversial new rent-supplement part of it be applied to the next-to-lowest income group rather than to the lowest — those with incomes just too high to qualify for low-income public housing, and a sizable and needy group.

It was felt that this would be both more acceptable to conservatives and less threatening to traditional public housing groups. Nevertheless, "They figured it exactly wrong," as one observer said to me. Conservatives from small towns could not see subsidizing the rent of persons making as much as $6000 a year. That sounds like a lot of money in Laramie or Hutchinson. Liberals did not want to support these moderate-income folk while there remain the really poor people who need housing. So the bill was remade to apply the rent supplement to *low*-income individuals, and thereby perhaps opened up possibilities not at first quite foreseen. By making projects like Florence Virtue available to the poorest group (those who are handicapped, elderly, displaced by government programs, victims of natural disasters, or living in substandard housing), this program opens up the possibility of putting units of what is essentially low-income housing out into the suburbs. Churches, human relations councils, and other civic-minded organizations that sponsor such projects presumably can *scatter* them throughout the metropolitan area, zoning permitting. No public housing authority is needed, and no public hearing.*

When President Johnson signed this Housing Act into law in August 1965 he gave one pen to Mayor Lee. Eight minutes later the Mayor was in the office of Marie McGuire, the head of public housing, making application for the first rent-certificate program in the country.

* Alas! 1966 was another year. The rent-supplement proposal was to have a rocky history. In an up-and-down battle over its appropriation, new restrictions were written into the bill that may prevent its being an instrument for penetrating the suburbs.

14. Antipoverty

*"If I had been a dropout yet, I'd be worth
my weight in gold."*

A FELLOW ALDERMAN who went with me on the CORE
tour of bad housing said to me later that some of the houses
weren't so bad. It depends, he said, on the people — whether
they fix up the house, or tear it down. Some of them, he said,
could take the best house you could give them and in a few
weeks it would be a slum. I don't agree with the conclusions
that he might draw from this — he is an antagonist to the city
programs — nor do I accept the tone of voice in which he said
it, with an edge of contempt. But I think we have to admit
that the conservatives have been partly right when they
insisted that people, not houses alone, make slums.

The causes of slum life are in large part environmental, but
you must include the cultural environment. That is a far deeper
thing than simply the tenement or the physical slum. It takes
more to break this hold than the provision of "decent, safe,
and sanitary" housing, important as that is.

New Haven's CPI has been a leader in the national effort
to eliminate slums and poverty. It started early and has been
successful, showing the way to others. All that talking and coffee
drinking by bright young fellows seems to have resulted in
something impressive. CPI has combined the possibility, at
least, of a profound social effect with broad social support.
The city takes the initiative to "open opportunities."

Let it be noted how significant an expansion of the purposes of an American city government this initiative is. The government — or, rather, let us say the society, of which government is the instrument — has set itself the objective of making war on poverty, indeed of eliminating poverty. Before the Great Depression Americans did not expect the national government to do much in that line, even in a palliative way and even in a time of a very general distress. We seldom used government to "care for the needy," let alone to help them stop being needy altogether. We have now had the experience of the PWA and WPA, and we expect the central government in Washington to prevent major depressions and we accept the Social Security system and we expect governments to provide welfare checks and unemployment benefits. But until the poverty program of 1964 we did not expect government to take *the initiative* to bring people up out of the condition of poverty. And certainly we have not hitherto expected that such a thing be done by the city government.

CPI, although itself technically not a part of the city government, helped set the pattern for the community-action section of the national antipoverty bill. Top CPI people, in fact, helped conceive and draft that section, and one of them is now an independent consultant to cities trying to qualify for such grants.

Technically CPI is a nonprofit agency of the unclassifiable quasiprivate, quasipublic kind that we Americans are good at inventing. When it was originally financed, in 1962, primarily by a grant of two and a half million dollars from the Ford Foundation, it was expected that the city could attract matching funds from other sources. Actually, CPI has been granted much more than matching funds, chiefly by the federal government. The Ford grant was to last three years to see if the agency succeeded. In the spring of 1965 the agency received another huge grant from the Ford Foundation for three more years of work — $2,550,000. One may reflect that this use of

Ford money must be a difficult part of American capitalist culture for the Marxists of the world to understand. It is hard enough for them to fit the Ford Foundation itself into their scheme — a great philanthropic research and humanitarian venture supported by capitalist profits. That this foundation should turn around and give great sums of money to arouse and organize the poor must make Marxists absolutely intellectually cross-eyed. By the end of 1965, CPI had received nearly $10 million, from Ford plus the federal government plus lesser amounts from other foundations and the city.

The nine-member Board of CPI has three representatives appointed by the Mayor and also representatives of Yale, the Redevelopment Agency, the Board of Education, the Community Council, and the United Fund.* Although it is not precisely an agency of the city government, one possible future arrangement might be that it become one, with a Deputy Mayor parallel to the Development Administrator (Logue and Appleby) taking care of the "human renewal" things. In any case, CPI would never have come into being had it not been for Mayor Lee, with whose administration it is closely related. CPI now receives over 60 percent of its funds from the federal government, from eight agencies, the initials of which I give without translating: OJD, OMAT, OED, URA, PHA, NYC, PHS, and VRA.

One can say that most of the actual elements of the antipoverty program existed before. It is a collecting together under this heading of efforts in education, employment, and social services that were mostly either already under way or already thought of. Putting them together and directing them toward a newly defined and enlarged goal — eliminating poverty — is important.

The expansion and clarity of purpose makes possible a con-

* In the fall and winter of 1965–1966, after much discussion of the "participation of the poor," the board was enlarged to sixteen, with seven added members chosen from and by the residents of the seven areas served.

certed action, cutting across and subordinating the several
special fields and goals to achieve the overriding objective. I
did not really grasp this point when I read it in CPI literature
or heard it in the speeches. This paragraph in Glazer and Moynihan's book gave me a sense of the difficulties that need to be
overcome: "Perhaps the worst misfortune of this bottom layer
in New York," they write, and no doubt something similar is
true on a smaller scale elsewhere, including New Haven, "is the
need to deal with large numbers of harried city employees
who have no contact with each other, or, in truth, with their
clients, except for the specific malfunction which brought
them into action. The school teacher or principal can do nothing about what goes on at home; the welfare investigator's role
must be simply one of testing whether the family is qualified;
the probation officer is supposed to keep in touch with his case,
not the case's family, and can do nothing if the home in which
the probationer is located is a tenement that is a center for
drug addiction or thievery; the housing project employee (if
the family is lucky enough to be in one) is concerned with
financial eligibility, the payment of rent, and the maintenance
of the physical property; the hospital hands out drugs and
treatment; and so on and so on. And social workers and others
now and then set up a joint project to see if out of the welter of
bureaucratic confusion there can be fashioned an instrument
that responds to families and individuals as full human
beings."

CPI comes much closer to being such an instrument than
anything that existed before. It does have its "bureaucratic"
restrictions and problems, too. Originally it limited itself to
six "gray areas" of the city where poverty was concentrated,
and some people moved over into these areas by giving the
address of an aunt or cousin in order to receive the services.
The government funds have many restrictions: for ninth-grade
work-study programs you go to the Department of Health, Education, and Welfare or to Sargent Shriver's poverty office, but

for tenth grade and above you go to the Office of Manpower and Training in the Department of Labor. CPI, in its operations, is not like that. It deals, if not quite with "the families and individuals as full human beings," at least with the family or individual's condition of poverty, which is a very large and important fact about their life.

CPI has been able to devise flexible new instruments intended to cut through the frustrating overdivision of labor that Glazer and Moynihan describe. It isn't merely some overhead "co-ordinating" agency that is needed; this would be the first bureaucratic instinct. It is effective, particular instruments that can themselves cut directly through to the problems — red-tape-beating instruments, so to speak. The three discussed below illustrate these possibilities.

The neighborhood worker is a person who ordinarily lives in the part of town where he works, and in many cases comes from it himself. His job is to do those things the special people like teachers, social workers, and police cannot do — make new opportunities for the poor. As the county agent used to be a very valuable fellow in rural areas so now a city agent, a neighborhood agent, can be one in the urban setting. He knows whom to call, what to do, what's available. He is somebody you can talk to, and indeed one who seeks you out. Like the old ward politician as well as the county agent, he knows the people and the telephone numbers and the programs. This contemporary type of ward heeler has a new set of programs with which he can connect his client: a job, an on-the-job training program, a work crew. Or he can persuade him to go back to school. The neighborhood worker is an indigenous, nonprofessional social worker; before long and perhaps unfortunately, from association, he begins to pick up some social worker language.

The neighorhood employment center is another instrument. Glazer and Moynihan might have listed among those who have one limited relationship to the poor the person at the Employment Service. He may try to match the poor person to the available list of jobs, but he has no relation to the limitations of that poor person's schooling and of his home life which make him unable to fit into that job. There are as of this writing about 6500 unemployed in the Greater New Haven area — down from 8000 in the early sixties. There are at the same time about 3500 jobs that are going begging. The trouble is that the former, who are unskilled and perhaps not literate, don't fit the latter, which are jobs for draftsmen, engineers, electronics experts. CPI's neighborhood employment centers differ from the old employment service, first, in that they are closer and much more approachable, being nearby rather than downtown or acrosstown in an imposing and unlocatable office building. They differ, second, in that the centers in addition to finding jobs will also find out what it would take to get a person a job. He may come in to the center looking for a job and receive a test instead. He may be encouraged and helped to go back to school. Or he may be put in on-the-job training, or directly into a job. And many of the persons helped by these employment centers do not walk in of their own accord; they are brought in by neighborhood workers or other CPI folk.

The community school is the third illustration of the new instruments. This means that the school serves as an all-year, all-week, all-day, all-around center of the activities of the community. In the evening the Conte Senior Citizens building is brilliant with light as older citizens play pinochle in a room across from the library for both adults and schoolchildren and many groups meet elsewhere in the building. A CPI team works out of the school. Reading in Jacob Riis's *The Battle with the Slum* of 1902, I was impressed to find on page 398 a description of what was to become in New Haven in 1962 the community school. Riis tells of a letter he has received from a settlement worker who wants to "make of the school truly the neighborhood house and soul" for young and old; "something to take the place, as far as anything can, of the home that isn't there; a place to meet other than the saloon; a place for the young to do their courting . . . a place to make their elders feel that they are men and women, something else than mere rent-paying units." Put the school to neighborhood use. Riis goes on with considerable enthusiasm to describe adult lectures, libraries, concerts, union meetings, political meetings, games, clubs, and dances at the school.

Some of the professionals in the affected fields have been wary about CPI's use of nonprofessionals; teachers worry about nonaccredited persons doing tutoring and assisting and social workers worry about untrained persons doing what looks like social work. A training valuable within a narrow frame set by defined professional goals may in a broader setting, beyond the profession's limits, be inadequate and sometimes even rigidly resistant with respect to larger aims and more complex objectives. CPI is concerned with the larger tasks of keeping students in school, salvaging dropouts, remedying the neglect of the education of Southern Negroes now moved North, connecting education with employment possibilities, reaching children even before formal schooling begins, making the school a center of leisure activities for adults. All of these are tasks ordinarily beyond and outside the teacher's training, and some are ones at which the school and the educators have notably failed. One of James Bryant Conant's points about American education is that professional educators have until very recently almost totally ignored the distinct problem of the education of the Negro — kept ignorant, neglected in segregated Southern schools, now moved North to be neglected and segregated again in a city slum.

And although there are many family and emotional and social problems that CPI cannot touch which need the care of professional social workers, there is also much that CPI can do which social work is not doing — finding jobs, giving training, keeping young people in school, helping people lift themselves out of the generation after generation of poverty.

One of the most impressive features of CPI is its use of *non-*professionals. I had mistakenly assumed that the organization was a collection of sociologists and other social scientists, of professional social workers and professional social reformers. I discovered, though, that a sizable and impressive part of CPI's staff are the nonprofessionals whom CPI has found and trained in its own way. There is the Negro woman who is work crew leader for the girls doing a kind of subnursing at a convalescent home; she herself was on ADC (welfare Aid to Dependent Children) before CPI hired her. There is a Negro man in his fifties who was laid off by Winchester Arms when the contract for the M14 rifle was canceled. He was spared the difficult time of finding a job by his job as a CPI work crew supervisor. There is a former maintenance worker for the Park Department who now leads work crews in fixing up park property, on which several of the crews work. There are a high linesman laid off by the bankrupt New Haven Railroad and a partially disabled former policeman and a former seminarian who stopped just short of becoming a priest. The neighborhood workers, who mostly come from the poverty areas, are an impressively nonprofessional group, too. Mitchell Sviridoff noted at this point: so far, not a single neighborhood worker has quit. "They like what they are doing. They get interested in it. It's a meaningful and rewarding job." They are not highly paid, by the way — $90 or $100 a week.

More than forty members of the CPI staff of a hundred plus have not gone beyond high school. "Who are they?" I asked. "Oh, they are spread through the organization. Neighborhood workers, work crew leaders — and the executive director," said Mr. Sviridoff, the executive director. "If I had been a dropout yet, I'd be worth my weight in gold," he added. He is one of these Americans, like Dick Lee, who have gained the full advantage out of never having gone to college.

CPI represents an initiative by society, of going out to the poor rather than waiting for appeals for help; it is an effort to break people loose from the grip of poverty rather than simply to treat the hurtful effects of it.

"Welfare" is one thing, and a rather discouraging business, I gather. The CPI type of antipoverty program is quite another. The slogan that has accompanied the effort nationally expresses this: they would "turn taxeaters into taxpayers" (thus an appeal to our purse rather than to our heart — we have both, but the purse is more tender). People now receiving checks for their dependent children and for unemployment, and young people now breaking and entering and costing time to the police and the courts, will be changed, we hope, from these expensive taxeating activities, or nonactivities, into working and taxpaying members of the social order.

CPI is to be distinguished also from the regular agencies of social service and social work like family service, though they have participated in its formation. Those worthy activities provide in the main a help to the victims and to the losers, to the disturbed, needy, and upset. CPI, in its different way, is trying to help people get out of the trap in which they need those services. It is trying to "break the cycle of poverty."

The main instruments for doing that are education and employment; "full education and full employment," said Willard Wirtz. The biggest part of CPI's money next after that for employment goes into the schools in the poor parts of town. The aims are to try to raise the horizons of children who have been given low ones, to extend the school down into the important prekindergarten ages, and to keep youngsters in school by giving them a part-time job in the cafeteria or library. The "prekindergarten" is perhaps the most successful of all the programs. The part-time work plan is the work-study program of the antipoverty legislation. It resembles the NYA for which Lyndon Johnson was once the Texas director. Much of these programs is a remedy or substitute for failures of the schools.

We didn't teach people to read at seven, said Moynihan of the Department of Labor, so now we have these programs to teach them to read at seventeen.

Then there are the young who drop out of school. James Bryant Conant's book of 1961 on *Slums and Suburbs* sharply contrasted the schools in those two areas and presented the picture of the "social dynamite" piled up in the former — disaffected, alienated young people dropping out of a school they hated, at sixteen, without a job or prospect of a job. One might say that the riots of the summer of 1964 were an explosion of the dynamite Conant had described in 1961.

CPI tries to bring dropouts and other young people sixteen to twenty-one years of age into its work crews, groups of four to six young people who work with a leader on a job, learning at least some work habits of punctuality and persistence. These work crews are now mostly made up of young persons; there are also to be adult crews. A very small dose of very basic education goes along with the work crew program, and embarrassed, silent kids struggle to learn to read.

I remember the work crew idea being described to me by a New York friend back in 1960, when the big lower East Side effort called Mobilization for Youth was being set up. The idea, he said, is to give these youngsters, who often have no notion of work as a manly thing to do, a model in the crew leader — one whom they can respect and with whom they can identify, and whose ability to work they can emulate. CPI has fifteen such crews now. A new federal grant will enable them to double that number. The young people in these crews are among the most difficult in the city, 60 percent of them being "known to the law," as Adam Festa, the work crew director, puts it. They are recruited by neighborhood workers from the school dropouts, from Selective Service rejectees, and from the streets. There is therefore a high ratio of disappointment. "It's getting so I hate to pick up the paper Monday morning," Mr. Festa said. "Too often some kid of ours has been arrested for breaking and entering over the weekend."

Providing on-the-job training, by CPI subsidy, is another device to get the unemployed into a job. Actually, what it turns out also to be, says Mr. Sviridoff, is a help to the expansion of small businesses that might expand if they could afford to train an extra hand or two. They don't do it on their own and are happy to have it done by CPI. And somebody gets a job.

CPI has three neighborhood employment centers. New Haven, with CPI assistance, has seven community schools. Like CPI as a whole, they are not simply a service waiting for customers but a base for an attack force to go out into the territory to battle poverty.

These antipoverty efforts may be about as significant for racial justice in New Haven as anything that happened all year. Civil rights ordinances are important, and scattering public housing would be important if we could do it, and correcting segregated schools — whether by "busing" or otherwise — is important, too. Perhaps more important than all of these, even from the standpoint of the impact on Negro life and on Negro-white relations, are actions to bring jobs and better schools to the city's poor. That is what the civil rights books are saying now, from having looked mainly at the situation of American Negroes. One gets the same results, reinforced, if one looks also at the white resistance.

What does it take to make an ordinary, not very prejudiced but quite unheroic Northern white man favorably disposed, or at least acquiescent, toward strong action for Negro rights? Not just moral appeals. It takes education and economic security, as well as integration: integration, so that he knows Negroes and sees Negroes distributed throughout the society's institutions to break his stereotypes; but also economic security so that he does not fear any direct loss from it to himself;

and perhaps specific education on the Negro's peculiar plight, but, much more important, a higher level of general education to increase empathy and knowledge and the capacity to take a larger view.

And what does it take for the American Negro's ancient injustice to be removed? Not merely civil rights. It takes the same three things. Integration, so that doors into the society are open; this includes doors to education and economic security. Not only an "integrated" education; also a *good* education. Not only "fair employment practices"; also jobs and training for jobs, full employment as well as fair employment. Without expanding employment and improving education the Negro's new ability to sit at Southern lunch counters surely will not suffice.

Education and employment are the two chief fields in which CPI concentrates its work. And, of course, the point is not alone to help Negroes or to improve intergroup relations. The point is to unbend the social warp of poverty for all its victims. CPI has worked in six — just recently, seven — sections of New Haven that have most of the city's low-income, unemployed, and problem people. Two of these areas (Dixwell and Newhallville) are predominantly Negro; four (Dwight, the Hill, West Rock, and Wooster Square) though predominantly white have substantial fractions of Negroes; one (Fair Haven, where the most notorious antibusing hearing was held) is overwhelmingly white. The staff of CPI includes many Negroes. One local Negro observed that a big contribution of CPI was that it brought numbers of intelligent Negroes to the city, and it certainly did. Notwithstanding, the people helped are the poor — white and Negro. The interracial aspect and the help-to-the-Negroes aspect are subordinate, incidental, taken for granted.

Although CPI receives a continual flow of praise, and additional grants, there is also muttering against it in New Haven. The national celebrations and local cursings must make for a confusing emotional atmosphere at CPI. And, one is told, there are also at least the normal internal rivalries.

A steady stream of visitors from other poverty programs and other countries, of journalists and photographers, and of foundation executives and government people gives forth regularly with more praise and more money for CPI. Both Sargent Shriver in Washington and the Ford Foundation in New York cite it as their banner program, and *Look* and the *New York Times* celebrate its pace-setting efforts in the whole national poverty program. At the same time CPI has become "controversial" in New Haven, especially since the busing affair. At one busing hearing an opponent of the plan asked everybody who worked for CPI to stand; my wife heard another opponent sourly explaining on a street corner some evil-doing by saying, "That's CPI." The Republican antibusing group kept up steady drumfire of press release criticisms of CPI; the aldermen grumbled a little in private even about giving CPI a variance for window screens over a sidewalk.

The biggest and worst and most predictable part of this opposition comes from the know-nothing or Goldwater right, and is composed of race feeling, anti-intellectualism, resistance to change, bully-boy authoritarianism, lack of pity for the poor. A columnist in a New Haven paper expresses this attitude, and it is not unusual to find the point of view in the letters to the Editor. One joke of this group is that CPI stands for "Colored People's Institute"; there are many fears about the new CPI people moving into town, and all the programs and changes and advanced ideas.

The muttering about CPI is by no means confined to this group on the unintelligent right. Since CPI is a catalyst for change, it produces resistance from many established interests, even some not ordinarily included under that phrase — some social workers, for example, and teachers. Some teachers and school administrators are uneasy about the educational programs that use nonaccredited people. And some teachers would say that what Bassett and Troup and the other junior high schools in New Haven now need is not a lot of community-school activities in the evening that knock the erasers onto the floor and mess up the classroom, nor a lot of extra programs, but just smaller classes.

One can wholeheartedly agree with the positive part of this, if not the negative. An unfortunate result of our long national failure to enact a general national aid-to-education bill has been that the money the schools badly need has had to come in "categories." It has been available for "national defense" education, or for programs to fight juvenile delinquency but not to hire more teachers, pay them better and build more classrooms. The slum school, especially, needs small classes and well-paid teachers and a good plant — in order that these children receive something like an "opportunity."

There are also critics on the left. One criticism from that side is to be expected, that the antipoverty effort is too small.

Passionate reformers' tracts like Michael Harrington's *The Other America,* called by Walter Lippmann, "that noble book," characteristically are strongest on exhortation and diagnosis. Their concrete prescriptions usually are weaker, and the tracts end in great swirls of rhetoric about "massive" efforts and "bold, new" programs and "the conscience of America." Characteristically they find that every actual thing any real and responsible agency has actually done is far too small, inadequate, piddling. This is what some say about CPI: too few people are helped, and the program "barely scratches the surface." Although CPI reaches only 20 percent to 30 percent of the people it should reach, according to Mr. Sviridoff, yet that is more than a surface-scratching, and well worth doing. Moreover, one cannot start off with massive programs. First one must find out what works, and what does not, and do what is politically and financially possible.

Some fraction of the public complaint that CPI is merely enriching bureaucrats, and that it is a fierce power-struggling "can of worms," comes from the program's liberal friends. Unquestionably there is no rule that requires anyone to fit consistently under some ideological label. The labels are very loose and baggy anyway. Furthermore, liberal or leftist criticisms of the poverty program may be directed to improving it and not destroying it, although this isn't always clear. I think that there may also be some new patterns forming. Radicals and militants are set to be against authority, even reforming authority, and against established agencies, even agencies set up for purposes they endorse. *Especially*, perhaps such agencies and such authority.

In New Haven the men of the left are faced with a notably progressive and activist city government, a very progressive school board under severe attack from masses of conservatives, and the country's most celebrated antipoverty program. What do people committed by doctrine and temperament to being against the Establishment do in that case? It is a problem. Mostly they go ahead and oppose this one, too.

CPI has been attacked for its large salaries and for the absence of the poor themselves from the governing board. It also has been charged with "taking over the city." One critic said that, although he had often heard of a town being run by a corporation, and perhaps occasionally by a union, this is the first time he'd heard of one being run by a social agency. One Negro leader in a struggle over the presidency of the NAACP accused the other side of being dominated by people from CPI.

I think these criticisms and antagonisms are easy to understand. There *is* a lot of money being spent, there are many new people coming into town, and there are many new ideas being tried. One surely can explain internal rivalries and larger struggles over control when one thinks of the money, of the newness of the program, of the rivalries of the specialists. Here is a well-financed agency devoted by definition to social change; no wonder that it rouses fears. And here is an agency that cuts through a host of professional, academic, bureaucratic specialties to try to do a new job; it is not surprising that there are rivalries.

Then, too, hopes and expectations expand faster than performance possibly can. A war on poverty! To eliminate poverty! A program not just to feed and care for the poor — but to bring them out of poverty! That is beyond the dreams even of utopians in the past, and it is no wonder, with hopes aroused in every idealist and many also of the poor, that there is disillusionment. "You had us up on cloud nine," said a New Haven Negro reproachfully to a top CPI man. "You told us about these neighborhood workers, who were going to be poor people right out of the neighborhood themselves, and they were going around to the bars and the homes and find jobs and do all these things . . . You had us up on cloud nine." The man seemed particularly disillusioned because one of the employees of CPI, when CPI became a reality, turned out to be a woman whom he knew. The antipoverty saints in his dream apparently had not looked like that woman who worked at the telephone company.

Certain difficulties and embarrassments recur in efforts to deal with the poor — in the poor law, the poor law reform, the "new law" tenements, public housing, or the war on poverty. Ostensible helps to the poor keep slipping upward to provide more help for those already better off, if not indeed for alert entrepreneurs, than for those most in need. Programs to aid the poor often introduce unintended side effects that are much to their detriment — the minimal dole that makes the pauper. Such programs often are carried out in such a way as to be degrading and inhuman.

Some part of these difficulties are inherent and inescapable, having to do with human nature and social complication. Another part of this nest of historical difficulties comes from the failure of social intelligence and the limitations of men's theories and knowledge of fact. But another source of the difficulty in effective poverty-warring, complicating all the efforts, lies in moral attitudes. Although there are characteristic attitudes on the part of many who are poor which do not help, such as cynicism about all institutions and living strictly for to-day, the great impediment lies in the moral attitudes of the nonpoor who must support such a "war." One rich Yale boy said that he is a conscientious objector to the war on poverty.

This moral attitude includes many familiar parts. There aren't any poor people any more; besides, it is their own fault; also, it's their own choice; and if you try to help them they'll take advantage of you. Also it won't work. Also it will just make things worse for the poor themselves. Deeper down is the in-clination to regard the poor as fundamentally a different sort of being from ourselves, one with a set of particularly disgust-ing habits. Also, deep down, we nonpoor are quick to resist any interpretations that imply we don't necessarily deserve the advantaged position we hold. In our more humane but also richer and more complacent society, the first of those listed above is by all odds the greatest barrier now — ignorance and inattention. One constant feature in the relationship of the pros-perous to the disadvantaged patently is the former's steady ef-fort to keep from thinking about the latter. I remember a wid-owed landlady of ours on Cottage Street, a good woman, saying fifteen years ago as I was going out to campaign, "There aren't any poor people any more." Then, when I told her what ward I was going to, she admitted, "Well — maybe over *there*." Ini-tially that part of town somehow hadn't counted.

Dickens' character Podsnap, in saying, with a sweep of his arm, "It doesn't exist; I won't hear of it," epitomizes the re-sponse of much of the comfortable world to the condition of the poor. Although contemporary Americans would generally be more humane than the upper classes of Dickens' time, it is easier today to be inattentive. I previously mentioned the large and salutary change in the foci of national attention which has taken place since the fifties; changing the agenda — focusing attention, altering the atmosphere — is already something important. The poverty program has certainly done that.

I have said that this defective moral attitude comes partly from human egotism and partly from American individualism. In other words, the general selfishness of mankind is given particular American additions. Basically there is our very strong disinclination to identify with the poor — or, to put the same point another way, to grant the role of environment. Characteristically and *en masse* we resist the idea that the difference between the very poor and ourselves is largely luck. Self-made, self-making Americans are particularly unwilling to grant the role of environment. I do not mean to say that Americans are therefore *worse* in their attitude toward the poor than other peoples. On the contrary; in some regards we are almost certainly better, in idealism, sympathy, and straight-out voluntary charity. Gunnar Myrdal says that no country has as many cheerful givers as the United States. In myriad philanthropies and voluntary association an enormous number of good deeds have been done for the poor. When the action no longer fits under the heading of charity, when it is regarded as a matter of justice, when it is no longer voluntary and becomes a work of law, government, and force — then the wind changes and our American record is not so good.

Among the perennial tangles in the poor laws and slum clearances are those having to do with the "means test" and what used to be called the "deserving poor." We the public feel strongly that the "undeserving" must be kept from taking advantage of our programs, those who either are lazy and won't work and will blow the money on whiskey or else are secretly well-fixed chiselers trying to get something for nothing. We have this aching fear that somebody somewhere is going to get something for nothing, and at our expense. Therefore we guard and restrict these programs very carefully: the families whose income rises above the limit must move out of public housing; welfare rolls must be carefully protected against chiselers; Medicare must have a "means test," according to conservatives. To some extent these attempts rest on sound reason. We don't want people who don't need help to crowd out those who do, nor do we want them to discredit the whole effort. But the wariness and the restrictions go further and reflect this other less creditable root — our suspicion that somebody is going to take advantage of us.

The spirit of the means test and looking for the deserving poor then adds a humiliation to the burden of the poor. Humiliation anyway — as Shaw said somewhere — is the problem of the poor as much as hunger, and it must be particularly humiliating to be poor in a country that is as rich as ours and attaches as much significance to money-making and now to money-spending as ours does.

Recent writings have identified the peculiar difficulty of the "first minority poor in history" — that of being in poverty when almost everybody else is prosperous, and when everybody is expected to be. I remember the large billboard that loomed up over a desperate block in East Harlem in the middle fifties, showing some happy white faces and carrying the ironical injunction to "Be a Two-Ford Family." This sign offered great homiletical possibilities to the social prophets in the area. The people on that block would not be able to be a part of a two-Ford family, and the social order that would blandly enjoin them to become one is callous. In addition to this bit of cruelty there is the spiritual significance that our America attaches to having, and to not having, Fords and multiples of Fords. In the crudest Americana this is supposed to prove something about your manhood.

Some writers on American values rightly point out that Americans are not exactly "materialistic" in the sense of being exceptionally attached in a possessive and immediate way to material goods, however obtained. We give money generously to charity; we have not been characteristically a nation of

misers or stingy people; we do not have the tradition of the
dowry; we do not particularly honor — or we have not in the
past — men who become rich through marriage or the lottery
or inheritance. The distinctive American point, at least in our
past and formative period, has been on *making* money, and
thereby proving oneself. We have never examined very closely,
of course, how much of luck and chance, or how much of sharp
practice, went into the money-making. We have roughly
equated wealth with hard work, honest dealing, and frugality,
with the Puritan-Yankee and Horatio Alger virtues of our past.
The devotion to these virtues has faded, but the feeling remains
that money-making establishes some sort of superiority.

So the poor in such a society have their humiliation
doubled, and tripled if then the programs intended to help
them suspiciously sort them out, restrict them, and stamp a
label on them, to be sure they aren't loafing. A program such as
the CPI seems to have taken another tack entirely: to turn
the American system of values not against the poor but in
their favor. Instead of offering some tangible material benefit
(money, house, medicine), suspiciously and grudgingly given
and hedged with restrictions to avoid abuse, CPI offers only
what every American ought to have — opportunity.

Some conservative criticism of CPI says that if a city does
such a thing well, then that city will attract the poor and Negroes and welfare seekers from around the country. I have
heard two citizens make this point about New Haven. To my
ears it says more about the fearful, restrictive, and ungenerous
attitude of the speaker than it does about the objective situation. And as to that, I doubt very much that the communication
system of the poor is that efficient, even assuming people in
large numbers moved from city to city with that motive.
People coming from southern Italy had garbled and long-out-
dated ideas about the kind of gold offered in the streets of
New Haven, and in counties of North Carolina rumors about

work in New Haven persisted in the late fifties that dated back, insofar as they had a basis, to World War II.

Even if it were true that this attraction worked, what does CPI offer? Not a "handout"; just an "opportunity." Just a job or chance to go to school or a chance for one's children to go to school. And though Americans are very suspicious of anyone's getting anything for nothing, they do believe that everyone ought to have an opportunity.

These acts and agencies in the field of poverty-fighting, as also in the field of Negro rights, regularly have that word "opportunity" in their titles. In the civil rights field it is usually accompanied by the word "equal." The New Haven ordinance against discrimination in housing and employment was called the Equal Opportunities Ordinance. Title VII of the United States Civil Rights Act of 1964, also directed against discrimination in employment, has the heading "Equal Employment Opportunity" and provides for an Equal Employment Opportunity Commission; there is a President's Committee on Equal Opportunity in Housing and also a President's Committee on Equal Opportunity in Employment. The New Haven school board's plan had as the first part of its extensive title, "Proposals for Promoting Equality of Educational Opportunity." The volunteer human relations group working to find homes for Negroes and to integrate neighborhoods calls itself H.O.M.E. — Housing Opportunities Made Equal. The national antipoverty agency, headed by Sargent Shriver, is called the Office of Economic Opportunity; an early booklet explaining CPI was called *Opening Opportunities,* and Mr. Sviridoff refers to the efforts of his organization as "opportunity programs."

This terminology, although somewhat repetitious, has a solid reason behind it, because the idea of equality of opportunity is firmly planted in our American system of values. That planting, in fact, is one of the best things about this country. It has been our way of reconciling freedom with equality, and pretty much overcoming, with the help of an expanding economy, the ancient warfare between individual liberty and equalitarian measures. This is no small accomplishment in the history of the human struggle. The American's idea is not strictly equalitarian and certainly not leveling, and "freedom" is his first word (even for progressives, as Myrdal says in the first chapter of *An American Dilemma*). He does think, however — at least at his best — that freedom ought to be equally spread, the freedom to make one's way in life, and especially in the career-making worlds of work and school. "Equally" is not interpreted in its literal meaning; it signifies that there should be no major blocks — that there be "opportunity" for everybody. Its realistic meaning, in other words, is that nobody should be categorically shut out. Everyone should have a chance at the start. There should be, as David Potter explains it in his book *People of Plenty*, "parity of competition" — some measure of a fair start in the race, and an open road ahead. Log-cabin boys (in American principle, presumably *all* log-cabin boys) should have the opportunity to become President, and office boys (presumably *all* office boys) should have a chance to become president of the company.

"Equality of opportunity" used to have a much more limited meaning: the absence of restraint by law upon what an ambitious lad could accomplish on his own hook. Now we are doing something considerably at odds with that, but all within the frame of the one broader American social-moral commitment. We are recognizing, as the old Americans certainly did not, the way circumstances, the social environment, can block opportunity or make it unequal. To go to a rural Southern Negro school or a Northern inner-city school, not to be effectively literate, to be rejected by a company because of racial prejudice, even to have low aspirations and little motive because one has never been exposed to stimulation and possibility — these are indeed grave restrictions on "opportunity," but hardly of the kind that the Horatio Alger man would have acknowledged.

And we have gone a step farther. We have said that society through its agencies, including government, shall take it upon itself to overcome these opportunity-denying circumstances.

15. Election, 1965

*"What my brother hoped to do with the New Frontier
Dick Lee is doing in New Haven."*

On a Monday night in August 1965, just as the five days of
rioting in the Watts section of Los Angeles were coming to an
end, the Republicans of New Haven nominated Joseph Einhorn, the antibusing man, to be their candidate for mayor. Mr.
Einhorn spoke, as candidates do, of a new community college,
new industry, new jobs, a new sports arena. He pledged himself, as opposition candidates do, to "free the people of New
Haven from the vicious stranglehold of the City Hall political
machine." He also promised "to oppose turning over our city to
outsiders, consultants, advisers, goldbrickers, and the like."
Among the agencies filled with these outsiders, consultants,
advisers, goldbrickers, and the like, in Mr. Einhorn's view,
the most significant obviously was CPI, with its "high-priced,
self-styled experts." "The few superficial efforts made by CPI,"
he said, ". . . are, for the most part, worthless." He declared
that he would take steps immediately to insitute an elected
school board, and he received his loudest cheers when he said
that if he was elected "all appropriations for forced, involuntary busing will be stopped."

The town Republicans adopted a written platform, as the
Democrats, who met two days later to renominate Mayor Lee,
did not. One feature of this Republican platform had to do with
Yale University: to examine whether civic justice would require Yale to make payments to the city in lieu of property

taxes. And another had to do with what I had come to think of as "income integration." This is the question of where to put the poor, a question as serious for the future, I have become convinced, as that of racial integration, to which it was very closely linked. I had noticed that the Fifteenth Ward resident who became Einhorn's brain trust had shifted on this subject. At the hearing at Hooker School he had testified *for* the Willow Street scattered house, but then later, at a city-wide discussion meeting, he had said he was for integration of all races and creeds *income permitting*. And this is what the Republican platform now endorsed. That seemed to me significant. The economic segregation of neighborhoods — in the first place — works to maintain racial segregation and — in the second — is undesirable in itself.

On the last day of August the Republicans picked as their candidate for Probate Judge a young lawyer who promised reform. Under the prevailing statewide system politicians are appointed appraisers of estates, and get a percentage of the estate as their fee. That can mean a lot of money. It is obviously an undesirable system, and this reform promise by the Republican candidate later grew into the liveliest issue in any of the races.

I went to Washington early in September to watch President Johnson sign the Act establishing the new urban affairs department. He had signed the Act establishing Medicare in Independence, Missouri, in the presence of Harry Truman; he had signed the Elementary and Secondary Education Act of 1965 in his Texas schoolhouse; he had signed the Voting Rights Act of 1965 in the Rotunda of the Capitol. Aides in Washington were speculating, in that early September of 1965, whether he might sign the Higher Education bill — just then on the point of being passed — in Monticello, in honor of Jefferson the educator. When the time came, though, he

signed it at Southwest Texas State College in San Marcos,
Texas. Wits suggested that the Act establishing the new department of urban affairs might be signed in a New York city
subway station.

The President signed the Act, instead, in the Rose Garden of
the White House. Urbanism was well represented by the beefy
crowd that watched the signing, and by its heavily interracial composition. Whitney Young, Jr., was there, a big,
handsome dark man with a mustache, standing on the White
House lawn with his arms folded across his chest and watching the President. Roy Wilkins was there, slight and bald and
scholarly in appearance. "Is that Dawson?" I asked, indicating
one of the Negroes standing behind the President. "Yes," said
Wilkins. "He's a silent congressman, you know. Never makes a
speech."

In the crowd on the President's right there was another Negro, also bald — Robert Weaver. Weaver had nearly become
the first Negro Cabinet member back in 1961, when President
Kennedy prematurely let it be known that he would appoint
Weaver to head an urban affairs department if one were set up;
it wasn't set up then, nor was it in 1962, partly because of Southern votes. Now Weaver was being dangled over the possibility
again, with newspaper speculation and presidential silence.
He looked cheerful enough, smiling and joking. (The Department of Housing and Urban Affairs, then being signed into law,
had originally been proposed by John F. Kennedy in his first
State of the Union message on January 30, 1961.)

At the signing there were fifteen mayors standing around in
various states of hope that *they* might be chosen for the Cabinet
post. Mayor Wagner of New York stood with his new wife on
the grass with us observers until he was called up into the crowd
around the President. Mayor Daley of Chicago, red-faced and
jowly, was there; he would shortly thereafter tangle with the
Office of Education over Chicago's de facto school segregation.
Mayor McKeldin of Baltimore, one of the few big city Repub-

licans and last seen on television orating powerfully but in vain for Rockefeller in San Francisco, towered up from the crowd.

Richard C. Lee of New Haven was not there. He had been invited, but at the last minute didn't come because of illness in the family. The President sent him one of the pens used in the signing — the third such pen in Lee's collection — and a letter saying, "Your urban development program in New Haven has earned national recognition. You deserve a lion's share of the credit for efforts leading to the new department which will advance the progress of our cities."

Citizens for Lee later reprinted this letter from the White House in a campaign advertisement.

I stopped in at the headquarters of the HHFA, the federal housing agency of which Weaver was the head and the main component, the only one at the time, of the department to be. On the bulletin board by the elevators there was a solitary item, a clipping from the *New York Times* of the previous Tuesday under the headline "New Haven Pursuing the American Dream of a Slumless City." I then went over to the office of Washington's own city renewal agency and found the same story on its bulletin board. Back home in New Haven, the *Times* story was reproduced for distribution by the Citizens for Lee. "Ten years ago Court Street in New Haven was a skid row," said a caption under one of the four pictures accompanying the article; "now it is a prestige address." "I think New Haven is coming closest to our dream of a slumless city," Robert Weaver was quoted as saying. "About a third of this city — six square miles — is being renewed, at a cost that will exceed $500 million in public and private investment," the story said. Farther along it gave the per capita figures on federal urban renewal grants: "New Haven ranks first in the country . . . with $438 for each resident. The figure for New York City is $31."

"It is like a dream. Everything is done with so much style," said a member of a New York City community planning board after a recent tour. "If only New York had half of New Haven's imagination and a quarter of its spirit."

Meanwhile back in the Fifteenth Ward of this dreamlike city the Republicans were showering voters with campaign letters like this:

What you should know about PAUL P. F. BUJALSKI, RE-PUBLICAN candidate for alderman of the 15th Ward:

that he is 35 years old — a native of New Haven — life long resident of the city . . .

that he is a communicant of St. Stanislaus R. C. Church . . .

that he represents the political thinking of the 15th ward on the following issues:

1. He is for true representation of the people in the 15th Ward at the Council meetings.

2. He is for an elected Board of Education.

3. He is for increased police protection on our streets and in our parks.

4. He is opposed to forced busing of our children to schools in other parts of town.

5. He is opposed to scattered housing as proposed by the present administration.

This letter was signed by Frank Carpinella, the new Fifteenth Ward Republican chairman who had led the attack on the scattered house, and who was also, as I knew very well, strongly against both the busing and the Equal Opportunities Ordinance. Like all the letters that were to follow, the letter carried this motto at the bottom of the page: "It is time the voters of the fifteenth ward elected an alderman who represents the majority."

Mr. Einhorn stayed away from a controversial rally in the New Haven arena sponsored by Connecticut's conservative Republican group and featuring the rising star in the Goldwater world, Ronald Reagan. (Some of the subjects that Mr. Reagan attacked were urban renewal, the antipoverty program, aid to education, welfare, and LBJ's "fiscal irresponsibility.") Einhorn's campaign was different from that, and also from local Republican campaigns in the past. There was more of a national connection, and a broader program. To me it seemed that the part of Einhorn's campaign which followed the high road was modeled on Lee's, or the new city politics since Lee — endorsements by national figures, pictures of new buildings and new housing projects, broad discussion of unemployment, housing, schools, warring on poverty.

On the day after Labor Day the New Haven papers carried a story about Candidate Einhorn's having had a conference with former President Eisenhower in Washington. There was a picture of the two men sitting side by side on a sofa, Einhorn talking, Eisenhower, arms folded, gazing off just beyond Einhorn's head. They discussed, the story said, "problems confronting the nation's urban centers," in a conference lasting "nearly a half an hour." Mr. Einhorn after the conference said he and Mr. Eisenhower agreed that "true integration will come about only through raising economic abilities." The story commented that Einhorn was the first Republican mayoralty candidate to call on national party leaders for help. Later he was shown shaking hands with Everett Dirksen and talking with Richard Nixon.

His campaign had also, of course, its negative content. The Redevelopment Agency pays $829,000 annually in salaries, he said, which means "lack of skill or gross wastage," considering what we get for it. He went to Pennsylvania to confer with Governor Scranton and his urban renewal people about how renewal really should be done. He attacked Mies van der Rohe's design for Church Street South as "flat, sterile, functional." He said the Church Street South site should have been used for industry rather than housing. And he promised that if elected he would fire the school board.

During the previous summer the school board had been caught in yet another major civic battle, this one about the principal of Hillhouse High School. Irregularities had been found in student transcripts sent by Hillhouse to various colleges, and the principal was suspended. The case quickly reproduced much of the conflict of the previous summer's busing battle. The Hillhouse irregularities had first been noted by Yale's admissions officer, so Yale was again an object of attack; the high school was located in the section of town (Westville) most annoyed by the busing, and the principal had been an opponent of busing, so many antagonists of Paquin and the school board looked on the suspension as vengeance. To supporters of the board, on the other hand, its action seemed an obvious necessity, since there had been hanky-panky with the transcripts of grades.

Now Einhorn promised to return the principal to his post. And he accused the Democratic Party of injecting the "ethnic issue" into the campaign. He said Democrats are "spreading the word that I am supporting the cause of the much maligned [principal] because he and I are both of the Jewish faith."

Mayor Lee uses polls; in fact, he introduced pollster Lou Harris to John Kennedy. His polls showed that he was not in trouble with New Haven voters. The only serious question had to do with Westville. He had a lunch at Mory's with Westville aldermen, to talk about busing, Einhorn, and Westville resentments. "Tell the people our record in education," he said. Two of these Democratic aldermen from Westville later demanded publicly that the school board resign, because it had "lost the confidence of the public."

Later in the campaign the Mayor was to announce appointments to the school board: C. Newton Schenck, the widely respected lawyer who was head of the Public Housing Authority, became the new president; William Celentano's brother, a physician (and a Republican) was named vice-chairman. Schenck lives on Everit Street, which meant a total of three members of the board living on that one street in the Fifteenth Ward. As the campaign progressed, attention shifted away from the education controversies.

The Mayor invited me to meet with his campaign staff as a volunteer speech writer. These meetings took place on Sunday nights in the Mayor's office, with his Honor sitting at one end of the long table and carrying on a monologue. His secretary sat with her stenographic machine at his side, and often he dictated then and there letters he suddenly thought of writing. The meetings were a mixture of much campaign gossip and discussion, mostly by the Mayor, with some businesslike consideration of the week's schedule of press releases, speeches, and campaign trips. They would end with the week's advertisements spread on the floor and the Mayor down on his knees inspecting them.

Lee's campaign featured a stream of press releases and systematic visits to plants and factories. "No more teas," he said, at one of the staff meetings. "Tomorrow morning Pepsi-Cola and Hull's Brewery; Tuesday morning, Sero shirts." At the end of the campaign Lee estimated that he had shaken the hands of 20,000 citizens, and less than 70,000 voters were registered for this election. He spoke with special affection about the labor leaders who had gone with him, stood with him, introduced him, at those early morning visits to the gates of the plants and factories. Toward the end of the campaign I was meeting people in my ward who said, "Oh, yes, the Mayor came to the plant yesterday."

At the Sunday night meetings the Mayor and his staff would go over the press releases for the following week. There was something, usually more than one item, for noon and for 6 P.M. of each day. "These releases!" said a local reporter. "I've never seen anything like it!"

The first major announcement showed the plans for the new building that would be the national headquarters for the Knights of Columbus, a twenty-six-story skyscraper, the highest in the city, designed by Kevin Roche of the Saarinen firm, "the most exciting building ever to rise in New Haven," according to the Mayor.

The city was seeking a Class I fire rating, which no city has ever achieved. There would be a half-million-dollar improvement in the city airport. The city's unemployment rate was at a new low, 3.7 percent. Lee admitted that plans for a coliseum were in the works (Einhorn had come out early with his "sports arena"). Lee announced a new Dixwell nursing home. He opened the new $850,000 Helene Grant Elementary School, the new school in the Dixwell area near the Florence Virtue Homes. He dedicated two new buildings of housing for the elderly on Wooster Square, the one named for William Celentano eliciting from the Mayor the comment, "Whoever thought fifteen years ago I'd be saying these nice things about him?" He broke ground for a new central services building, which, because it would house among other things the city health services, was helped along by federal Hill-Burton funds. A new "skill center" for CPI, a job-training place for the poverty program, was opened, with appropriate speechmaking. He broke ground for the Dixwell Plaza shopping area. He dedicated Winter Gardens, another 221(d)3 project adjacent to Florence Virtue. He cited figures showing a 10 percent reduction in class size in the city's elementary schools, and a large amount of adult education. Retail sales of $550 million were predicted for New Haven stores in 1965, up $46 million and a new record, "reversing the loss of shopping dollars to suburban shopping centers."

The Mayor tossed the ball to me one night, asking me to write a Columbus Day speech. I was impressed that in the middle of a local election he wanted to spend his Columbus Day speech on a piece of national legislation: the Immigration Act of 1965, which President Johnson had signed into law in front of the Statue of Liberty a few weeks before. That Act brought to an end the old national-quotas system, the system that — as the speech said — "kept thousands of people from Italy and other countries on the waiting lists for years" and "kept families from being reunited in this country."

On the Monday on which I was busily drafting this speech the Yale University Press elsewhere in New Haven was stealing Columbus Day. They announced the finding of a map indicating that Leif Ericson, not Columbus, discovered America. Humorous news stories and angry Italian-American comments quickly followed. John Lindsay in New York City took this instructive position: "Saying Columbus didn't discover America is as silly as saying Di Maggio doesn't know anything about baseball, or that Toscanini and Caruso were not great musicians, or that La Guardia was not a great mayor of New York."

I remarked later that the release of the map the day before Columbus Day showed Yale's distance from the affairs of ordinary people. "Don't kid yourself," said a more realistic faculty member. "They knew perfectly well what they were doing. They'll sell the book."

When Mayor Lee got up to give his Columbus Day speech to five hundred Italian-Americans at the Waverly Inn, he began this way, "Fellow Norwegians!"

New Haven's busing program, in that fall of 1965, went into its second year. Bassett Junior High was now a giant ninth grade — nothing more. Sheridan held an enlarged seventh and an enlarged eighth grade. The ninth-graders of the previous year had gone on to high school and the eighth-graders had become the sole inhabitants of Bassett, as ninth-graders. The new seventh-graders had all been sent to Sheridan. In 1966–1967 the

present eighth-graders at Sheridan will go presumably not to
Bassett but to high school, because in that year the new Hill
High School would open and the students would be freshmen
in a four-year high school rather than ninth-graders in a junior
high. Bassett thus would be left unoccupied, and the Board of
Education suggested that it might be taken over as another
skill center for CPI.

My daughter Cindy was in the sixth grade at Hooker with
essentially the same bused-in group of Negroes who had been
there in the fifth. Cindy got a solid Negro vote when her Halloween costume (Mary Poppins) was chosen the best in her
room. Next year, supposedly she will be bused to Sheridan, or
perhaps to Bassett, if it is used again as a school.

It is reported that about 80 white students who would have
gone to Bassett from the Westville area have dropped out, and
only eight students now go there from the Hooker area.

The integrationist organization called HOPE was preparing
during the fall a report on the busing and related school matters that would recommend changes and priorities in the Sargent Plan to meet population shifts, and say that, because of
delay in building projected new schools, "we can expect at
least two more years of busing." The report would also say that
its authors "question the value of busing lower-class Negro children into lower-class white schools. This is not likely to raise
the sights of the Negro or the white children." "The Board," it
said, "and others who propose racial balance should be realistic enough to accept more limited goals." The report would acknowledge as inescapable the fact that white parents resist
having their children bused into a Negro section of town, or
sent to a school that is more than half Negro. In each case the
whites tend to move out of the public schools, and policy must
take account of that fact.

The HOPE report would then turn its eye to the suburbs. On
August 10, 1965, the report said, Hartford was presented with
its "Sargent Plan," written by a Harvard specialist, and "this

up-to-date plan calls for busing Negro children to the suburbs." The Harvard man is quoted as having said that this is "the only genuine long-range solution to racial imbalance." "We have seen," the report went on, "that New Haven also is getting close to the limits of how much busing it can do within the city." The coming rise in the proportion of Negro children will press against these limits. Therefore, *"Any long-range school plans for New Haven must include the suburbs to achieve racial balance."* This sentence in HOPE's report was underlined. The report went on to give a rather broad hint to the suburban brethren: "Residents of our wealthier suburbs, such as Woodbridge, Orange, and large parts of Hamden and North Haven, might well ask themselves the same questions as people in other parts of the nation have been asking. So far, we know of no definite action on the part of New Haven's suburban towns to aid in the solution of educational problems of New Haven's poor and racial minority."

In New Haven's election the busing issue pretty much faded away. We were glad it did. I was told at one of the Mayor's meetings the results of a private poll. Among Einhorn supporters, 92 percent opposed busing. Among Lee supporters, 76 percent opposed busing. It was scarcely a winning issue.

On October 19 the American Institute of Planners, meeting in St. Louis, gave its annual citation to the city of New Haven, for "outstanding achievement in urban planning and redevelopment."

In a touring display of American architecture, shown in Moscow and at the Museum of Modern Art, twenty-five of the seventy-nine separate displays were done by architects connected with New Haven in some way: "a fantastic showing," according to the *New Haven Register*'s business editor, "for an area which contains roughly one-half of one percent of the nation's population." Among the structures shown in the exhibit were New Haven's Temple Street Garage and Central Fire Station, and

Yale's Beinicke Library and Art and Architecture Building.

On the Orange Street bus one night in early September I talked with a sponsor about a proposed cultural center for New Haven. A new building would be built on Audubon Street, as part of the State Street renewal project, to house a music school, symphony, theater, arts workshop, opera society, and the like; a federal government loan of nearly $2 million would pay for acquisition of the land, clearance, and relocation. The sponsor reported, "Dick says 'it's our one chance in a hundred years to build such a center.'"

The window of a storefront location in the center of town that used to be a Christian Science Reading Room now bears the legend "Commission on Equal Opportunities." The young teacher who was the senior Negro alderman when I joined the board is one of its executives. From time to time the papers carried reports of its cases, mainly in the field of housing.

Fifteenth Ward voters kept receiving letters from Carpinella or Bujalski. A typical one had "Opposed to Forced School Busing" and "Opposed to Scattered Housing" in heavy black enlarged type on its first page; all of the letters and other materials without exception emphasized those two issues. All of the letters also bore the motto "It is time the voters of the 15th ward elected an alderman who represents the majority."

Further statement on school busing went like this: "The discriminatory policy of 'forced' cross town school busing of our children must be terminated. The reason advanced by the Board of Education as to why our children are being bused will not be discussed at this time.

"Our immediate concern is that the 'forced' busing program is a deliberate contradiction to the generally accepted concept of neighborhood schools. The nearness and availability of a neighborhood school is one of the chief reasons why many of the parents have originally moved into the area.

"When elected, I will do everything in my power to end the

'forced' busing and will insist that children of the neighborhood attend *their* neighborhood schools."

On scattered housing the letter said: "The houses in the 15th
ward have a very high value on the real-estate market. To im-
pose the scattered housing program in the neighborhood would
immediately lessen the market-value of the houses in the area.

"Many home owners have labored hard and have put forth
great efforts to purchase and maintain houses in this area. Scattered housing is definitely a threat to the established high market-value of the houses and the rentals *in the 15th Ward.*

"I am firmly opposed to the 'scattered housing' program. The
Democratic aldermanic incumbent has leaned in favor of this
program. When elected alderman, I will see that the petition
opposing scattered housing, signed by over 300 residents of the
ward, will be continually recognized. The will of the majority
of the people on this very critical issue should and will be respected. 'Rigged hearings' on vital issues within the ward will
be a thing of the past."

This and other materials also talked about Mr. Bujalski's being "opposed to increased tax rate." And another theme was
"increased police protection." On his visits around the ward
Mr. Bujalski gave out police whistles with his name on them.

Supporters of mine were worried and began to complain that
I wasn't campaigning.

Among Yale students of the new left, at the same time, I was
encountering attitudes that seemed to come from some other
planet. I would see around town a car with this astonishing
pair of stickers on its bumper: the SNCC slogan "One man, one
vote," plus "Einhorn for Mayor." I knew the impressive young
couple who drove this car — an earnest and idealistic white
former Yale student and his quiet, intelligent Negro wife. I had
eaten peanut butter and tunafish sandwiches in their kitchen,
and talked enough politics to know we weren't quite on the
same wavelength. Still, that pair of stickers came as a bit of

shock. With all due respect to the more serious motives that were also present, I cannot avoid the conclusion that *one* motive was to give the "white liberals" a jolt. This couple and their group, with whom I had a long luncheon conversation during the campaign, were opposed to Lee and opposed to CPI, and for that matter to President Johnson and the poverty program and even perhaps to civil rights laws — from the left. They were living and "organizing" in a poor section on the Hill, and their "new radical" ideology seemed to me to include a new parochialism of the left. One night before his death, Malcolm X had come to New Haven, and after his speech a distinguished liberal professor at Yale had argued in some agitation with this young man — the young man of the two stickers — because he had seemed to be in sympathy with Malcolm's black nationalism and black segregationism. At the lunch I had with the group they snorted when I mentioned a Negro politician I approved of; "He's certainly no black nationalist," one white boy said.

Einhorn, to our further astonishment, visited with this group more than once during the campaign. In Lee's camp this was regarded with amusement, since it was an obvious waste of Einhorn's time; this group had very few votes and almost no influence, and they were way out in left field, and would be vigorously rejected personally and ideologically by the vast majority of New Haven's population, especially including Einhorn's normal Republican constituency. And yet there was a curious semimeeting of minds at these conversations. The young left group was so far left that it was right — radical enough to come around full circle and agree on many points with the conservative candidate. And they, rather innocently, as it seemed to me, took all he said to them at face value. They all were anti-Lee. They all were opposed to CPI and Mr. Sviridoff (the young man of the two bumper stickers had worked briefly for CPI — I had given him a recommendation, when the agency asked — and then had quit in a complicated quarrel over the legitimacy of a CPI worker doing political organization). They were all opposed to busing. Most important, they all wanted each neighborhood to work out its own problems, with much "participatory democracy," without centralization in City Hall.

A conference of New England mayors was held in New Haven shortly before the election, with Vice-President Humphrey as the feature attraction. While we waited outside the Jewish Community Center on Chapel Street for the conference to begin, a girl I knew to be part of this "young left" on the Hill was handing out a mimeographed statement.

TO THE MAYORS OF NEW ENGLAND [it said],

Mayor Lee and other city officials tell you what great things they've done for New Haven. But there is another side to the same story. Here are some of the things that the poor people of New Haven said about some of the conditions in this "dream city."

We are tired of waiting for the city to correct the problems in our housing. Would you like to come and live in one of the "slumless" dwellings of Mayor Lee's city?
— The Hill Neighborhood Union, a group active in rent strikes because the city will not enforce its own Housing Code.

We charge and register complaint of . . . Excessive force. . . . Vulgar and abusive language — including racial slur and discriminatory statement . . . Neglect of an injured person.
— From a complaint against police brutality offered by New Haven CORE following a sit-in at the Mayor's Office, May 1965.

We urge that CPI's pending application for federal funds be refused acceptance until CPI provides in that application for the resident participation required by law.
— From a complaint filed by the Hill Neighborhood Union, New Haven CORE and prominent local clergy and community leaders. July 23, 1965.

The New Haven Redevelopment staff has insisted on placing liquor outlets in this (Dixwell) plaza. The citizens of the Dixwell area are opposed to these liquor outlets because we are determined to change the image of the past. Yet the Redevelopment Agency insists. Where is citizen participation in New Haven?

— The Dixwell-Newhallville Program Planning Committee, a group trying to represent the citizens against the Lee Machine.

Men, women and children are demoralized and embittered by having to call "home" a building whose sidewalks are strewn with garbage, whose hallways are dingy, decrepit and ill-lighted, whose basements are filthy and filled with stench, whose apartments are dirty, decaying and over-run with roaches. Yet, New Haven claims that it has no serious relocation problems.

—"The Shame of Our City," New Haven CORE, 1965.

There is more to New Haven than the beautiful buildings downtown. Ask the Mayor to show you the Hill, Dixwell Ave., Newhallville, and the projects. You may have to ask directions. He might not know that they are there.

In the penultimate week of the campaign Ladybird Johnson, Richard Nixon, Vice-President Hubert Humphrey, and Senator Robert Kennedy one after another visited the city. The Kennedy visit was explicitly political; he was in New Haven, he said, on a nonpartisan visit to help Mayor Lee. Mrs. Johnson flew into the city completely unexpectedly; the Citizens for Lee had thought of inviting her, since she had been making kind remarks about New Haven, but then they decided not to do it because the President was at that time in the hospital recuperating from his gallstone operation. Mrs. Johnson suddenly appeared one morning on an Allegheny Airlines flight, quite on her own and without warning. She wanted to see the Beinicke

Library, because she was considering architects for a Johnson library in Texas. The Mayor also showed her some of the redevelopment, including Conte School.

"How do you get the local architects to put up with this?" Mrs. Johnson, apparently a direct and realistic woman, asked the Mayor, "Don't they object to your having all these national figures?"

Vice-President Humphrey arrived at two o'clock, light glowing from his smile and his bald head, for the conference that was to have begun at twelve-thirty. "I selected New Haven," he said, "because it is one of the best examples — if not the best — of creative federalism."

Bureaucrats spoke, mayors asked questions, Humphrey made colorful, knowledgeable summaries. "I know it sounds like a lot, Mom, I said to her, but it costs me more to park my car each week than it did for Dad to feed the family." . . . "When I was mayor of Minneapolis it cost seven times more per block for public services in the poorest section than in the richest." . . . "These four lanes came right up to the edge of the city, and then — bang! — there was a two-lane bridge." . . . "I come from the land of the sky-blue water, but I don't want to tell you what color some of that water has turned."

Humphrey brought with him sub-Cabinet officers from Commerce, Agriculture, the poverty program, HEW, and the housing agency — William Slayton, head of the Urban Renewal Agency — and introduced each for a short speech followed by mayoral questions. The mayors said things like "We do not have a *exit ramp* that will bring people down into our town and allow people to spend money on their way to the Cape."

Repeatedly mayors and selectmen asked when they could get the application forms for federal aid for "water and sewage" facilities, apparently now a weighty concern. The answer was not quite yet; the appropriations bill was just that week going to pass the Congress. Humphrey said, "We can't give out the forms until we've got the money. You don't say, 'come and look into the cookie jar' until you've got the cookies."

The most effective presentation was that of Ralph Huitt, a former teacher of political science at the University of Wisconsin, just forty-five days on his job as Assistant Secretary of HEW for legislation — "I've been making speeches since I was thirteen years old, but this is the first time I've been important enough to have a speech written for me." He praised the historic measures passed by the session of Congress just then concluding its work, any one of which alone, he said, would make it a great Congress. It could be called the Health Congress, or the Education Congress, or the Clean Environment Congress (air and water pollution were main topics of the conference). This was the year, he said, of the great harvest; we have been talking aid to education for seventy years, and this is the year we made the breakthrough. Twenty-five thousand school districts are eligible for funds under Title I (the weightiest part of the Elementary and Secondary Education Act of 1965, which gives funds to districts with numbers of poor people). This great harvest is the result of the planting done by heroes throughout the years — and none deserves more credit than one named Hubert Humphrey. Mr. Huitt's tribute was a more graceful one than I have here reproduced.

Mr. Huitt went through many of the major bills passed during the season — 21 so far of the 22 the President asked for he said, and the 22nd (aid to higher education) was just about to be passed. On the rubber-stamp business he told a joke. A member of Congress said, "We keep passing these bills and shoving them up to the President, and he has signed every one of them. He's a rubber-stamp President."

Robert Kennedy, in four and a half hours, went from New Haven airport to the Knights of St. Patrick to the Mayor's home on McKinley Avenue to a Polish Democratic Club rally in St.

Stanislaus Church to the Fair Haven Junior High School and back to the airport, with female "jumpers" — young, middle-aged, and old — knocking the buttons off police uniforms all the way.

St. Stan's, which is in the Thirteenth Ward, was the point nearest our ward. Robert Kennedy said a few words of greeting in Polish, and then shifted to English because, he said, he noticed that the Mayor didn't understand. This brought laughter. He led the crowd in a Polish song. He then modulated to the serious and touching statement that was to be quoted many times in the days thereafter: "I stand here today in place of my brother. If he were alive today, he would be here. What my brother hoped to do with the New Frontier Dick Lee is doing in New Haven."

Kennedy's visit helped us Democrats in the Fifteenth Ward, where I needed help. "I'm not worried about the Mayor, and I'm not worried about Probate; I just want to be sure we win the alderman," said Pat Cassidy.

Bujalski posters had appeared on bumpers. There were even big pins with Bujalski's picture. A car down the street from us had a big Bujalski sign on its top. All of this was quite unusual for an aldermanic campaign. A Bujalski letter, signed by Carpinella, on the last weekend said that the Republican Fifteenth Ward committee had "waged without a doubt the most intensive and impressive aldermanic campaign that has ever been witnessed in the entire city of New Haven." The letter gave statistics: "More than one thousand police whistles and 500 picture pins will have been distributed, not to mention several hundred calling cards, picture posters, and bumper stickers . . . This letter will have completed the mailing of over 7,000 first class letters to your entire area, averaging one letter every seven days . . ." On Halloween night, the Sunday before the Tuesday of the election, Bujalski and some of his supporters gave out whistles, picture pins, and trick or treat bags of candy with campaign literature attached to them. My son David, aged eight, came back from the Bujalskis' house (we live on the same large block) with a load of candy, whistles, and pins and a good deal of sympathy for my opponent. "Bujalski's nice," he said.

Downtown nobody took my mutterings about the ward very seriously. One city-wide Democratic politician laughed and said, "Can you imagine a Polak winning in that ward?" My answer was yes. I did not like the question, not alone because it reflected an objectionable ethnic politics, but also because it was mistaken. Bujalski proved to be a personable Yale graduate, a pleasant and well-spoken bachelor in his thirties, who in his energetic campaigning won sympathy from many persons more relevant to his political objectives than my son David.

Friends who knew the ward, differing from complacent city-wide types who contemplated a huge Lee victory, were predicting that I would lose. When it came right down to the moment of truth in that voting booth, would the old-line Democrats really split? One group said No, they won't. They don't know how. It's too hard to do on the machines. So this was my situation as a professor of ethics who had ventured into politics: to hope that enlightenment had not yet progressed so far as to allow the traditional straight-party Democrats to split their ticket. But the antibusers had a strong motive for splitting (Carpinella's last letter had spoken of "the most important issues ever to face our ward"). The Republican campaign in the ward quite frankly encouraged splitting; it was all Bujalski, with scarcely a mention of Einhorn. The advertisement for their ward rally had Bujalski's name in large black type as the feature attraction; in small type down along with the mention of refreshments it said, "Also meet Joseph Einhorn, candidate for mayor." And the Fifteenth had shown itself before to be the splittingest ward in the city. In 1962 the three major races resulted in one Republican victory, one Democratic victory, and one tie.

That was very nearly to be the result in 1965, too.

Working with the Mayor's staff beats doorbell-ringing in glamour and in working conditions, but I could see that I had to tend to my home fires. In the last two weeks I worked hard in the ward. One of Mr. Carpinella's letters spoke of my "late and last desperate effort to get votes." At first I worked mainly on the working class side, on the theory that I could thus win back traditional Democrats tempted to split. Then I began to wonder.

"You didn't help us on this busing, you know, Mr. Miller. You didn't help us at all. I have to pay $500 for my children's education, Mr. Miller, and I can't afford that. I ought to be allowed a free education for my children, Mr. Miller, like everybody else, and not have to pay all that money. We couldn't see that Bassett, Mr. Miller. We weren't going to have any of that." This woman, a registered and lifelong Democrat, said this with heat as we stood on her doorstep. She named the two parochial schools to which her children were now being sent. I hadn't realized how steep the tuition for nonparishioners could be in parochial schools.

Perhaps campaigning on that side of the ward wasn't such a good idea, after all. People in the Hooker PTA who gasped when they saw the alderman vote against the antibusing resolution, or who saw their alderman at the scattered-housing hearing, would be reminded of these unpleasant experiences when they saw me personally. Perhaps it was better to leave them unreminded — to hope that, undisturbed by any actual contact with the candidate, they would vote for him inadvertently just by pulling that habitual lever.

A fellow alderman gave me advice. Leave that side of the ward alone, he said, and concentrate on the apartments on the other side. The people over here have their minds made up, one way or another, he said, but in the apartments they don't have any kids, they aren't involved in city affairs, and they can be influenced by a visit. So I tried that.

In one of the apartments a woman came to the door in her housecoat, chewing her dinner, at three-thirty in the afternoon, and we joked for a pleasant moment or two. I handed her my materials. She took one look at the names on it, and the atmosphere abruptly changed. "Dick Lee!" she said, in some agitation. "I wouldn't vote for Dick Lee under any circumstances. I am a schoolteacher. Dick Lee had me removed from my school three years ago and a Negro put in my place." The agitation increased as she spoke. "That school has gone downhill ever since. Dick Lee did that, just so he could get the Negro vote. So let the Negroes vote for Dick Lee." She ripped my materials, threw the pieces at me like confetti, and slammed the door.

But not many of the encounters on the Whitney side of Orange Street were like that.

A young architect's wife, smoking a cigarette in a holder, said, as we sat in an Eames chair and a Le Corbusier chair in her bare living room, "You're fighting a sociological thing here, aren't you?" She explained that she and her husband — lifelong Republicans — had decided to vote Democratic in this election. "It's hard to do, you know," she added.

While we were worrying about the city election in New Haven delegates to Connecticut's constitutional convention — including Mrs. A. Whitney Griswold from the Fifteenth Ward — were working on the constitution for the state, up in Hartford. The main point, of course, was reapportionment. The Supreme Court in 1964 had specified "one man, and one vote," and the new constitution would give legal basis for the new arrangement of districts the two parties had finally agreed upon. (A Goldwater faction opposed the arrangement, and later opposed the whole new constitution in the referendum.) This new apportionment would reduce New Haven's delegation to the Senate, which had slightly overrepresented the cities and the Democrats, from four to two in a smaller Senate. But it would increase New Haven's delegation in the House, which had vastly overrepresented rural areas and Republicans, from two to *ten*, in a House reduced in size from 294 to 177 members. Under the new plan the Fifteenth and Eighteenth Wards, plus the Twenty-eighth (the first ward east into Fair Haven) will compose a district and send a Representative to Hartford.

While writing the constitutional language that allowed for this new set of districts the constitutional convention also made other changes in the state's basic document, establishing a new constitutional guarantee of free public education for all Connecticut citizens, for example. It grants "home rule" to cities, in general, and provides for such regional and intermunicipal and metropolitan government as may someday arise. It makes it a "right" rather than a "duty" for Connecticut citizens to worship a Supreme Being and it included for the first time a specific antidiscrimination clause in the state's Bill of Rights. It eliminated the *mandatory* party lever that we Connecticut politicians, almost uniquely, had managed to foist on our state's voters; henceforth, the party lever will be optional.

While the convention was cranking out these and other more or less minor changes in the state's machinery something bigger was slipped in, too. On Yom Kippur, when important Democrats were absent from the drafting committee, a leading Republican had inserted in the section on eminent domain an innocent-sounding new phrase that no property shall be taken for public use unless that taking be "necessary." The convention itself swallowed this phrase when the committee made its report. But knowledgeable people around the state — prominently including the redevelopment staff in New Haven — spotted the change and pointed out its dangers. The phrase would, or it might, hamstring redevelopment and also interfere with the finding of sites for schools and for highways, and interfere with all the projects and agencies that make use of the powers of eminent domain. There could be lots of litigation over what "necessary" meant. A fight over "eminent domain" developed that seemed to me to reflect some future divisions in political philosophy. On the one side as an unusual assortment of supporters of strong powers of land-taking, ranging from the NAACP to boards of education and the public utility companies, and featuring most especially a pair of agencies to whom many in the Fifteenth Ward had quite contrasting reactions — the urban renewal agencies and the State Highway Commission. The opposition found support not only on the right but also among some on the left, who were worried about governmental powers.

There was a separate vote on this land-taking amendment, when the referendum on the new constitution was held a month after the city election, and the amendment lost. Voters in the New Haven area, nevertheless, favored it. Opponents of urban renewal could point out that the city that had had most urban renewal voted for restrictions on land-taking powers. The evident reason for the amendment's success in New Haven, however, was the power, in the absence of competing sources of influence, of the *New Haven Register.* "VOTE YES FOR YOUR HOME," it said in a front-page editorial.

But all of this was an anticlimactic epilogue to the city election. Late in the afternoon of the Thursday before election day I got word that the *New York Times* would run an editorial praising Lee and urging his re-election. I called to find out where the Mayor was, and found him in a steam room on the fourth floor of the Payne Whitney gymnasium, lying stripped on the table getting a massage. While the massage man rubbed his Honor at one end, I told the other end the news. "Wonderful!" said Lee, and he began thinking immediately what political use might be made of the editorial.

The editorial did not appear the next morning, Friday, but the word had been that it might be Friday or Saturday. The Mayor's aides got ready to grab the first copy of the *Times* to come into the city on Saturday, to reproduce the editorial, and to spread it around a few of the city's wards (the Fifteenth, for one). Saturday morning I got up early, snatched the *Times*, turned immediately to the editorial page, and found there a very satisfying piece of reading under the title "The Vote in New Haven." It was three hundred words long, the second editorial, and it was a solid endorsement: pretty good for a local election in a medium-sized Connecticut city sixty miles from New York! "Next Tuesday's municipal election in New Haven," it began, "provides a reminder of what can be done by a community when it addresses itself vigorously to solving its local problems." Farther along the editorial said that "under the forceful leadership of Mayor Richard C. Lee, New Haven has in recent years become an inspiration to other cities trying to solve these problems," and "On his record, Mayor Lee deserves re-election . . ." and, in the final sentence, "Mayor Lee's defeat would not only block progress for New Haven but would dishearten people working for reform and innovation in many other American cities." I thought the editorial was excellent.

I waited, on that Saturday morning, for a call from the Mayor's staff about the distribution of reprints — but it didn't come. I telephoned, and learned that the Mayor had decided not to reprint the editorial, largely because of material in the last paragraph. Those who "had religion" would see it in the *Times* anyway, so the story went, and elsewhere it might cause trouble. I looked again at the last paragraph. It mentioned "a controversy over the school board's interim plan for busing some students while new schools are being built," and said that "Mayor Lee has properly stood up for the autonomy of the school board . . ." Too much about schools and busing.

On Canner Street, the workingclass side of Orange, I stopped in to see a voter who turned out to be a graduate student in philosophy at Yale. There was a big library copy of Descartes in French open on his desk. His thesis was in progress in an electric typewriter beside a paper-strewn desk. "What do you think of this 'compulsory busing,'" he asked, his accent revealing a trace of the South. "Are you for 'forced integration'?" His own argument kept turning back to the insincerity of integrationists: "They have their *own* children in private school. Or they live in suburbs with only a token of Negroes in the schools." I told him I thought a philosopher ought to make up his mind on the merits not on his opinion of a policy's proponents. Forty-five minutes of dialectics followed. This was three days before the election, and I could have used the time more profitably.

The last weeks of Mr. Einhorn's campaign featured attacks against Lee and his administration. He charged that Lee would not serve out his term. Lee in answer denied that he had heard anything about the urban affair Cabinet post. Einhorn charged a conflict of interest on Lee's part: Lee had been a part-time consultant to the Pepsi-Cola Company, and a director of that company was also director of the construction firm that built Florence Virtue. He returned, although only briefly, to the busing theme. He issued one extraordinary statement about the city being "gripped with fear" of the "Lee machine," including as his evidence that businessmen were not contributing money to his (Einhorn's) campaign. On the last weekend he proposed "security call boxes" on corners throughout the city, by which citizens could summon the police or fire department by pushing a button.

In a talk with student reporters, Mr. Einhorn said, or was quoted by the *Yale Daily News* as having said, that "Yale has been a luxury to New Haven, and one that we can ill afford. It has not accepted its obligations to the community." Mr. Einhorn was further quoted as having said "Yale cannot be a jewel in a swamp." The headline on the *Yale Daily News* story reporting these extraordinary statements said, "Einhorn Criticizes Yale; blasts Lee Administration." The story carried a picture of Einhorn, and under it the quotation "Jewel in a Swamp?" Citizens for Lee reprinted this story as a flier, and added at the bottom "Dick Lee has said: Yale is one of New Haven's most important resources. The University's contributions to the life of our city have been invaluable." This flier was handed out at the Yale-Dartmouth game at the Yale Bowl on the Saturday before election.

Crawford Manor, the 106-unit high-rise housing for the elderly designed by Paul Rudolph, was dedicated on the morning of the day that Hubert Humphrey came to town. Crawford Manor stands next to University Towers and is named for George Crawford, a venerable Negro lawyer who was the Lee administration's first corporation counsel, and who helped to inspire Constance Baker Motley to enter the civil rights fight. Marian Anderson, an old friend of Crawford's, came to the dedication. "No city in New England has done more than New Haven to create a variety of attractive low cost housing to meet the needs of our senior citizens," said the Mayor at the dedication.

Mayor Lee used television spots extensively, too. His final one showed him standing on top of the Paul Rudolph garage, pointing out the hotel, the office building, Crawford Manor, the Crown Towers, the site for Church Street South — new buildings built, cranes at work, sites for further projects all around him. Finally, in the last days of the campaign, there was the climax to it all: the topping out of the new hotel in the front block — a moment of deep satisfaction to the Mayor. Three conventions, the papers said, were tentatively booked on the spot.

By then the only question was how big his victory would be.

That wasn't the only question in my campaign, though. At five minutes to six on the evening of election day I came home from the ward headquarters, gathered up my wife and children, and walked with them once more to the basement of Hooker School, to watch the opening of the machines. It had been a brisk, clear election day in New Haven and in New York, with slow voting in both places. "There's lots of splittin'!"

"You've worked hard," I said to Bujalski, when he came into Hooker.

"In a minute we'll know whether it was worth it," he answered.

I got paper and pencils for my children to follow the results. Bob Reilly, once again the moderator, closed the polls and the workers gathered around the back of the first of the three machines. The Probate Judge election was on the first line, Mayor on the second, Alderman on the ninth, following the city slate. Once again there came that portentous silence. Then: first machine, 287 Democrats, 425 Republicans. The poll watchers and party workers gasped. The Republican's candidate for Probate Judge was way ahead. What would that mean for the rest? Then: Mayor Lee 413; Republican Einhorn 297. Again there was murmuring, although this time mainly murmuring of a recovered assurance on the part of Democrats.

One for the Republicans, one for the Democrats. What would it be now for Alderman?

"Is there anybody who wants to hear the rest of the offices, before we skip to Alderman?" asked Mr. Reilly. A chorus of noes.

"Line nine." The readying of pencils. "Nine A — 359. Nine B — 353." That meant Miller 359, Bujalski 353, for a margin of six. A still different kind of murmuring from the crowd. I had no assurance of victory, because I knew that Pat Cassidy, hospitable to Democrats, had been on the first machine; I might do better there than on the second and third.

"Second machine. One A — 184; one B — 306." Another big Republican lead on Probate Judge. "Two A — 276; two B — 216." Another slightly narrower lead, in the other party direction, for Mayor Lee. "Nine A — 251; nine B — 241." A ten-vote margin for me — but what about the third machine?

"One A — 149; one B — 251. Two A — 230; two B — 169."

The pattern once again, on Probate and Mayor. "Nine A —
195. Nine B — 205." There came here a slight pause in my
breathing. For the first time in my experience a voting machine
had got out of line with its fellows, and against me. But then
I started breathing again. The ten-vote loss on that machine
just canceled the ten-vote gain on the second; there was still a
six-vote margin on the first.

"Did you win, Daddy?"

"Congratulations, Bill."

A rather subdued group of wellwishers gathered around to
congratulate me. Pat Cassidy looked battered, tired, and happy.
I had won, on the machines, by six votes. I had a twenty-one-
vote plurality on the absentees (mostly straight party votes)
so that I was re-elected alderman by the thumping margin of
six plus twenty-one — twenty-seven votes.

As we walked home my daughter's transister radio was already telling us about the large victory Mayor Lee was winning.
She had sent to a radio station's contest a card with our semi-
scientific estimate of the outcome: Mayor Lee by a plurality of
14,360. I knew what the Mayor's last polls had shown. Lee won,
when it was all added up, by a plurality of 16,893. The more
striking figure was his percentage of the unusually low vote:
66.5 percent, a new record. He had demolished Einhorn by a
margin of nearly 2 to 1. Even more impressive, he had carried
every Democrat into office with him. The Democratic candidate
for Probate Judge ran way behind Lee, but won. And for the
first time in New Haven's history one party won every single
seat on the Board of Aldermen — 33 Democrats, turning out
all of the three lonely Republicans.

We didn't have a victory party in the ward this time, since I
wasn't sure that we would have a victory. Instead my wife and
I went to two city-wide parties, the Citizens for Lee at the Taft
Hotel and the Democratic Party at the Ambassador Restaurant.
We took along, as it happened, two co-workers from the ward
— Mrs. A. Whitney Griswold, the widow of the late President

of Yale, and Pat Cassidy, the brother of the late Democratic chairman of the ward.

In New York City, Yale man John Lindsay was elected to succeed Yale man Robert Wagner despite, or conceivably even because of, the efforts of Yale man William Buckley. Mr. Lindsay soon thereafter named Edward Logue of Boston (and once of New Haven) to head a group examining his urban renewal program, and Mitchell Sviridoff of CPI to head a group studying the antipoverty and human relations efforts of the city. Rumor had it that both these New Haven alumni had been offered top jobs by Lindsay. Perhaps New York had found its Lee.

In Boston Mrs. Louise Day Hicks, the chairman of the school committee who had promised "never to vote to destroy the neighborhood school system," led all candidates and was overwhelmingly re-elected. She had said she was opposed to "shipping children all over the city," that is, to busing. Other candidates who supported Mrs. Hicks and her position were re-elected; the one incumbent who opposed her was defeated.

In Cleveland Carl Stokes, a Democrat, missed by only 2731 votes becoming the first Negro mayor of a major American city. Stokes got 36 percent of a vote that was divided among four candidates; Negroes constitute 37 percent of Cleveland's population.

In Louisville as in New York City the Republicans won the mayor's office, and in Philadelphia they won the attorney-general's office, when the number of Negroes voting for the Republican candidate increased markedly over 1964. In Louisville Republican mayoralty candidate Schmeid received 50 percent of the Negro vote, whereas Republican presidential candidate Goldwater had received only 5 percent one year earlier.

As New Haven digested its election results, I came to realize that I had the distinction of being the incumbent Democrat who came nearest to having been beaten.

In two wards — the Thirty-second and Thirty-third — in which Democratic candidates turned out Republicans, there were margins of victory even smaller than mine; margins of eleven votes and fifteen votes respectively. (In those two wards and mine there were uneventful recounts.) But I had by far the narrowest victory among the incumbents — a much closer call than, say, the two Democrats in Westville who had been so concerned about the antibusers, and who had publicly called for the school board's resignation. I took a perverse satisfaction in the closeness of my victory. People had said complacently that I wasn't in any trouble. By golly, I showed them. Nevertheless, I did feel a bit defensive when people talked about coattail candidates and "Landslide Miller."

The primary topic of political conversation in New Haven soon became whether Mayor Lee would be named by the President to be the first Secretary of the Department of Housing and Urban Development. A Washington editor of a national newsmagazine said Lee would be a shoo-in if it were not for his health. Lee's name appeared regularly in the national news stories about the new department, and later on Ed Logue's name did, too. (Other cities also had their parochial gossip; "In Detroit," somebody said, "they are talking about Mayor Cavanaugh heading the department just the way we are talking about Lee.") Shortly before Christmas Mayor Lee had a couple of long conversations with Senator Ribicoff about the appointment, and as a result of these conversations in effect withdrew his name from consideration. Lee said that it looked as though the Secretary would be the man on the spot for every urban and racial crisis — every eruption in Watts — and would spend his time putting out fires rather than building something. In January the President named Robert Weaver to the post.*

During the time of intense speculation about Lee's future, much thought, or at any rate much discussion, was devoted to

---

* Lee later declined to be considered for an Assistant Secretaryship in the Department of Housing and Urban Development.

the question of possible successors to him. To face that question was to perceive how unique his mayoralty had been; he had set a new standard of expectation for mayors, and there wasn't anyone visible in New Haven politics who came up to it. Some think that after Lee New Haven will fall back into the unimaginative and conventional ethnic politics of an industrial city. Others say no; the agencies, and the personnel, and — most important — the expectations on the part of the citizenry will still be there.

The other large topic of political conversation in New Haven was the embarrassing completeness of the Democratic victory on the Board of Aldermen. Editorials and lunchtime conversations anxiously discussed the future of the two-party system in the city. Voters began already to grumble about next time, when almost on principle they would support some Republicans. We aldermen began to talk about how we would conduct ourselves without any "opposition." A Negro alderman joked that he would now have to be "the new minority leader." The charter provides for aldermanic representation from both parties on some boards and commissions; presumably the Republican slot would simply be left vacant. When it came down to it, though, there was to be at least as much opposition on the new board as on the old. There is plenty of difference of opinion, as a matter of fact, within the diverse group who are all nominally members of the one party.

The deeper problem of the board, I think, is how to make it a significant participant in city government, which it isn't now. I would grant — as everyone, including the Mayor, was saying — that it might have been better had the victory been just a shade less total. It would have presented a less disturbing appearance had at least one Republican somewhere been elected. But I am glad that didn't happen in the Fifteenth Ward.

Acknowledgments
and Sources

IT IS IMPORTANT that the reader of a book like this one really believe that, despite all the help he had, the author alone is responsible for what is said. Mayor Lee was most gracious and co-operative in every way, and was kind enough to read an early version of two chapters, but of course he is in no way responsible for the interpretations or for any errors printed here. Neither are any of the members of his administration or of the Democratic Party, or of the citizenry of the Fifteenth Ward, or the others from New Haven and elsewhere who have helped me, sometimes inadvertently.

I wish particularly to thank L. Thomas Appleby, who magnanimously allowed me to take over as my own material in Chapter Thirteen which was originally a collaboration between us, and who has helped this book in many other ways. I wish also to thank the able literary critic from Morse College, Yale University, Richard Ruland, for a most careful and helpful reading of the entire manuscript, and for much encouragement. In addition the following persons kindly granted specific requests for interviews or for readings of drafts of chapters, and I thank them all: Mel Adams, Roger Armstrong, Richard Dowdy, Tom Lord, Al Myers, William Muehl, Sam Nash, Eric Sandall, Al Science, June Shagaloff, Mitchell Sviridoff, Orville Sweeting, Allan Talbot, and Robert Wolfe.

Mrs. Pat Sorrells typed the book, with the utmost efficiency and helpfulness to the writer. She is, incidentally, one of the white parents on Mansfield Street — from Berkeley Seminary — who in the midst of the busing furor quietly moved her children from Hooker, to which they had hitherto gone by permissive and dubious zoning, to the nearer, largely Negro Winchester School.

The *New York Times* kindly granted permission to reprint in altered form in Chapters 6 and 13 material that originally appeared in its magazine section. The text indicates that I relied on Robert Dahl's *Who Governs?* and on *Beyond the Melting Pot* by Nathan Glazer and Daniel P. Moynihan. I also used *City Politics* by Edward Banfield and James Q. Wilson, *New England State Politics* by Duane Lockard, *Governing New York City* by Wallace Sayre and Herbert Kaufman, *Three Centuries of New Haven, 1638–1938* by Rollin G. Osterweis, and other books about cities, politics, and race.

A book like this, however, does not come out of other books but out of conversations. Most of these I had with my wife, Betty Horton Miller, who deserves far more than the routine husbandly acknowledgment. In addition to typing and living this book, she talked it all over with the writer, and probably deserves credit for any merit it may have. The errors, I repeat, are my own.

W.L.M.

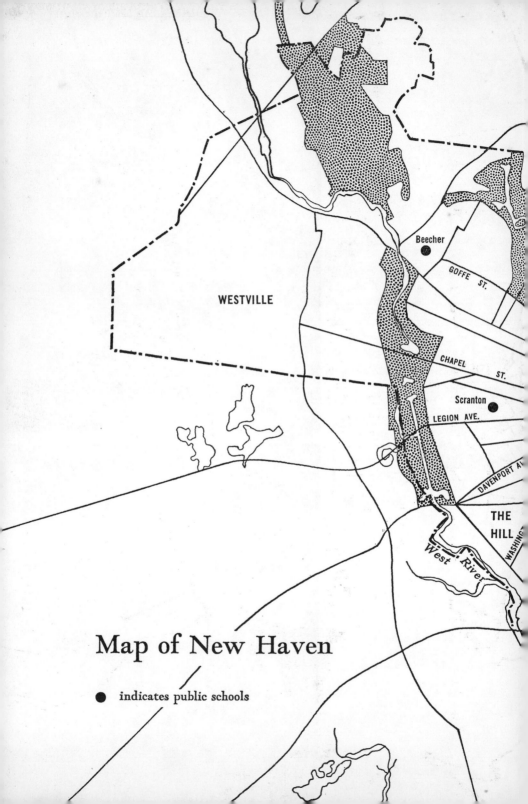

Beecher

GOFFE ST.

WESTVILLE

CHAPEL
ST.

Scranton

LEGION AVE.

DAVENPORT AV

THE
HILL

WASHING

West River

Map of New Haven

● indicates public schools